T0305432

Competition and Sustainability

Economic Policy and Options for Reform in Antitrust and Competition Law

Justus Haucap
Professor for Competition Economics, Düsseldorf Institute for Competition Economics (DICE), Heinrich-Heine-Universität Düsseldorf, Germany

Rupprecht Podszun
Professor for Competition Law, Chair for Competition Law, Heinrich-Heine-Universität Düsseldorf, Germany

Tristan Rohner
Postdoc, Chair for Competition Law, Heinrich-Heine-Universität Düsseldorf, Germany

Anja Rösner
Düsseldorf Institute for Competition Economics (DICE), Heinrich-Heine-Universität Düsseldorf, Germany

With contributions by
Philipp Offergeld (Part II Chapter 3)
Prof. Dr. Charlotte Kreuter-Kirchhof/Prof. Dr. Rüdiger Hahn (Part III Chapter 1)
Prof. Dr. Charlotte Kreuter-Kirchhof (Part III Chapter 4)
Prof. Dr. Rüdiger Hahn, Alexandra May (Part III Chapter 5)

Edward Elgar
PUBLISHING

Cheltenham, UK • Northampton, MA, USA

Cover image: Mathew Schwartz on Unsplash.

Published by
Edward Elgar Publishing Limited
The Lypiatts
15 Lansdown Road
Cheltenham
Glos GL50 2JA
UK

Edward Elgar Publishing, Inc.
William Pratt House
9 Dewey Court
Northampton
Massachusetts 01060
USA

A catalogue record for this book
is available from the British Library

Library of Congress Control Number: 2024930488

This book is available electronically in the **Elgar**online
Law subject collection
http://dx.doi.org/10.4337/9781035325399

ISBN 978 1 0353 2538 2 (cased)
ISBN 978 1 0353 2539 9 (eBook)

Printed and bound by CPI Group (UK) Ltd, Croydon, CR0 4YY

Contents

Boxes

Contributors

Rüdiger Hahn is Professor for Sustainability Management at the Faculty of Business Administration and Economics, Heinrich-Heine-Universität Düsseldorf, Germany.

Justus Haucap is Professor for Competition Economics at the Düsseldorf Institute for Competition Economics (DICE), Heinrich-Heine-Universität Düsseldorf, Germany.

Charlotte Kreuter-Kirchhof is Professor for German and International Public Law, International Law and European Law at the Faculty of Law, Heinrich-Heine-Universität Düsseldorf, Germany.

Alexandra May is a PhD Researcher at the Faculty of Business Administration and Economics, Heinrich-Heine-Universität Düsseldorf, Germany.

Philipp Offergeld is a PhD Researcher at the Chair of Civil Law, German and European Competition Law, Heinrich-Heine-Universität Düsseldorf, Germany.

Rupprecht Podszun is Professor for Competition Law, Heinrich-Heine-Universität Düsseldorf, Germany.

Tristan Rohner is a Postdoctoral Researcher at the Chair of Civil Law, German and European Competition Law, Heinrich-Heine-Universität Düsseldorf, Germany.

Anja Rösner is a Postdoctoral Researcher at the Düsseldorf Institute for Competition Economics (DICE), Heinrich-Heine-Universität Düsseldorf, Germany.

Preface

In this study, we look into all aspects of competition and sustainability. It is an intriguing field: How do we resolve the need for more sustainable solutions with our traditional model of a market economy with competition at its heart? Free markets are often seen as the cause, not the solution to problems such as climate change. Our aim when writing this book was to develop options to integrate sustainability concerns into the legal area that provides the fundamental structure of doing business – competition law. Making the magic of markets work for sustainability! At the same time, we were firm in our belief that competition as the driving principle of the market economy must not be forfeited.

The study is based on the understanding of sustainability as expressed in the Sustainable Development Goals (SDGs) of the United Nations. This concept of sustainability is broad and comprehensive including a heterogeneity of contents. The concept includes economic, ecological and social goals – and it is entrenched in international law as well as in EU and national law. Companies are actors of sustainability; their activities are of fundamental importance for sustainable development.

From an economic perspective, in principle, there is no tension between competition and sustainability. Sustainability deficits can go hand in hand with a lack of competition and other market failures and can be exacerbated by such market failures. Competition can even be seen as a factor of sustainability, as trust is created in markets, the other market is protected, and a social balance is maintained.

In Part I of this book, we identify the economic reasons for a useful intervention with competition law tools in markets when sustainability concerns are at stake. Often, market failures exist that affect sustainability issues. Some of these can be cured with antitrust. In individual cases, the cooperation and mergers of companies can be an effective instrument for achieving sustainability goals, if sovereign market interventions are not sufficient (e.g., due to 'regulatory failure') or if companies need economies of scale and scope while at the same time considerable irreversible investments are required to be able to realise sustainability goals. But this requires a measuring of sustainability indicators which is a difficult quantitative exercise. We present the methods in this book.

Competition law can be further developed with a view to sustainability goals. However, proposals must be economically justifiable in that they must be competition-related or explicitly recognise non-competitive interests. There are many options for a further development of competition law, we set these out in Part II of the book. In the Annex, all options are summarised briefly for a better overview. They cover diverse aspects such as the scope of application of competition law, the prohibition of anti-competitive agreements, exemptions from such prohibitions, abuse of dominance cases, merger control, sanctions and procedural issues.

For a better understanding and a more systematic approach, we developed four patterns of competition law reform:

* Ensuring a sustainability-sensitive application of competition law, which exclusively continues to follow the logic of competition (Sustainability Awareness);
* Expand competition law to include legislative clarifications so that sustainability goals, which are fully in line with the competition rationale, can be better promoted through competition law (Sustainability Boost);
* Orientation of competition law toward the protection of ecologically and socially sustainable competition on the merits, so that sustainable business becomes an inherent part of the application of competition law (Sustainable Competition);
* Consideration of non-competitive interests in competition law by creating areas of exception or by integrating these interests into the application of competition law as explicitly non-competitive (Levelling Approach).

The various proposals tie in with the current discussion on competition policy between the Post-Chicago School, Progressive Antitrust and the Neo-Brandeis School on the limits of competition law. This points to the fact that the debate has some overarching issues such as the risk of greenwashing or questions of legitimacy. We look into some of the overarching issues in Part III.

Competition law in all areas can be more strongly oriented toward sustainability goals than has been the case to date. Competition will not solve all the world's problems. But where competition is lacking, the prospects are bleak. So this study may brighten the outlook.

Acknowledgments

This book is based on a study that was commissioned by the German Federal Ministry for Economic Affairs and Climate Action (BMWK). The authors and contributors are part of the Future Group Competition & Sustainability of Heinrich Heine University Düsseldorf, an interdisciplinary research group. The BMWK is not bound in any way by this study.

The authors would like to thank Zeinab Ansah, Can Degistirici, Sarah Deutschmann, Klara Dresselhaus, Stephanie Faust, Anna Kronenberg, Anna Patzer and Jennifer Rontganger for their support in preparing the manuscript.

PART I

Basics: the relationship between competition and sustainability

1. *Competition and Sustainability*: an introduction

In this study, we address the question of how sustainability goals can be better taken into account in competition law and what changes are required for this at the German or European level. For the definition of sustainability, we are guided by the Sustainable Development Goals of the United Nations, the *UN SDG*, a comprehensive, internationally consented catalogue of goals, which are defined in more detail by indicators.

So far, sustainability goals have only been taken into account in competition law in isolated cases and within narrow limits. This is true both when sustainability goals are used to justify restrictions on competition (competition law as a shield) and when competition law is used proactively to enforce sustainability goals (competition law as a sword). If legislators and practitioners want to charge competition law with sustainability references more strongly than before, this can be done with varying degrees of intensity. In this study, we present options for doing so. They range from a sustainability-sensitive application of competition law without any change in the law to far-reaching changes in the protection of competition, whether by internalising certain effects or opening competition law to the balancing of interests with non-competition aspects. In order to assess the reform options, however, it is first necessary to illuminate the fundamentals of the complex relationship between sustainability and competition. Second, it must be discussed under which circumstances antitrust instruments are well suited to achieve or at least support sustainability goals and under which circumstances policy instruments from other areas of law (such as environmental law, tax law, consumer protection, labour law, energy law, and other areas of law) are better suited to achieve sustainability goals. Otherwise, an isolated consideration of antitrust instruments, without accounting for other policy measures and the overall framework, can easily lead to wrong conclusions.[1]

---

[1] The idea can be illustrated through the following example: if, for example, the legislature has decided to address the negative externalities of eating meat through a meat tax, meat-free days at schools, and legal advertising restrictions, it is at least questionable whether an antitrust exemption of price fixing in the meat industry could be socially desirable, even if additional price increases would further reduce meat con-

THE TENSION BETWEEN SUSTAINABILITY AND COMPETITION

If the urgent problems of our time are to be solved, this cannot be done without private businesses: CO_2 emissions are to be reduced in all areas of life; buildings are to be constructed more sustainably; textile traders are to organise their supply chains in such a way that child labour is prevented; supplier companies from the Global South are to pay fair wages to employees.

Policymakers are faced with the task of finding the best instruments or setting incentives to achieve such sustainability goals. From a competition point of view, it would be ideal if companies had sufficient incentives to pursue such goals autonomously, even without government intervention. If the market does not provide these incentives on its own, then – from an economic perspective – it is necessary to generate these incentives through government intervention, for example, by defining pollution rights (such as emission certificates), through taxes, subsidies or even prohibitions and bans. This corresponds to classical legal ideas of regulation, according to which state intervention with laws, prohibitions, taxes, subsidies, and similar means is the way to achieve political objectives. Yet, we also see the limits of such a government-focused regulatory approach: setting incentives in markets is difficult; policymakers often lack the power or the necessary information; there is regulatory capture. This prompts the question whether companies can help and push ideas of sustainability on their own or through coordinated efforts. In some instances, and this is true for sustainability, companies see the need to do more than is required by regulation, for instance since they fear litigation or are under pressure from shareholders, customers, employees, or NGOs. Why should managers not simultaneously agree to switch to sustainable production processes in a sector or to jointly develop new technologies? Should business associations set standards? Would the impact not be particularly high if companies with market power unilaterally enforced their conditions in the market – in favour of sustainability?

The experience of competition experts makes it hard to embrace such an approach: collusion by companies and the unilateral enforcement of conditions harm competition, and, ultimately, the consumer. When companies cooperate 'for the common good' they often agree upon a minimum, even though some

---

sumption. The reverse case is also not unproblematic: if, for example, a majority in Parliament decides against the introduction of a meat tax, it is not clear without further ado that a hypothetical price agreement by meat producers can be interpreted as serving the common good, even if this would lead to a decline in meat consumption. At the very least, an antitrust exemption of such an agreement would not be easily justified.

companies would be willing to take things further. Innovation is often the result of competition, not of coordination. When competitors meet, they may not limit their agreements to joint efforts for the pursuit of sustainability goals but go further and engage in clearly detrimental activities such as price fixing. Collusion between companies can lead to market mechanisms being overridden, resulting in inefficient solutions. Market players with market power are often characterised precisely by their lack of consideration for sustainability goals. Restrictions on competition regularly lead to higher prices, less innovation, less choice for consumers, and a spiralling concentration in markets that exacerbates negative effects. Competition law is designed to protect against this.

So far, authorities and courts in Europe have been reluctant to link competition law to sustainability goals. While there is a mounting awareness that corporate actors are key to achieving sustainability goals, competition law is seen as distant from this topic. An 'opening up' of competition law is often viewed with concern, not least because of the danger of 'greenwashing' by companies. In some cases, there is also concern that well-intentioned regulatory interventions in the economic process, which are not committed to a narrow focus on competition, go too far or go wrong.

The urgency of the ecological problems and the extent of the social distortions do not need to be explained. The climate catastrophe is calling into question economic activity according to outdated patterns. Human rights violations along the supply chain are now felt everywhere in the world. Do competition law and competition economics have anything to say about this? The answer can only be 'yes', and this study aims to provide an impetus for formulating that answer. The implications extend beyond detailed questions of competition law: competition law and competition economics define the economic order. It is in this area where the framework for the market economy is set. Competition rules are the essential outer boundaries within which companies develop their activities. Defining this framework requires political decisions, but of course these decisions need to be based on scholarly research.

There is one other aspect that makes competition law an interesting feature for policymakers in the field: antitrust is often seen as an efficient tool to regulate markets. The variety of enforcement instruments and the experience of the enforcing agencies are in high esteem. There is also an EU-wide, well-functioning pattern of cooperation in the multi-level-framework of EU, states, and even regional levels. Can this institutional and enforcement design help to solve the problems we face?

We are not so sure about the second aspect, the belief in the salvific power of antitrust. Yet, it seems clear to us that only a strong market economy is in any way capable of producing the innovations needed for climate protection and of generating the profits with which protective measures and social compensation are to be financed. In any case, restricting free competition in favour of sustainability goals is not an unproblematic approach. Probably the most important argument against anchoring sustainability goals in competition law is that other policy instruments, such as taxes, subsidies, or regulatory interventions, are often much better suited to achieving sustainability goals. Whether in some situations competition law can play a complementary role, or even a more central one is an open question. It is controversially discussed in antitrust circles.

The protection of competition through competition law does not conflict fundamentally with goals of sustainable development – on the contrary: when a competition agency steps in to stop companies from raising prices, when a mega merger is prohibited, when a powerful company is told not to exploit customers, then trust in markets is preserved and the economy is made to work for the benefit of consumers. It is the rule of law at work here, the taming of corporate power, the establishing of a level playing field between actors of different size. Competition, if based on a rivalry of merits, has important social functions. All these aspects of competition support sustainable development. The protection of competition and the fight against abusive or collusive behaviour ensures trust in markets. Achieving a basic level of competition, of fairness, or equity is a prerequisite for making the exchange of goods and services in a society sustainable. A sustainable economy requires strong competition law.

However, the underlying assumption that the economy should be organised as a free market economy, with competition as its driving force, is no longer generally shared – especially with regard to sustainability issues. There are voices in society that radically question competition as an end or at least as a means: the representatives of the degrowth movement see the possibility of a sustainable way of life only when the 'system' changes.[2] In their view, climate protection and other sustainability goals fundamentally conflict with the profit-making interests of companies and the competition paradigm of the market economy. *Consumerism* as a social ideal and as an economic driver for the functioning of the market economy is seen as outdated.[3] The market

---

[2] See Matthias Schmelzer and Andrea Vetter, *Degrowth/Postwachstum zur Einführung* (3rd edn, Junius 2021); Giorgios Kallis, Federico Demaria and Giacoma d'Alisa, 'Degrowth', in Giacoma d'Alisa, Federico Demaria and Giorgios Kallis (eds), *Degrowth – Handbuch für eine neue Ära* (oekom 2016) 17 ff.

[3] The role of consumption was pioneered by Thorstein Veblen, *The Theory of the Leisure Class* (first published 1899, Dover 1994) and John Kenneth Galbraith, *The Affluent Society* (Houghton Mifflin 1958).

economy, which is geared toward growth, has allegedly robbed itself of its own foundations by recklessly overstepping its boundaries.[4]

There is a less radical alternative to degrowth, namely the Common Good Economy. It is critical of both the existing mechanisms of the market economy and centralised intervention by the state. Proponents of this approach often refer to *Elinor Ostrom*'s pioneering research, which has demonstrated the benefits of decentralised self-organisation, especially for local cooperation problems.[5]

There is some truth in the criticism of degrowth activists or the common good movement: the use of fossil fuels in recent decades has contributed greatly to climate change, while at the same time driving consumption and profits. The wealth of Western societies today can arguably be attributed to the unsustainable exploitation of resources. But is this a necessary link?

What distinguishes our approach in this book is not so much a difference in assessing the past but a belief in the possibilities of the future: the transformation of the economy and the society is possible! And to be more exact, it can only be achieved if we use the power of competition, innovation and markets – not by restraining this power.

Turning away from the competition paradigm does no more justice to the complex relationship between competition and sustainability than does an exclusive efficiency orientation of the economy, such as that advocated by the Chicago School in the 1980s and 1990s and still prevalent today. In the current legal framework, which is characterised by fundamental rights and binding targets, positions that seek to eliminate or unilaterally exaggerate free enterprise are hardly justifiable. The legally constituted, competitive market economy has proved to be an effective mechanism for allocating scarce resources and stimulating innovation. In our view, it remains the way forward. Entrepreneurs, with their inventiveness and drive, are indispensable for achieving ambitious sustainability goals. Competition law protects the freedom of companies to compete and the freedom of consumers to choose. It defines the outer limits of what is necessary for markets to function.

Nevertheless, the complex relationship between competition and sustainability must be rebalanced. In the medium term, climate change and the reaching of planetary boundaries will call into question the ability of markets to function. Persistent sustainability problems jeopardise market efficiencies if this leads to a loss of confidence in markets and deteriorating conditions for

---

[4]   The 'limits to growth' were first prominently highlighted in the seminal report for the Club of Rome, Donella Meadows et al, *The Limits to Growth* (Universe Books 1972).

[5]   Elinor Ostrom, *Governing the Commons: The Evolution of Institutions for Collective Action* (Cambridge University Press 2015).

the market framework. Climate catastrophe leads to severe economic damage; disregard for social standards leads to problems in the supply chain. Both topics have become legal risks for companies due to more and more laws and successful claims. Sustainability issues are therefore also economically relevant issues. Sustainable development in the twenty-first century is the basic prerequisite for permanently stable market framework conditions. At the same time, market mechanisms are the most effective means of making rapid progress toward achieving the United Nations' Sustainable Development Goals.

RESEARCH QUESTIONS AND COURSE OF THE PRESENTATION

The authors of this study are concerned with the sustainable transformation of the economy. The path to greenhouse gas neutrality, the development and expansion of new infrastructures for the energy turnaround, the increasing demand for corporate responsibility for compliance with human rights or animal welfare standards raise the question of how this transformation can be achieved within a competition framework.

This study is based on a report that was commissioned in 2023 by the German Federal Ministry for Economic Affairs and Climate Action. The Ministry asked us to explore options for policy reform in the field of competition and sustainability. We presented the report (in German), where it is to serve as a basis for further legislative steps.[6] For this book, we not only translated the study, but substantially reviewed our findings and updated it. This has become a different, new study.

The two key questions of this study are:

- How does competition law affect the achievement of sustainability goals?
- What are the options for further development?

These two questions will be answered in this report with a particular view to EU law. Since competition law is largely based on economic principles, we begin by answering the following question:

- What is the link between sustainability and market failure? (Chapter 2)
- What patterns of reform can be identified on a general level? (Chapter 3)

---

[6]   For the German report see HHU Zukunftsgruppe Competition & Sustainability, 'Wettbewerb und Nachhaltigkeit in Deutschland und der EU' (*BMWK*, 2023) available at www.bmwk.de/Redaktion/DE/Publikationen/Studien/studie-wettbewerb-und -nachhaltigkeit.pdf accessed 18 August 2023.

We next turn to concrete policy options, exploring how competition deals with issues of sustainability at present and what is conceivable in the future. These options are presented in Part II (and in a short version in the Annex to this study). We sorted them according to the fields of competition law: its scope of application, the prohibition of restrictive business agreements (cartels), exemptions, abuse of dominance (monopolisation), merger control, and procedure and sanctions.

Of course, we also answer some of the 'issues' that often come up in discussions (Part III):

- What is meant by the term sustainability? (Chapter 10)
- Which test criteria seem reasonable to legitimise interventions in competition? (Chapter 11)
- How can the achievement of sustainability goals be measured or quantified? (Chapter 12)
- How do we resolve the problem of legitimacy for certain government actors? (Chapter 13)
- How do we deal with the danger of 'greenwashing'? (Chapter 14)

This study thus provides a comprehensive overview of the discussion on competition economics, concrete reform options in the entire field of competition law, and difficult problem areas that arise when competition law and sustainability goals are more closely intertwined.

Interim results of this report were discussed with a sounding board consisting of representatives from public authorities, companies, research institutes, associations and law firms. We also received some comments from staff members of the German Ministry for Economic Affairs and Climate Action who funded this study, but who gave us all the freedom we needed and claimed as independent researchers. We thank all these people for their suggestions and comments – even if not all of them could be taken into account. The work on this book would not have been completed without the dedicated help of the student team at Heinrich Heine University Düsseldorf.

STATE OF THE DEBATE

The consideration of sustainability aspects in the application of competition law has become a highly debated topic in competition policy.

Initiatives on the National Level

Let us take a look at a selection of initiatives in different states:[7]

- The Austrian legislator clarified in the Cartel and Competition Law Amendment Act 2021 that a fair share for consumers can also lie in the fact that the profit generated by an agreement 'contributes significantly to an ecologically sustainable or climate-neutral economy' (Section 2(1) sentence 2 Cartel Act 2005).[8]
- The Netherlands Competition Authority has submitted a proposal in the form of guidelines on sustainability agreements which, in the opinion of the authority, can also serve as a model for a European initiative to give companies further scope for action.[9]
- In Greece, the Hellenic Competition Commission has proposed a so-called 'Sustainability Sandbox' to allow companies to develop initiatives in a protected manner.[10]
- The French Autorité de la concurrence made 'Développement durable' cases a priority in 2021.[11]
- The Nordic competition authorities published a working paper on 'Competition Policy and Green Growth' in 2010.[12]
- The British CMA has published a guidance paper.[13]

---

[7] Cf Simon Holmes, 'Sustainability and Competition Policy in Europe: Recent Developments' (2023) JECLAP Survey, 1; Jurgita Malinauskaite, 'Competition Law and Sustainability: EU and National Perspectives' (2022) 13 JECLAP 343.

[8] Austrian Federal Competition Act, as amended effective 10 September 2021, Federal Law Gazette I No 176/2021. See, in more detail, Chapter 6.

[9] Autoriteit Consument & Markt, 'Second draft version: Guidelines on Sustainability Agreements – Opportunities within competition law' (26 January 2021) www.acm.nl/en/publications/second-draft-version-guidelines-sustainability-agreements -opportunities -within -competition -law accessed 22 June 2023. See, in more detail, Chapter 6.

[10] Hellenic Competition Commission, 'Sustainability Sandbox' (July 2021) www .epant.gr/en/enimerosi/sandbox.html accessed 22 June 2023. See, in more detail, Chapter 6.

[11] Autorité de la Concurrence, 'After a very active 2020, the Autorité de la concurrence announces its priorities for 2021, which will focus on the digital economy' (23 December 2020) www.autoritedelaconcurrence.fr/en/communiques-de-presse/after-very -active-2020-autorite-de-la-concurrence-announces-its-priorities accessed 22 June 2023.

[12] Martti Virtanen et al, 'Competition Policy and Green Growth' (2010) Report from the Nordic Competition Authorities 1/2010 https://en.samkeppni.is/media/skyrslur -2010/competition_policy_and_green_growth_final_version.pdf accessed 22 June 2023.

[13] Competition & Markets Authority, 'Environmental sustainability agreements and competition law' (27 January 2021) www .gov .uk/ government/ publications/

- The German Federal Cartel Office dedicated the 2020 meeting of its competition law working group to the issue.[14] In recent years, the authority has also dealt several times in case practice with joint initiatives which serve the realisation of sustainability objectives.[15] As part of the amendment to the Act against Restraints of Competition in Germany, one parliamentary group proposed including climate protection as a purpose in the competition act – the party behind this is now in government.[16]

Initiatives on the EU Level

The topic is also high on the agenda at the EU level: Executive Vice-President Margrethe Vestager gave the starting signal for a debate that ties in with the European Green Deal, with a conference on 'Competition Policy Contributing to the European Green Deal' on 4 February 2021.[17] Over 200 submissions were made as part of the debate.[18] For the agricultural sector, a provision was adopted in December 2021 with Article 210a CMO, which excludes supra-legal sustainability standards in the food supply chain from the scope of the ban on restrictive business agreements under Article 101 TFEU.[19] In July 2023 the Commission published a revised version of its guidelines on the applicability of Article 101 TFEU to horizontal co-operation agreements – including a controversial chapter on sustainability initiatives.[20]

---

environmental -sustainability -agreements -and -competition -law/ sustainability -agreements-and-competition-law accessed 22 June 2023.

[14]   Bundeskartellamt, 'Open markets and sustainable economies – public interest objectives as a challenge for competition law' (25 November 2020) www.bundeskartellamt.de/ SharedDocs/Publikation/EN/Diskussions_Hintergrundpapiere/2020/Working_Group_on _Competition_Law_2020.html;jsessionid=64966C0F895A80866845252AA887FDE0.2 _cid378?nn=3590872 accessed 22 June 2023.

[15]   See, in more detail, Chapter 6.

[16]   Materials of the German Bundestag, 'Antrag Verbraucherschutz und fairen Wettbewerb stärken' (BT-Drucks. 19/23705, 27 October 2020).

[17]   Programme and recordings available at https://ec.europa.eu/competition-policy/ green-gazette/conference-2021_en accessed 22 June 2023.

[18]   A collection of the submissions is available at https://ec.europa.eu/competition/ information/ green _deal/ contributions .zip accessed 22 June 2023, cf Jurgita Malinauskaite, 'Competition Law and Sustainability: EU and National Perspectives' (2022) 13 JECLAP 341.

[19]   See, in more detail, Chapter 4.

[20]   European Commission, 'Guidelines on the applicability of Article 101 of the Treaty on the Functioning of the European Union to horizontal co-operation agreements' [2023] OJ C 259/1. See, in more detail, Chapter 6.

The European Commission summarised the challenges, its main conclusions, and possible demands as follows:[21] there are three transformative challenges, namely to achieve environmental sustainability (with a focus on climate neutrality), a green growth (a clear distancing from a degrowth-approach), and a fair and just transition (pointing to the social problems). Three findings from the consultation process stood out for the Commission: competition has a complementary role and can do more; competition and enforcement are part of a smart industrial policy that aims at innovation and a level playing field; the approach must be gradual, taking into account the very different landscape in the EU. The Commission also identified what stakeholders thought of when looking into the more specific instruments:

'State aid: Favouring funding of non-fossil fuels; simplifying the rulebook; enhancing possibilities to support innovation.
Antitrust: Clarifying whether and how to assess sustainability benefits; improving guidance and open door policy.
Mergers: Strengthening enforcement concerning possible harm to innovation, including 'green "killer acquisitions". Reflecting sustainability aspects/features prevailing in the markets and consumer preferences for these.'[22]

In sum, sustainability is defined as a transformative challenge that should go hand in hand with 'green growth' in terms of industrial policy and a fair distribution of costs and benefits in terms of social policy. The Commission will hold on to a competition-driven market framework. It wants to clarify the eligibility of sustainability gains and examine mergers and acquisitions more strictly when green innovation is targeted. In addition, sustainability aspects are to be better taken into account in markets and consumer preferences.[23]

Beyond the European Union, the topic is also discussed internationally – in fora like the OECD. The OECD has put the topic on the agenda with a round table in its Competition Committee.[24]

---

[21]   DG Competition, Competition Policy Brief 1/2021: Policy in Support of Europe's Green Ambition, p. 3.
[22]   DG Competition, Competition Policy Brief 1/2021: Policy in Support of Europe's Green Ambition, p. 3.
[23]   The field of state aid is not part of this study.
[24]   See OECD, 'Sustainability and competition' www .oecd .org/ daf/ competition/ sustainability -and -competition .htm accessed 22 June 2023; see also OECD, 'Sustainability and Competition, OECD Competition Committee Discussion Paper' (2020) www .oecd .org/ daf/ competition/ sustainability -and -competition -2020 .pdf accessed 22 June 2023.

State of Research

The further development is intensively discussed in the literature on competition economics and competition law. In particular, debates on the objectives of competition law are being taken up. The relationship between public welfare objectives and competition protection has regularly been a subject of debate. The focus on issues of (especially ecological) sustainability in competition law is a more recent phenomenon. It follows in real time the more intensive societal discussions on combating climate change. In this respect, the antitrust discussion is a kind of 'antitrust for the future'.

As particularly frequently cited elaborations the texts of *Monti*,[25] *Quellmalz*,[26] *Roth*,[27] *Townley*,[28] *Kingston*,[29] and *Monti/Mulder*[30] have to be mentioned. In addition, there are many other contributions to the discussion.[31] In 2015, the influential German Monopolies Commission dedicated an anthology to the

---

[25] Giorgio Monti, 'Article 81 EC and Public Policy' (2002) 39 CML Rev 1057.

[26] Jens Holger Quellmalz, 'Die Justiziabilität des Art. 81 Abs. 3 EG und die nicht-wettbewerblichen Ziele des EG-Vertrages' (2004) Wettbewerb in Recht und Praxis 461.

[27] Wolf-Henning Roth, 'Zur Berücksichtigung nichtwettbewerblicher Ziele im europäischen Kartellrecht – eine Skizze' in Christoph Engel and Wernhard Möschel (eds), *Recht und spontane Ordnung: Festschrift für Ernst-Joachim Mestmäcker zum achtzigsten Geburtstag* (Nomos 2006).

[28] Christopher Townley, *Article 81 EC and Public Policy* (Hart Publishing 2009).

[29] Suzanne Kingston, 'Integrating Environmental Protection and EU Competition Law: Why Competition Isn't Special' (2010) 16 *European Law Journal* 780; Suzanne Kingston, *Greening EU Competition Law and Policy* (Cambridge University Press 2011).

[30] Giorgio Monti and Jotte Mulder, 'Escaping the Clutches of EU Competition Law' (2017) 42 EL Rev 635.

[31] By way of example only, Okeoghene Odudu, 'The Wider Concerns of Competition Law' (2010) 30 OJLS 599; José Carlos de Paz, 'Protecting the Environment Without Distorting Competition' (2012) 3 JECLAP 248; Christopher Townley, 'Is There (Still) Room for Non-Economic Arguments in Article 101 TFEU Cases?' (*SSRN*, 17 October 2012) https://papers.ssrn.com/sol3/papers.cfm?abstract_id=2162864 accessed 22 June 2023; Julian Nowag and Alexandra Teorell, 'Beyond Balancing: Sustainability and Competition' (2020) 4 Concurrences – On-Topic 34; Thomas Lübbig, 'Sustainable Development and Competition Policy' (2013) 4 JECLAP 1; Ioannis Lianos, 'Polycentric Competiton Law' (2018) 71 CLP 161. Also cf the helpful antitrust reading list provided by the Sabin Center on Climate Change Law and the Columbia Center on Sustainable Investment, available at https://blogs.law.columbia.edu/climatechange/2023/07/11/antitrust-reading-list-competitor-collaborations-and-sustainability/ accessed 18 August 2023. The institutions published the report by Denise Hearn, Cynthia Hanawalt, and Lisa Sachs, 'Antitrust and Sustainability: A Landscape Analysis' (*Columbia Center on Sustainable Investment*, 2023) https://ccsi.columbia.edu/content/antitrust-and-sustainability-landscape-analysis accessed 18 August 2023.

topic of non-competition goals.[32] For the German-speaking area, the background paper of the German national competition agency (Bundeskartellamt), in 2020 excellently summarised the discussion at the time.[33] The OECD has done something similar at the international level.[34] In addition to more academic elaborations, there were a large number of conferences and postings that have significantly driven the political debate.

For a long time, the debate focused primarily on the question of whether sustainability cooperations could be exempted from the prohibition of Article 101(1) TFEU. Only a few contributions shed light on other aspects of competition law.[35] In their work, *Breuer* and *Müller* have comprehensively discussed the tension between protection of competition and other Union objectives.[36]

In the past, sustainability issues have largely been treated separately from competition economics. However, the contributions of environmental economics go back a long way. The main focus has been on measuring the impact

---

[32] See therein Daniel Zimmer, 'Begrüßung und Einführung: Wettbewerb und Politik – eine Einführung in das Thema' in Monopolies Commission (ed), *Politischer Einfluss auf Wettbewerbsentscheidungen* (Nomos 2015); Wolfgang Kirchhoff, 'Außerwettbewerbliche Aspekte bei Entscheidungen nach Art. 101 AEUV, insbesondere im Licht der Querschnittsklauseln des AEUV' in Monopolies Commission (ed), *Politischer Einfluss auf Wettbewerbsentscheidungen* (Nomos 2015); Juliane Kokott and Daniel Dittert, 'Die Pflicht zur Berücksichtigung außerwettbewerblicher Belange im Rahmen von Art. 101 AEUV und ihre praktische Umsetzung' in Monopolies Commission (ed), *Politischer Einfluss auf Wettbewerbsentscheidungen* (Nomos 2015); Heike Schweitzer, 'Die Bedeutung nicht-wettbewerblicher Aspekte für die Auslegung von Art. 101 AEUV im Lichte der Querschnittsklauseln' in Monopolies Commission (ed), *Politischer Einfluss auf Wettbewerbsentscheidungen* (Nomos 2015).
[33] Bundeskartellamt, 'Offene Märkte und nachhaltiges Wirtschaften – Gemeinwohlziele als Herausforderung für die Kartellrechtspraxis' (1 October 2020) www .bundeskartellamt .de/ SharedDocs/ Publikation/ DE/ Diskussions _Hintergrundpapier/AK_Kartellrecht_2020_Hintergrundpapier.html accessed 23 June 2023.
[34] OECD, 'Environmental Considerations in Competition Enforcement: Background Paper by the Secretariat' DAF/COMP(2021)4 (1 December 2021).
[35] See on the prohibition of abuse: Marios C Iacovides and Christos Vrettos, 'Falling through the Cracks No More? Article 102 TFEU and Sustainability' (2022) 10 *Journal of Antitrust Enforcement* 32; on merger control see: Jonas Zenger, 'Public Interest Considerations in Merger Control: The Case of Biodiversity' (2018) 39 ECLR 336; Tilman Kuhn and Cristina Caroppo, 'Sustainability in Merger Control – Time to Broaden the Discussion' (2020) 41 ECLR 596.
[36] Ludger Breuer, *Das EU-Kartellrecht im Kraftfeld der Unionsziele* (Nomos 2012); Thomas Müller, *Wettbewerb und Unionsverfassung* (Mohr Siebeck 2014).

and effects of externalities.[37] In addition – and also awarded the 2018 Alfred Nobel Memorial Prize in Economics – there are various models for measuring climate damage, for example by *William Nordhaus*.[38]

As a rule, economists assume that in the case of, e.g., environmental concerns a market failure can easily result. This literature is widespread and started more than a century ago with *Arthur Cecil Pigou*.[39] In contrast, the focus on the specific relationship between competition and sustainability is still in its infancy. However, there are initial expressions of literature related to various aspects that are closely related to sustainability. The competition economics literature on possible collusion with respect to sustainability aspects has developed considerably in recent years. For example, *Myles/Hashimzade*,[40] *Schinkel/Spiegel*,[41] *Schinkel/Toth*[42] and *Inderst/Sartzetakis*[43] in particular examine the topic intensively. In addition, *Inderst/Thomas*,[44] *Inderst/Rhiel/Thomas*[45] and *Inderst*[46] provide new evidence not only on the measurement of willingness to pay (WTP), but also on the measurement of consumer benefits that can arise

---

[37]   Richard Schmalensee, *Measuring external effects of solid waste management* (US Environmental Protection Agency 1975).

[38]   William Nordhaus, 'A Review of the Stern Review on the Economics of Climate Change' (2007) 45 *Journal of Economic Literature* 686; see also Gunnar Luderer et al, 'Economic Mitigation Challenges: How Further Delay Closes the Door for Achieving Climate Targets' (2013) 8 (3) *Environmental Research Letters*.

[39]   Arthur Cecil Pigou, 'The Economics of Welfare' (1920). Also see Francis Michel Bator, 'The Anatomy of Market Failure' (1958) 72 *The Quarterly Journal of Economics* 351.

[40]   Nigar Hashimzade and Gareth D Myles, 'Do Corporate Environmental Contributions Justify the Public Interest Defence?' (2017) CESifo Working Paper Series No 6755 www.cesifo.org/en/publications/2017/working-paper/do-corporate-environmental-contributions-justify-public-interest accessed 18 August 2023.

[41]   Maarten Pieter Schinkel and Yossi Spiegel, 'Can Collusion Promote Sustainable Consumption and Production?' (2017) 53 *International Journal of Industrial Organization* 371.

[42]   Maarten Pieter Schinkel and Lukas Toth, 'Balancing the Public Interest-defence in Cartel Offenses' (2016) Amsterdam Center for Law & Economics Working Paper 2016-01 www.bruegel.org/sites/default/files/wp-content/uploads/2016/02/SSRN-id2723780.pdf accessed 23 June 2023.

[43]   Roman Inderst, Eftichios S Sartzetakis and Anastasios Xepapadeas, 'Firm Competition and Cooperation with Norm-Based Preferences for Sustainability' (Working & Discussion Papers, 2022) EconStor http://hdl.handle.net/10419/254323 accessed 23 June 2023.

[44]   Roman Inderst and Stefan Thomas, 'Integrating Benefits from Sustainability into the Competitive Assessment – How Can We Measure Them?' (2021) 12 JECLAP 705.

[45]   Roman Inderst, Felix Rhiel and Stefan Thomas, 'Sustainability Agreements and Social Norms' (2022) ZWeR 225.

[46]   Roman Inderst and Stefan Thomas, 'Integrating Benefits from Sustainability into the Competitive Assessment – How Can We Measure Them?' (2021) 12 JECLAP 705.

from sustainability aspects. These issues are very helpful for considering how sustainability aspects can be integrated into competition law.

Recently, numerous other contributions have appeared, also on more specific issues. Here, we can only refer to individual contributions by way of example.[47] Critical voices that largely reject adjustments in the application of competition law should also not be disregarded.[48]

---

[47] Anna Gerbrandy, Willem Janssen and Lyndsey Thomsin, 'Shaping the Social Market Economy After the Lisbon Treaty: How "Social" is the Public Economic Law?' (2019) 15 (2) *Utrecht Law Review* 32; Edith Loozen, 'Strict competition enforcement and welfare: A constitutional perspective based on Article 101 TFEU and sustainability' (2019) 56 CML Rev 1256; Onno W Brouwer, 'Sustainability and Competition Law: Living Apart Together' in Tobias Klose, Martin Klusmann and Stefan Thomas (eds), *Das Unternehmen in der Wettbewerbsordnung: Festschrift für Gerhard Wiedemann zum 70. Geburtstag* (C.H.Beck 2020); Jordan Ellison, 'A Fair Share: Time for the Carbon Defence?' (*SSRN*, 2020) https://ssrn.com/abstract=3542186 accessed 23 June 2023; Simon Holmes, 'Climate Change, Sustainability, and Competition Law' (2020) 8 *Journal of Antitrust Enforcement* 354; Roman Inderst and Stefan Thomas, 'Reflective Willingness to Pay: Preferences for Sustainable Consumption in a Consumer Welfare Analysis' (2021) 17 (4) JCLE 1; Eva van der Zee, 'Quantifying Benefits of Sustainability Agreements Under Article 101 TFEU' (2020) 43 (2) *World Competition* 189; Maurits Dolmans, 'Article 101(3) TFEU: the Roadmap for Sustainable Cooperation' in Simon Holmes, Dirk Middelschulte and Martijn Snoep (eds), *Competition Law, Climate Change & Environmental Sustainability* (Concurrences 2021).

[48] Cf Maarten Pieter Schinkel and Yossi Spiegel, 'Can Collusion Promote Sustainable Consumption and Production?' (2017) *International Journal of Industrial Organization* 371; Cento Veljanovskim, 'The Case Against Green Antitrust' (*SSRN*, 2021) https://ssrn.com/abstract=3955340 accessed 23 June 2023.

2. Economic justification of further developments in competition law

The question to be addressed is, on which economic basis can competition law be extended and/or restricted? This analysis delves into situations where conflicts between competition law and sustainability arise, specifically, the question of whether and under what conditions competition law should be restricted (I.). In the case where competition and sustainability align, the question arises under which conditions it is justified to utilise competition law to advance sustainability goals or to relax antitrust enforcement in order to facilitate the pursuit of sustainability goals (II.).

COMPETITION LAW AS AN OBSTACLE TO SUSTAINABLE CONDUCT

Competition law essentially serves to protect competition, thereby upholding individual freedom of choice and action.

Competition, Consumption and Use of Resources

Hence, from the outset, competition law may, to a certain extent, lead to tension with some sustainability goals. The underlying rationale is as follows: in general, reduced competition often leads to higher prices, subsequently reducing demand, and consequently decreasing production and thus lower resource consumption.[1] In monopoly and oligopoly situations, supply is regularly artificially reduced to achieve the highest possible prices. To the extent that competition law protects competition, it prevents this artificial shortage, thus indirectly fostering an expansion of supply.[2] If consumption and the associated utilisation of resources are considered as a sustainability problem, the direct impact of competition can be seen as quasi-detrimental to sustainability.

---

[1]   Cf Jean Tirole, *The Theory of Industrial Organization* (The MIT Press 1988).
[2]   Cf Massimo Motta, *Competition Policy: Theory and Practice* (Cambridge University Press 2004).

Nobel laureate in economics, *Robert Solow*, expressed this nearly 50 years ago as follows:

> The amusing thing is that if a conservationist is someone who would like to see resources conserved beyond the pace that competition would adopt, then the monopolist is the conservationist's friend.[3]

However, it should also be noted that companies operating without competitive pressure often tend to adopt inefficient production methods that result in a waste of resources (the so-called X-inefficiency).[4] Furthermore, companies in non-competitive markets generally exhibit lower levels of innovation compared to their competition-driven counterparts.[5] As innovation plays a pivotal role in achieving sustainability goals, increased monopoly and cartel formation conflicts with sustainability goals.[6]

Companies with market power frequently tend to leverage this power into procurement markets as well, aiming to obtain better conditions from suppliers. In this way, buyer power can have a negative impact on suppliers' incentives to innovate.[7] Considering that sustainability also affects a fair balance between suppliers and consumers, the increased formation of monopolies and oligopolies on markets, which competition law is currently trying to prevent, is likely counterproductive.

The question also arises as to whether facilitating increased market concentration and cartelisation through a more generous interpretation of competition law vis-à-vis companies (resulting in higher prices for consumers and less favourable conditions for suppliers) can be deemed socially acceptable and align with the broader concept of sustainability. If the promotion of market concentration and cartelisation is indeed a political aim, the present stance of competition law may indeed present an obstacle.

---

[3]   Robert M Solow, 'The Economics of Resources or the Resources of Economics' in Chennat Gopalakrishnan (ed), *Classic Papers in Natural Resource Economics* (Palgrave Macmillian 2000).

[4]   Harvey Leibenstein, 'Allocative Efficiency vs. "X-Efficiency"' (1966) 113 (8) AER 392.

[5]   Cf Philippe Aghion, Christopher Harris and John Vickers, 'Competition and Growth with Step-by-step Innovation: An Example' (1997) *European Economic Review* 467.

[6]   See Giulio Federico, Fiona Scott Morton and Carl Shapiro, 'Antitrust and Innovation: Welcoming and Protecting Disruption' (2020) 20 *Innovation Policy and the Economy* 125.

[7]   European Commission, *Buyer power and its impact on competition in the food retail distribution sector of the European Union – Final Report* (EU Publications 1999) 160.

Competition, the Common Good and Sustainability

However, the notion that competition should be universally restricted with the aim of compelling individuals to reduce consumption through market monopolisation and consequent price escalation, is likely extreme. In principle, competition is considered a framework worth protecting in the social market economy as it endows market participants with greater choices, thereby opening avenues for improved exchange and reduced market dependencies. Nevertheless, competition is not welfare-promoting per se. Instances where competition occurs at the expense of uninvolved third parties (e.g., due to externalities)[8] or exploits one party unknowingly taken (e.g., in the case of information asymmetries),[9] there will be a need for regular market interventions. In actual markets, unregulated competition is a rarity; competition always operates within the legal framework applicable to a given market. Competition always takes place within the legal framework applicable to a market. This includes the general legal framework, such as the German Civil Code (BGB), competition law, and labour law, and also special regulations for particular industries (such as the Energy Industry Act, the Telecommunications Act, hygiene regulations for food processing, special rules for financial markets and the banking industry, etc.). These regulations generally aim not to eliminate competition entirely but rather to channel it and steer it so that competition serves the common good.[10]

From an economic perspective, corrective measures become particularly important when there is a threat of market failure in the absence of certain rules. In contrast to common usage, the concept of market failure in economics is rather broad. In economic terminology, market failure not only denotes a complete market collapse but also encompasses situations where market outcomes fail to optimise for the common good.[11] Efficient market outcomes, as understood in economics, align with outcomes that maximise the collective welfare. In other words, a market outcome is said to be inefficient when it falls short of maximising the common good – a phenomenon referred to as market failure in economic theory.

A range of instruments is available for addressing such market failures. These tools range from taxes and subsidies to concrete rules or the regulation

---

[8] Cf Jean-Jacques Laffont, 'Externalities' in John Eatwell, Murray Milgate and Peter Newman (eds), *Allocation, Information and Markets* (Palgrave Macmillan 1989).

[9] Cf George A Akerlof, 'The Market for "Lemons": Quality Uncertainty and the Market Mechanism' (1970) *The Quarterly Journal of Economics* 488.

[10] Cf Massimo Motta, *Competition Policy: Theory and Practice* (Cambridge University Press 2004).

[11] Cf Francis M Bator, 'The Anatomy of Market Failure' (1958) *The Quarterly Journal of Economics* 351.

of products and production processes as well as information obligations and transparency requirements to bans (cf Part III.B.III.).

From an economic perspective, competition law, along with its instruments, can be perceived as a mechanism to prevent market failures stemming from competition deficits. This is based on the view that competition fundamentally promotes the common good, while monopolies and cartels undermine it.[12] Other forms of market failure, rooted in externalities or on information asymmetries on the demand side, are typically addressed by distinct legal provisions, such as environmental or consumer protection regulations.

Yet, the question arises as to whether circumstances exist so that competition law impedes the socially desirable attainment of sustainability goals, and whether instances arise in which sustainability goals can be more effectively realised through antitrust instruments compared to alternative market interventions available to policymakers.

Regarding government interventions in the market that potentially distort competition, EU State aid law provides a legal framework wherein potential distortions of competition are weighed against the pursuit of other public welfare objectives. The extent to which improvements can be made to various EU State aid directives for the enhanced realisation of sustainability goals is not the subject of this report, however, as we focus on private constraints of competition (i.e., agreements between companies, abuse of dominant positions, and mergers).

Unilateral Behaviour

From an antitrust perspective, nothing prevents companies from making unilateral efforts to operate more sustainably. If a company anticipates gaining a competitive advantage by transitioning towards more sustainability-oriented products or operational methods, competition promotes sustainability. If a company seeks to embrace greater sustainability for (supposedly) altruistic reasons, there are likewise no direct antitrust impediments to implement such initiatives.[13]

---

[12] Cf Massimo Motta, *Competition Policy: Theory and Practice* (Cambridge University Press 2004) 39 ff.

[13] In large parts of economics, it is doubted in principle that companies take sustainability measures that go beyond legislative requirements, if this action is not expected to bring at least certain advantages in product markets, labour markets or capital markets, at least in the long term. For this position, see for example Maarten Pieter Schinkel and Yossi Spiegel, 'Can Collusion Promote Sustainable Consumption and Production?' (2017) *International Journal of Industrial Organization* 371.

Even if adherence to sustainability standards does not lead to immediate rewards in the product market, such (possibly higher) standards do not inherently entail a competitive disadvantage. This may hold true, for instance, when they result in cost savings (e.g., in the use of energy-efficient processes), contribute to risk mitigation (e.g., upholding social standards in global value chains), increase a firm's attractiveness for employees in the labour market or offer benefits in capital markets (e.g., attracting demand from sustainability-conscious investors or securing lower insurance premiums for companies equipped with environmental management systems). However, if this is not the case, higher sustainability standards can lead to competitive disadvantages.

Unilateral actions by companies may face competition law constraints, particularly if a company holds a dominant market position and is subject to rules governing the abuse of market power. In specific cases, it is conceivable that conduct aimed at promoting sustainability could be classified as abusive under competition law. For instance, this could be the case if a dominant company discriminates against customers or denies access to certain facilities. While such discrimination and access denial could be deemed anticompetitive, they might align with sustainability goals.

Cooperation Between Companies

With regard to cooperation between companies, constellations must be identified in which antitrust regulations prevent private actions in markets that serve sustainability and are at the same time socially desirable. In these cases, consideration should be given to reducing the regulatory intervention under competition law or expanding the concept of efficiency defence. Collaborative efforts among companies geared towards sustainability may conflict with the prohibition of cartels. If this collaboration is contractually implemented under company law, it could potentially qualify as a merger subject to merger control.

Companies may have an incentive to cooperate with competitors to eliminate the risks resulting from competitive actions. Improvements in sustainability are sometimes accompanied by higher costs and subsequently decreasing sales if the market counterpart does not reward sustainability efforts. A 'first-mover disadvantage'[14] can emerge: the first company opting for more resource-efficient and environmentally friendly production may inadvertently place itself at a disadvantage in comparison to competitors adhering to lower-cost, environmentally damaging production practices. To prevent

---

[14]   William Boulding and Markus Christen, 'First-mover Disadvantage' (2001) *Harvard Business Review* 20 f.

disadvantages vis-à-vis competitors, there is a clear interest in reaching agreements with competitors to establish a unified approach to sustainability.[15] Such cooperation also mitigates the risk of being overtaken by competitors who achieve a sustainability-driven competitive edge that could sway the market. Thus, cooperation can function as an insurance policy against greater sustainability by eliminating competition in this dimension.[16]

These motivations for cooperation may not always be evident – they represent classic risk-mitigation strategies that unfairly restrict competition. It is important to distinguish them, in specific cases, from three motivations that are generally recognisable.

Exceeding legal requirements

Companies may consider cooperation when statutory regulations specify a 'sustainability level' that is perceived as insufficient, such as when government targets for reducing greenhouse gases fall short of internationally binding standards. Private objectives, exceeding governmental regulations, *can* serve as a corrective measure for this 'regulatory failure' or 'policy failure'. This approach aligns well with companies' role as the targets of sustainability goals. Pursuing sustainability goals can be directly consistent with profit-making, such as when sustainable production becomes a competitive factor. Moreover, access to the capital market has emerged as a tool for advancing sustainability goals ('sustainable finance', ESG). In certain instances, companies also pursue sustainability objectives without a direct impact on profits – whether driven by motives of personnel recruitment, long-term considerations, or a sense of corporate responsibility towards the common good.

Reaching a critical mass of customers

It is also conceivable that diverse customers may desire distinct sustainable products, for example, regarding livestock farming or production methods. However, laws typically establish only minimum requisites and, where applicable, mandate information disclosure. A challenge can arise if attaining higher sustainability levels than those legislated demands garnering a critical mass of customers (e.g., due to economies of scale), an objective that an individual company alone cannot achieve, and considerable irreversible investments are necessary to achieve the goals. In these cases, at least superficially, cooperation between companies may seem to make sense.

---

[15]   Cf Johannes Paha, 'Sustainability Agreements and First Mover Disadvantages' [2023] *Journal of Competition Law & Economics* 1, 3.

[16]   Jorge Alé-Chilet et al, 'Colluding Against Environmental Regulation' (2022) CEEPR Working Paper.

The example mostly cited in this context is a scenario where investing in or enforcing more environmentally friendly packaging system (e.g., reusable or other recyclable packaging and packaging materials) is not economically viable for a single company.[17] Rather, implementing such systems may require the collective commitment of multiple companies and other stakeholders. Even if a subset of consumers values environmentally friendly packaging, this alone might not suffice as a market incentive to establish the infrastructure for circular packaging or packaging systems. This could serve as an example where cooperative efforts between companies prove to be efficient.[18]

In other cases, systems that are inherently complex, as in the example of closed-loop packaging systems, lead to the failure of sustainability efforts by individual stakeholders. Occasionally, joint initiatives involving diverse stakeholder groups emerge then. The development process of the ISO 26000 guideline offers a case in point, involving over 500 experts from varied stakeholder groups (including, e.g., non-governmental organisations, companies, government agencies). In this standard, the expert panel, under the leadership of the International Organisation for Standardisation, developed non-binding guidelines for organisational responsibility.[19] At the national level, the Circular Economy Initiative Germany drafted recommendations for a comprehensive circular economy in working groups featuring a range of stakeholders.[20]

BOX 2.1   COOPERATION IN THE CIRCULAR ECONOMY

A circular economy is a production and consumption model that aims to use existing materials and products for as long as possible by extending the life cycle of products. In doing so, the model targets global challenges such as

---

[17]   Circular Economy Initiative Deutschland (ed), 'Plastics Packaging in a Closed Loop' (2021) www.circular-economy-initiative.de/plastics-packaging-in-a-closed-loop -potentials-conditions-challenges accessed 26 June 2023.

[18]   However, it should be noted that, particularly in the area of the circular economy, the German Federal Cartel Office has in the past repeatedly permitted cooperation between companies within the existing antitrust framework. In addition, Article 210a of the CMO Regulation already allows exemptions from competition law precisely for the promotion of the circular economy.

[19]   Rüdiger Hahn and Christian Weidtmann, 'Transnational Governance, Deliberative Democracy, and the Legitimacy of ISO 26000: Analyzing the Case of a Global Multistakeholder Process' (2016) *Business & Society* 90.

[20]   Circular Economy Initiative Deutschland (ed), 'Plastics Packaging in a Closed Loop' (2021) www.circular-economy-initiative.de/plastics-packaging-in-a-closed-loop -potentials-conditions-challenges accessed 26 June 2023.

climate change, biodiversity loss, waste and pollution. The challenges are to be overcome by sharing, lending, reusing, repairing, refurbishing, and recycling products. Ideally, the raw materials originally used are reused for new production after the product has been used or consumed.

The European Commission published 'A new Circular Economy Action Plan – For a cleaner and more competitive Europe' in 2020 (COM(2020) 98 final)). The aim is to promote a longer life cycle for products (with less obsolescence) and a circularity for the materials used so that waste is reduced and raw materials are preserved. Companies are increasingly required to design products for a circular use. Initiatives in this regard are the EU Ecodesign Regulation and the EU Right to Repair Directive. (At the time of finalising this manuscript, both legal acts were still in the draft stage.)

The Circular Economy is a major shift for many business models that are based on quick consumption and ignorance towards the waste generated. It also presents chances for new markets. From a competition perspective it will be essential to keep these markets open. That is also true for after-markets, e.g. for spare parts and repair services, that may become more important in times of repair and reuse. Original manufacturers may try to monopolise such secondary markets. This has been a topic for competition law enforcement for decades, but the phenomena may gain new ground and may become more important for businesses. Monopolisation may become easier with the use of data in many products since such data enable predictive maintenance (so that the company analysing the data can control who offers maintenance services) and require access to data which may again be controlled and only offered against a licence fee. For this problem, the EU Data Act may provide some competition-friendly solutions at the outset. It is also important to put competition safeguards into legal acts such as the Ecodesign Regulation or the Right to Repair Directive. Apart from that the provisions on abuse of dominance will remain crucial.

Change of preferences

In addition to the two reasons mentioned above, the literature discusses the possibility that social norms for the consumption of sustainable products develop (too) slowly and that these norms depend on how many other consumers also consume these sustainable products.[21] In other words, individual

---

[21] Roman Inderst, Felix Rhiel and Stefan Thomas, 'Sustainability Agreements and Social Norms' (*SSRN*, 2021) https://papers.ssrn.com/sol3/papers.cfm?abstract _id = 3887314 accessed 26 June 2023; Roman Inderst, Eftichios S Sartzetakis and Anastasios Xepapadeas, 'Competition and Co-Operation When Consumers' Sustainability Preferences Depend on Social Norms' (2021) www.wiwi.uni-frankfurt

preference and willingness to pay for sustainable products depends on whether a sufficient number of other consumers act in the same way and consume sustainably. Comprehensive sustainability standards are usually only consciously demanded by a few customers. Often, for example, there exists an 'intention-behaviour gap' among consumers,[22] whereby a positive attitude toward sustainability fails to translate into corresponding actions, such as actual purchasing decisions.

The introduction of a sustainable product by a single company might prove insufficient to induce a shift in buyer preferences. Therefore, at least in theory, a cooperative arrangement among companies could potentially be advantageous. However, this 'efficiency defence' presents a significant risk – cooperative agreements might be allowed based on the anticipation of a preference change that is not observable ex ante but is only hoped for. Whether such a shift in preferences will occur is challenging to predict with sufficient certainty in advance. This uncertainty poses substantial challenges for antitrust authorities should they need to assess predictions regarding possible preference changes. Instead, there is a risk that an alleged, hoped-for shift in preferences could serve as an unverifiable rationale for nearly any cartel formation.

Self-regulation

In various industries, codes of conduct are being introduced (e.g., at association level or on the initiative of individual companies) to commit the respective member companies to uniform minimum standards.[23] Voluntary commitments allow companies to act jointly in the interest of sustainability goals. The establishment of standards, for example, within the framework of industry associations, is ambivalent in terms of competition economics.[24]

.de/fileadmin/user_upload/dateien_abteilungen/abt_fin/Dokumente/PDFs/Allgemeine _Dokumente/ Inderst_Downloads/ Neuere _Arbeiten _seit2015/ Competition _and _Co -Operation_when_Consumers_Sustainability_Preferences_Depend_on_Social_Norms .pdf accessed 26 June 2023.

[22]   Pat Auger and Tomothy M Devinney, 'Do What Consumers Say Matter? The Misalignment of Preferences with Unconstrained Ethical Intentions' (2007) *Journal of Business Ethics* 361; Hyun Jung Park and Li Min Lin, 'Exploring Attitude-behaviour Gap in Sustainable Consumption: Comparison of Recycled and Upcycled Fashion Products' (2020) *Journal of Business Research* 623.

[23]   See also Shanti Gamper-Rabindran and Stephen R Finger, 'Does Industry Self-regulation Reduce Pollution? Responsible Care in the Chemical Industry' (2013) *Journal of Regulatory Economics* 1.

[24]   Cf Richard Gilbert, 'Competition Policy for Industry Standards' in Roger D Blair and Daniel Sokol (eds), *The Oxford Handbook of International Antitrust Economics* (Vol. 2, Oxford University Press 2015). For antitrust treatment, see, for example,

Various other aspects of sustainability management, including sustainability-related management systems and corresponding certified standards (e.g., for environmental, social, or occupational safety management systems) or consumer-focused labels, attempt to promote sustainability standards by addressing information asymmetries.[25] This can help to elevate sustainability to a more prominent factor in competitive decision-making, both in business-to-business interactions and end-customer markets. Nevertheless, these tools inherently contend with the limitations previously discussed, such as intention-behaviour gaps.

From a competition law perspective, self-regulatory measures are assessed not solely against the prohibition of agreements that restrain competition, but also in light of potential abuses, if applicable.

COMPETITION LAW TO PROMOTE SUSTAINABILITY GOALS

The previous section discussed the extent to which strict antitrust enforcement can hinder sustainability goals. This section shifts the focus to the converse: can stricter antitrust enforcement, i.e., more competition, be leveraged to enhance the attainment of sustainability goals?

Competition law interventions to achieve sustainability objectives can be economically rationalised if they (also) serve to protect competition. A firm's behaviour can infringe competition law *and can be* detrimental to the achievement of sustainability goals. In these scenarios, the alignment between competition and sustainability is not inherently conflicting; rather, they go hand in hand. Thus, antitrust action can stop action that simultaneously undermines both competition and sustainability. Consideration should be given to strengthening the application of competition law in such context.

Sustainability as a Competition Parameter

In a market economy, transactions within markets are based on voluntary agreements. Buyers generally acquire products and services when their

---

European Commission, 'Guidelines on the applicability of Article 101 of the Treaty on the Functioning of the European Union to horizontal co-operation agreements' [2023] OJ C 259/1, paras 439 ff; comprehensively Björn Lundqvist, *Standardisation under EU Competition Rules and US Competition Laws: The Rise and Limits of Self-Regulation* (Edward Elgar Publishing 2014).

[25]   Rüdiger Hahn, *Sustainability Management* (Rüdiger Hahn 2022) ch C1, C7.

perceived value matches or exceeds the price they pay.[26] Suppliers generally sell products and services because they derive a benefit from the sale. Thus, voluntary exchanges inherently yield mutual gain for both involved parties – a condition pivotal to the voluntary nature of the transaction.[27] Consequently, voluntary exchange fundamentally contributes to increase the welfare of both parties.

Competition in markets regularly creates incentives to make offers that are as attractive as possible to the counterpart.[28] In a competitive environment, a contracting party can only anticipate concluding an agreement if their offer is sufficiently attractive. Competition on one side of the market strengthens the other side, as a wider range of choices reduces dependency on single offerings.

Competition among entities facilitating exchange opportunities can take place in numerous dimensions. While the price is often a substantial parameter of competition, it is by no means the only factor determining the attractiveness of an offer. The dimensions in which competition – to the extent that it is workable or effective – ultimately takes place depend not only on legal regulations and technical possibilities, but above all on the preferences of the costumers. Consumers' quite differentiated desires are typically better fulfilled in competitive markets than in the absence of competition. In the absence of competition, suppliers have comparatively little incentive to offer consumers the products and conditions they want.

Sustainable production can constitute one of many competition parameters. If customers value environmentally and climate-friendly production, or if they value companies paying their employees a fair wage and providing decent working conditions, companies can gain competitive advantages by precisely delivering such offerings.[29] This holds true even when customers prioritise 'fair' prices for suppliers (like farmers) from retailers and manufacturers. Companies can enhance transparency regarding their practices through labels such as the 'Fair Trade' label or organic certification. If consumers view these labels as advantageous and higher sustainability standards are genuinely upheld, sustainability emerges as a decisive element of competition.

---

[26]   On market failures (information deficits, erroneous behaviour) that override this logic, see Chapter 11.

[27]   This benefit does not always have to be immediate, but can also manifest itself in the long term. Free samples, for example, are usually not distributed for charitable reasons, but in the hope of future sales.

[28]   This applies to competition in product markets as well as in procurement markets for production factors. For example, competition for scarce labour means that attractive offers have to be made in order to win them over.

[29]   Of course, this only applies if a sufficient number of consumers are actually willing to pay for it (and not only claim to do so publicly).

Competition tends to lead to a greater variety of products compared to what is typically observed in more concentrated markets. In cases where different consumers have different preferences regarding sustainability and are interested in diverse levels of sustainability, competitive markets are more likely to present suitable options compared to markets with limited competition. In addition, individual companies are more likely to make a competitive push in the 'sustainability dimension' in competitive markets than in markets with little competition. In this respect, strengthening competition also promotes sustainability.

Competition Law and the Promotion of Innovation

Competition is a driving force of innovation. Through so-called product innovations – i.e., the development of new or improved products – companies can set themselves apart from the competition and gain new customers and market shares. In industrial economics, product innovations basically mean all product changes and quality improvements that customers value. The same rationale can be extended to process innovations, through which companies save resources and thus produce more cheaply, ultimately securing competitive advantages on the cost side. Competition creates these incentives for innovation because innovations – both at the product level and in production processes[30] – translate into competitive advantages. In monopolies or highly concentrated markets, on the other hand, incentives to innovate are low because companies already enjoy high profits and market shares and there is, therefore, little to 'gain' – unlike in competition.[31]

---

[30] Production processes are to be understood here in a broad sense and also include management and logistics and thus the entire process required for entrepreneurial performance from purchasing to sales.

[31] There is an extensive economic literature on the relationship between competition and innovation with not entirely uniform findings. While some of the literature concludes that more competition in principle also leads to more incentives to innovate, most of the literature now concludes that there is not always a positive correlation, but that the correlation can be depicted as an inverted U. This means that the incentives to innovate are not limited to highly concentrated markets (as in the extreme case of monopolies). According to this, the incentives to innovate are low not only in highly concentrated, low-competition markets (as in the extreme case of monopoly), but also in very fragmented and extremely competitive markets with low margins. Accordingly, the highest incentives to innovate do not exist in the case of full or very intense price competition, but in markets with moderate concentration rates (see Philippe Aghion et al, 'Competition and Innovation: An Inverted-U Relationship' (2005) *The Quarterly Journal of Economics* 701; Philippe Askenazy, Christophe Cahn and Delphin Irac, 'Competition, R&D, and the Cost of Innovation: evidence for France' (2013) Oxford Economic Papers 293). From an economic perspective, we could also speak here of

The concept of innovation is initially neutral regarding sustainability objectives. However, it is clear that innovations can be particularly significant for climate protection. For instance, technologies urgently needed to reduce, store or remove CO_2 can only emerge from innovation efforts spurred by competition. Process innovations hold the potential to enable resource-conserving production methods; product innovations can extend the service life of products or introduce new drive technologies in transport (electromobility); business model innovations can drive the introduction of product-service systems (e.g., car sharing).

Furthermore, competition enables experimentation: what is a good idea and what is not, which forms of organisation are efficient and which are not, are best shown by competition. Above all, it ensures that the best possible response is made dynamically to evolving and changing consumer preferences, either through the adaptation of established providers or through market entry of new competitors. In essence, competition operates as a 'discovery process'[32] discerning individual preferences, timing, locations, methods, and the most efficient modes of production and organisation. As the importance of sustainability increases, this competition-driven process of experimentation and selection will reward economic activity that promotes sustainability. Overall, the promotion of innovation through dedicated antitrust enforcement can also be seen as positive in terms of sustainability goals.

Alignment of Sustainability and Harm to Competition

The two reasons for the increased application of competition law primarily address the market failure of imperfect competition. At the very least, it is also conceivable to use the instruments of competition law in cases of other market failures (see Chapter 11) if these failures are also detrimental to sustainability. In these instances, it could, in principle, be considered as enriching the competition law toolkit with non-competition considerations. In this case, competition law would be used for regulatory purposes, but outside the scope of its competition policy objectives. This may seem far-fetched from the point of view of competition economics, but it can be considered for three reasons:

First, competition law at the European level is an effective tool to address companies directly.

---

functional or effective competition – as distinct from complete competition or even ruinous competition.

[32]   Friedrich August von Hayek, *Freiburger Studien: Gesammelte Aufsätze* (Mohr 1969) 249.

Secondly, there may exist potential overlap between diverse objectives, which cannot always be clearly separated.

Third, from a competition perspective, it may be argued that market interventions should rather be made within the competition law framework which aims at protecting market competition, even if non-competition objectives are being pursued. In cases where specific market interventions, such as CO_2 pricing, taxes or general product and production standards, symmetrically apply to all market participants, they maintain competition neutrality by affecting all parties in a uniform manner, thereby avoiding distortions of competition. However, where sustainability initiatives risk distorting competition, the involvement of competition authorities should be warranted. This could lead to a more robust integration of sustainability and competition considerations.

Such an approach would be particularly evident where competition law deals with the same subject matter and its responsibilities overlap with those of other legal areas, such as environmental law. While competition law should not be primarily concerned with environmental issues, a basis for regulatory intervention could be created through judicious cooperation with other institutions. Based on the collective insights of all relevant authorities, regulatory intervention could then be assessed, taking into account competition economics considerations.

EVALUATION CRITERIA FOR OPTIONS FOR ACTION

The propositions outlined in this report (Part II) are subject to evaluation, underpinned by the economic considerations delineated above. Additionally, overarching legal and political evaluation criteria are applied.

From an economic perspective, the key factor is whether antitrust interventions, or conversely their absence, can be justified through the prism of market or policy failure. This rationale is essentially reflected in the European Union's state aid control framework: competition is inherently considered worthy of protection. However, in certain scenarios, competition can exacerbate a market failure or conflict with other social objectives (such as the reduction of interregional imbalances) cannot be achieved. In such circumstances, it may be economically rational to deliberately accept restrictions on competition to address a market failure. However, this requires a balancing of the constraints of competition against the benefits of addressing the market failure. This assessment paradigm is congruent with the European Commission's balancing test in state aid control. A similar balancing test is proposed below for sustainability cooperation:

- Is a market failure being addressed?

- In particular, the examination should cover the efficiency effects that arise and how they improve the position of consumers or overall welfare.

Relevant market failures that can be addressed include externalities, information asymmetries, and constrained rational behaviour. Market interventions to correct competition deficits (in extreme cases, for example, preventing the abuse of market power by a [natural] monopoly) are already generally covered by competition law (or sector-specific regulation) and do not need to be subjected to any new or additional test.

- Is the market failure already addressed by existing legislation?

An assessment must determine whether a recognised market failure is already being addressed by pre-existing legislative measures. If not, it must be demonstrated that addressing the market failure is genuinely in the legislative interest. Conversely, if the market failure is already addressed by legislative measures, it must be examined whether and to what extent the measures taken so far are insufficient to adequately address the identified market failure. This could be supported by case law or by a demonstrated gap between the objectives set out in laws or international treaties and their actual achievement. Consequently, competition law and antitrust exemptions are not intended to become the primary arena for sustainability policy, but rather an alternative to be used when the prevailing legal framework is manifestly inadequate to achieve the sustainability goals set by the legislator.

- What are the implications for sustainability?

In this context, it is imperative to identify the likely benefits for different stakeholders and whether these benefits are strong enough to outweigh any potential negative effects on competition (and market participants). This does not necessarily require a case-by-case analysis but can be based on a typological assessment. The quantifiability of sustainability effects must also be considered.

An option is only viable if it is lawful. From a legal perspective, it is therefore necessary to ask whether possible legal changes are compatible with higher-ranking laws and how they fit into the system of applicable law.

- Is the option for action compatible with higher-ranking law?

In this context, the higher-ranking law is to be applied as the standard of assessment. The more the legality is affected by a fundamental change in the case law of the higher courts, the less likely it is to be implemented. However, the aspect of system compatibility should not be overestimated: serious changes – such as the 'discovery' of sustainability as a topos of commercial law – are bound to lead to dogmatic distortions and further developments.

The next step is to evaluate the feasibility and practicability of the measures for the stakeholders.

- What are the regulatory costs associated with the action option?

Regulatory costs include expenses related to law enforcement, monitoring and compliance. These costs tend to be higher for complex sets of rules and standards that need to be created and then adhered to. The more complex a standard, the more difficult it is for authorities, courts, and companies to interpret and comply with it. This not only incurs costs, but can also lead to lengthy procedures, misapplication of standards due to complexity and, as a result, non-adoption of desirable or even undesirable behaviour. The effectiveness of a measure must therefore be assessed not only in terms of its results, but also in terms of its implementation.

It is then necessary to balance the positive and negative effects of measures. This balancing must be based on the political objectives, which cannot be determined in this report. Consequently, different objectives (such as functioning competition or the Sustainable Development Goals) may be given different weights. Costs may be allocated differently. Risks and uncertainties in the assessment of measures can be categorised and mitigated differently. This weighing and ultimate decision is an original political task that cannot be performed in this report.

3.   Patterns of antitrust reform options

In this book we develop policy options for integrating sustainability goals into competition law in a better way. All these options can be assigned to four basic patterns. The starting point is that competition law should not stand in the way of achieving sustainability goals. So far, competition law has been considered as largely 'agnostic' toward sustainability issues, even though it has already been shown above that competition and sustainability are interdependent. The four basic patterns move away from agnostic competition law in different ways and intensities. The approach that is chosen is a political decision. In practice, it is conceivable to combine different options to a limited extent.

SUSTAINABILITY-SENSITIVE APPLICATION OF COMPETITION LAW (SUSTAINABILITY AWARENESS)

The first pattern is what we call an approach of 'Sustainability Awareness'. Some sectors are particularly important for some specific sustainability goals. It is obvious, for example, that the energy industry is directly affected by climate protection measures to a high degree. In the application of competition law, there may be cases that directly or indirectly have significant effects for the achievement of sustainability goals.

One set of options aims to raise awareness of such sustainability effects of antitrust application. This is a sustainability-sensitive approach that follows the idea of 'Sustainability Awareness': awareness of the sustainability effects of competition law is raised, and this may be followed by increased vigilance or a change in attitude. Sustainability awareness is typically measured as individuals' knowledge, behaviour, and attitudes.[1] Competition law is applied in a sustainability-sensitive manner when decision-makers in public authorities

---

[1]   See Ibrahim H Garbie, 'Sustainability Awareness in Industrial Organizations' (2015) 26 Procedia CIRP 64; Janice Denoncourt, 'Integrating Sustainable Development Awareness in Intellectual Property Law Education' (2021), https://papers.ssrn.com/sol3/papers.cfm?abstract_id=3897254 accessed 26 June 2023; The European Investment Bank has issued a Sustainability Awareness Bond, see European Investment Bank, 'Sustainability Awareness Bonds' www.eib.org/en/investor-relations/sab/index.htm accessed 26 June 2023.

and companies are aware of the sustainability impact of their actions and know that there is a connection between their activities and the achievement of sustainability goals.

However, identifying such cases with a high sustainability impact is not a matter of course. Competition law application goes hand in glove with examining market structures and changing market behaviour. The impact of competition law on achieving sustainability goals varies significantly, depending on which case is investigated. For example, cases from the energy, waste management, or environmental tech sectors can become significantly relevant to climate action.

- For example, if a company's behaviour in trading carbon credits were to be examined, this could potentially have a significant impact on the market and thus on the achievement of Sustainable Development Goals.
- In the *ARA* case, the European Commission took action against a company that obstructed the market access of companies to waste disposal infrastructures (here: collection of household waste).[2] Stronger competition might have led to efficiencies in waste management.
- In her statement on the *Car Emissions* case, *Margrethe Vestager*, Vice President of the EU Commission in charge of competition, emphasised the connection between her action against the car manufacturers and the objectives of the Green Deal.[3] It is noteworthy, however, that these political statements in the press statement find no counterpart in the decision itself: the decision makes no reference to the fact that the conduct led to environmental harm.[4]

Currently, the effects of corporate competition strategies and antitrust interventions are not analysed in terms of sustainability impacts. Greater sustainability awareness does not affect the competitive logic of competition law, but it increases awareness of the extent to which free competition promotes sustainability and how, in individual cases, competition law stands in the way of achieving such goals.

---

[2]   *ARA Foreclosure* (Case AT.39759) Commission Decision 2016/C 432/05 [2016] OJ C 432/6.
[3]   See Vestager, Statement of 8.7.2021, available at https:// ec .europa .eu/ commission/presscorner/detail/de/statement_21_3583 accessed 26 June 2023.
[4]   Cf *Car Emissions* (Case AT.40178) Commission Decision [2021] C 458/11 [2021] 4955 final.

STRENGTHENING ENFORCEMENT (SUSTAINABILITY BOOST)

A second set of options for sustainability-oriented reform of competition law aims to further develop competition law on a selective basis in areas where a stronger enforcement of competition law leads to a better attainment of sustainability goals. We call this approach the 'Sustainability Boost' as a pattern for competition law development. Competition law would remain committed to the existing market and competition logic. However, the current antitrust framework would be adapted from case to case to better promote sustainability goals *by competition means*. Competition law and thus competition protection would be strengthened for those cases in which there is no fundamental conflict between competition and sustainability. By means of moderate adjustments and clarifications, competition law could be designed in such a way that sustainability elements can be better applied without breaking with the logic of competition. In this respect, sustainability would get a boost: where competition law can support the pursuit of sustainability, it is enforced with more vigour.

Market failures are the decisive starting points for this approach. According to the traditional economic rationale, these can justify interventions in the market and in competition. As long as sustainability goals can be achieved by remedying classic market failures, this can also justify an adjustment of the current legal framework without any conflict with more traditional advocates of competition principles.

SUSTAINABILITY AS AN INTEGRAL ASPECT OF COMPETITION (SUSTAINABLE COMPETITION)

A third set of options assumes a new competition model: competition as 'Sustainable Competition'. In this model, competition law remains true to its competition orientation and does not pursue objectives other than protecting competition. However, the notion of competition is interpreted in a new, different way – namely as ecologically and socially sustainable competition. The interpretation of competition as a purely economic concept that is solely focused on achieving lower prices is superseded by an interpretation that sees competition as a concept that inherently features the idea of sustainability: an economic model that does not respect the limits of resources needed to engage in economic activity (such as the planetary boundaries) and that does not link profits and risks is not a viable concept. To a certain degree, European State aid law follows this approach of integrating ecological goals into economic discretionary decisions as an integral part of the economy. Sustainable Competition means to reconcile economic activities with the achievement of sustainability goals.

There are various legitimations for such a stronger integration of sustainability goals into the concept of competition:

For some sustainability goals, this consideration is a practical, functional mechanism: if climate catastrophe is not averted, the economy will implode. Economic competition that promotes climate change cannot meaningfully exist – before this consideration – and cannot be protected. Climate protection is a functional prerequisite for economic competition, so only competition that respects climate goals is worth protecting.

From an economic perspective, in addition to this functional consideration, as illustrated by the example of climate protection, market players also increasingly understand competition as sustainable competition. On the one hand, this applies to consumers who are increasingly directing demand toward sustainable products and expressing a stronger interest in sustainability. On the other hand, there is also a need for companies to take sustainability into account as a competition parameter. This is happening, for example, against the backdrop of increased costs for greenhouse gas emissions, changing consumer demand, possible reputational losses, and compliance difficulties in the event of legal violations in the supply chain, or with a view to attractiveness as an employer. New economically motivated behaviours are emerging here, which may be reflected in a changed competition model. In addition, companies are called upon to play an active role in achieving sustainability goals as part of the various sustainable development strategies. Preferences and incentives in the markets have thus changed.

From a normative viewpoint, the sustainable competition model can be justified by reference to the legality of corporate behaviour: the law does not protect illegal competition. For instance, a competition agency would not step in to protect a criminal dealer who is exploited by a drugs cartel. Why not? Because competition law is geared toward the protection of legal development of economic activities. Regarding sustainability, it can be argued that some activities are violations of rules even though they may not be sanctioned – think of the violation of human rights standards abroad. For social sustainability goals in particular, this concept can be made fruitful. The extent to which obligations that are not designed as hard legal norms are also recognised is a follow-up question. These days, more and more non-sustainable economic activities become illegal, or liability is placed on economic actors (e.g., for climate damage). It may be important to take this normative assessment of activities in competition into account for the concept of what is protected under competition law.

On the basis of functional, economic, and normative considerations, it is therefore possible to call for a stronger orientation of competition law toward sustainability goals – one could also say: a stronger link between competition law and other values. Of course, competition law would then no longer be 'agnostic'. However, in the past, too, values have guided antitrust practice. The purely efficiency-oriented orientation of competition law in the sense of the Chicago School, for example, can be understood as such a setting of a value. The definition of which concept of competition should be enforced is a permanent task in the discourse of legislators, courts, authorities, academia, and the public.

Recently, courts and legislators have again increasingly relied on normative models of competition when they use the term 'competition on the merits'.[5] If competition on the merits (or performance-based competition) is protected, this means there is a modification compared to a more open concept of competition that does not focus on performance ('merits'), but accepts any advance in the market. A normatively charged concept of competition, on the other hand, can exclude unmerited competition. Similarly, competition can only be considered worthy of protection if it is sustainable. This is to be stipulated by legislation. With the guiding principle of 'sustainable competition', competition law becomes more value-based (which would certainly tie in with the ordoliberal tradition of German competition law in particular).

The model of an 'ecological-social market economy' is particularly relevant for the further development of the competition model with a view to sustainability.[6] The core of this model is often the true cost for ecological burdens. Coupled with the 'polluter pays' principle, which is laid out in *Hans Jonas*' 'Principle of Responsibility',[7] this must lead to sovereign control that internalises external costs and provides common goods with a stronger protection. Thus, the model ultimately remains committed to the competition order and faithful to a regulatory approach – market failures are consistently combated.

Such a transformation of competition law would mean that sustainability effects would be taken into consideration within the antitrust review grid. For example, in the context of abuse control, behaviour could be considered anti-competition that leads to an increase in anthropogenic climate change on the basis of market power. Sustainability effects would be considered part of the competition regime – whether to ensure the long-term viability of the market mechanism, for reasons of changing preferences and incentives, or

---

[5]   For example, in Section 20(3a) GWB; Case T-612/17 *Google Shopping* ECLI:EU:T:2021:763, [2021] para 157; BGH, KZR 55/19, 9.3.2021, NZKart 2021, 509, 513, para 45.

[6]   This term can be found, for example, in the Federal Ministry for Economic Affairs and Climate Action's Competition Policy Agenda to 2025, 2022; early on, Josef Riegler, *Ökosoziale Marktwirtschaft* (oekonom 1989).

[7]   Hans Jonas, *Das Prinzip Verantwortung* (Insel 1979).

because of a normative setting that competition can only be environmentally sustainable competition. It would be questionable, however, whether the integration of sustainability goals should go so far that cartels of producers of mineral oil, tobacco, sugar, and other products whose consumption is to be reduced for sustainability reasons should be prosecuted less strictly or possibly not at all under competition law, or whether price-level abuse for such products is more likely to be tolerated. Sustainability effects would always have to be seen in the context of economic actions in markets. The aim is not a primacy of sustainability over the economy, but a transformation of the market economy in which sustainability goals are better achieved through the internalisation of costs, regulatory requirements, and other genuinely market-based instruments.

However, such a turnaround can hardly be achieved without legislative intervention. The legislator must legitimise the realignment of competition law.

The 'sustainable competition' model contains a conceptual quantum leap for competition law: sustainability would be integrated into the competition assessment. This can be seen as a development of the competition model for the twenty-first century. This would probably be associated with a visible transformation of economic law, without abandoning the principles of the market economy. At the same time, this quantum leap could point the way to better achieving Sustainable Development Goals through competition instruments.

However, the classic protection of competition would be watered down. Innovations and efficiencies in the more traditional sense could be made more difficult in certain cases. Two risks in particular must be taken into account here: first, competition authorities, as part of the executive branch, would have to resolve the tension between competition and sustainability. So far, this has largely been the task of democratic discourse in parliaments and not of the executive branch, which could easily be overwhelmed by it. Secondly, the concept of sustainability is so comprehensive that it would be almost impossible to draw clear boundaries. It would virtually open the floodgates for diverse argumentations. This makes at least a limitation of this approach by the legislature imperative. On an even more fundamental level, the concept of open competition would be replaced by another concept of order.

CONSIDERATION OF NON-ECONOMIC INTERESTS (LEVELLING APPROACH)

Some of the policy options fit a pattern of opening up competition law to integrate concerns that are not primarily economic or competition-related.[8] These interests are placed on an equal footing with the original competition law ideas – we call this a 'Levelling Approach'. Two completely different strands can be identified.

On the one hand, there is the possibility of excluding certain conduct from the application of competition law from the outset because aspects are involved that claim priority over the protection of competition.

This option has the disadvantage that competition aspects no longer play any role at all. One of the advantages, however, is that the application of competition law as such is not affected and there is a clear hierarchy of interests. Such an exception from the scope of application of competition law is a 'clean' alternative to a model with 'dirty' compromises between competition law goals and other goals.

On the other hand, there are options for taking non-economic interests into account in competition law proceedings. In this case, the competition standard of review is mitigated within the proceedings. The established procedures and tools of competition law are partly converted to achieve other goals.

This option has the disadvantage of overriding the 'pure' competition law yardstick within the system. However, the procedures provide an established framework for addressing entrepreneurial behaviour in a sovereign manner. In some cases, competition interests can still be enforced. There may then also be a balance between the protection of competition and other goals, such as the protection of the Sustainable Development Goals in cases where the two are not complementary.

The displacement of antitrust standards has occurred time and again in the past, for example, when statutory exemption areas were created, or the scope of competition law was limited by judicial decisions. The reasoning behind this is that the protection of competition is not granted in absolute terms. Other legally anchored objectives can also shape the regulatory framework for doing business. We will discuss this in the course of exploring the options in more detail. However, it must be pointed out that the protection of competition has a special position in European law, since Articles 101 and 102 TFEU are directly applicable European primary law, which in its concrete form directly addresses companies. Most other provisions do not reach the same status

---

[8]   Cf Jean Tirole, 'Socially Responsible Agencies' (2022) 7 *Competition Law & Policy Debate* 171.

in the hierarchy of norms or are formulated in a much broader, less directly enforceable way.

THE CURRENT DISCUSSIONS ON COMPETITION POLICY

The four basic patterns identified here as four overarching ideas for the policy options discussed below are reflected in the current international debate on the state of competition theory. The debate on sustainability in competition law ties in with the ongoing fundamental debate on the state of antitrust concepts. This debate is raging in the United States and Europe. It started with the criticism of the lack of enforcement in the past years, partly due to economic concepts of the Chicago School and the legacy it left. Digitisation and the rise of digital gatekeepers, climate change, or inflation change the business world, and consequently lead to questions on the role of the basic mechanism of the market economy, i.e. competition. One important point in the debates on antitrust theory is the integration of non-competition goals in competition law enforcement, be it privacy, democracy or sustainability.[9]

At present, a distinction may be made – in broad outline – between three directions within competition theory:

- The proponents of post-Chicago economics remain faithful to a strict effects-based approach to competition law. They often align competition law with a narrowly defined consumer welfare standard.[10] Accordingly, antitrust interventions are only justified if increases in consumer welfare are expected, especially through efficiency gains (which theoretically should be passed on in the form of price reductions). This is calculated (in monetary terms) on a case-by-case basis. According to this view, other objectives play no role in competition law, so that, at best, exceptional areas are to be recognised (basic pattern 4) or priorities can be set in a pre-legal area (basic pattern 1).
- Other scholars, however, argue for a moderate extension of the consumer welfare standard.[11] From the point of view of this school of thought,

---

[9]   On the economic definition of goals, see the fundamental contributions in Daniel Zimmer (ed), *The Goals of Competition Law* (2012); David J Gerber, *Competition Law and Antitrust* (Oxford University Press 2020) 17 ff.

[10]   See Phil Gramm and Christine Wilson, 'The New Progressives Fight Against Consumer Welfare' *The Wall Street Journal* (3 April 2022); A Douglas Melamed and Nicolas Petit, 'The Misguided Assault on the Consumer Welfare Standard in the Age of Platform Markets' (2019) *Review of Industrial Organization* 741.

[11]   See Carl Shapiro, 'Antitrust: What Went Wrong and How to Fix It' (2021) 35 *Antitrust* 33; Herbert J Hovenkamp and Fiona M Scott Morton, 'Framing the Chicago

the assumptions of the Chicago and Post Chicago School have led to underenforcement, since the dangers of vertical mergers and abuses of monopoly power have been particularly underestimated. In some cases, the focus is on a 'total welfare standard'; in others, the freedom of choice and decision-making of the market counterpart ('consumer choice') is included. In Europe, there is a widespread conviction that competition must be protected as a process, regardless of concrete effects. The tendencies summarised here very roughly are occasionally characterised as 'progressive', 'modernist', or 'structuralist'. What they have in common is that they favour stronger enforcement. According to these views, sustainability considerations only play a role in competition law if they can be integrated into the competition framework. There seems to be an increased willingness to do so among some representatives of this school of thought, since the connection between sustainability and competition is recognised. In particular, basic patterns 1 and 2 correspond to this, with a fluid boundary to basic pattern 3.

- The so-called Neo-Brandeisians, who refer to the progressive US Supreme Court Justice *Louis Brandeis* (1856–1941), want to expand competition law to include broader objectives and sharpen it considerably.[12] They criticise the high level of concentration in markets, which leads not only to restrictions on competition but also to social inequality and other problems (e.g., lack of sustainability). Proponents of this view would particularly approve of options 3 and 4 in the sense that they advocate the integration of further objectives into competition law. However, they would probably be highly critical of both options at the same time, if mergers and cartels are treated more generously. The Neo-Brandeisians are calling precisely for stricter enforcement, not for a softening of antitrust enforcement.

The very brief spotlight on this discussion is intended to recall three aspects in particular: first, the debate is global. Second, the sustainability discourse is embedded in a broader debate over the system and purpose of competition

---

School of Antitrust Analysis' (2020) *University of Pennsylvania Law Review* 1843; Frédéric Marty, 'Is Consumer Welfare Obsolete? A European Union Competition Perspective' (2021) *Revista Prolegómenos* 55, 57.
   [12] Cf Lina Khan and Sandeep Vaheesan, 'Market Power and Inequality: The Antitrust Counterrevolution and Its Discontents' (2017) *Harvard Law & Policy Review* 235; Ariel Ezrachi and Maurice E Stucke, 'The Fight over Antitrust's Soul' (2017) 9 JECLAP 1; Joseph E Stiglitz, 'Towards a Broader View of Competition Policy' (2017) Roosevelt Institute Working Paper https://rooseveltinstitute.org/wp-content/uploads/2020/07/RI-Broader-View-of-Competition-Policy-201703.pdf accessed 17 August 2023.

protection. Third, it is ultimately a political choice, so that the selection of the 'right' options is not a scientifically technical question.

PART II

Policy options for a better integration of sustainability: status quo and possible developments in competition law

INTRODUCTION TO PART II

In this part, we show how extensively sustainability issues can already be integrated into competition law, and what policy options exist for further developments in the future. We explore the options according to the different instruments of competition law: we look into the scope of application of competition law so that some practices may be exempted upfront. We then turn to the prohibition of restrictive business practices (caught under Article 101(1) TFEU) and possible exemptions (as under Article 101(3) TFEU). We also check options with regard to the abuse of market power (Article 102 TFEU), merger control (as regulated under the EC Merger Regulation on the EU level), plus proceedings and sanctions across the fields. For a better understanding, these options have an abbreviation and a number:

- Scope of application: SC
- Prohibition of restrictive business practices: RE
- Exemptions under competition law: EX
- Abuse of market power: AB
- Merger control: MC
- Proceedings and sanctions: PR

The annex contains a brief overview of all options.

4. Scope of application of competition law

As a matter of principle, competition law extends to all sectors of the economy – it is universally applicable. Having stated that, there have always been exceptions and special rules for some sectors, limiting or modifying the scope of application of competition law. For instance, in many jurisdictions, agriculture, media, energy or health were subjected to specific rules due to the (alleged) importance or specificities of the sector.

The first set of options relates to this kind of regulatory intervention and explores the possibility to limit or modify the scope of application of competition law in order to better achieve the Sustainable Development Goals. For these options, it is necessary to identify sectors with a high relevance for achieving sustainability goals.

THE EXAMPLE OF THE EXCEPTION FOR AGRICULTURE

Various exceptions at the national and European level declare competition law inapplicable in some economic sectors that are closely related to sustainability. The most obvious example is the agricultural sector.

In the field of agriculture, there have always been considerable deviations from a pure competition law approach. The European Union established the Common Markets Organisation (CMO) as part of its common agricultural policy (CAP).[1] The CMO is a heavily interventionist framework for agricultural products. It aims at achieving the specific objectives of the CAP as defined in Article 39 TFEU. In this provision, it is stated that the CAP aims i.a. at increasing agricultural productivity, ensuring a fair standard of living for the agricultural community, and stabilise markets.

To this end, the CMO, in its Part IV, contains far-reaching exemptions from competition law. For instance, according to Article 209 CMO, farmers and

---

[1]   Current version: Regulation (EU) No 1308/2013 of the European Parliament and of the Council of 17 December 2013 establishing a common organisation of the markets in agricultural products and repealing Council Regulations (EEC) No 922/72, (EEC) No 234/79, (EC) No 1037/2001 and (EC) No 1234/2007.

farmers associations may forge agreements for the joint production or sale of agricultural products (as long as there is no price fixing).

In December 2021, a new Article 210a CMO was introduced containing a far-reaching exemption of sustainability agreements for the agricultural sector, including horizontal and vertical agreements.[2] The food supply chain, arguably one of the most important sectors for sustainability, now has a strong shield from competition law enforcement. Paragraphs 1 and 2 contain the broad exemption for agreements. In para 3, it is explicitly defined what sustainability relates to. Paragraphs 4–7 define procedural aspects. The exemption falls under the self-assessment rule; the parties have to define themselves whether their cooperation fulfils the criteria. Yet, they have a right to ask for an opinion by the Commission – a considerable help (and a partial return to the former 'comfort letter'-practice).

BOX 4.1   ARTICLE 210A CMO

Vertical and horizontal initiatives for sustainability

1. Article 101(1) TFEU shall not apply to agreements, decisions and concerted practices of producers of agricultural products that relate to the production of or trade in agricultural products and that aim to apply a sustainability standard higher than mandated by Union or national law, provided that those agreements, decisions and concerted practices only impose restrictions of competition that are indispensable to the attainment of that standard.

2. Paragraph 1 applies to agreements, decisions and concerted practices of producers of agricultural products to which several producers are party or to which one or more producers and one or more operators at different levels of the production, processing, and trade in the food supply chain, including distribution, are party.

3. For the purposes of paragraph 1, 'sustainability standard' means a standard which aims to contribute to one or more of the following objectives:

---

[2]   Regulation (EU) No 2021/2117 of the European Parliament and of the Council of 2 December 2021 amending Regulations (EU) No 1308/2013 establishing a common organisation of the markets in agricultural products, (EU) No 1151/2012 on quality schemes for agricultural products and foodstuffs, (EU) No 251/2014 on the definition, description, presentation, labelling and the protection of geographical indications of aromatised wine products and (EU) No 228/2013 laying down specific measures for agriculture in the outermost regions of the Union.

(a) environmental objectives, including climate change mitigation and adaptation, the sustainable use and protection of landscapes, water and soil, the transition to a circular economy, including the reduction of food waste, pollution prevention and control, and the protection and restoration of biodiversity and ecosystems;

(b) the production of agricultural products in ways that reduce the use of pesticides and manage risks resulting from such use, or that reduce the danger of antimicrobial resistance in agricultural production; and

(c) animal health and animal welfare.

4. Agreements, decisions and concerted practices that fulfil the conditions referred to in this Article shall not be prohibited, no prior decision to that effect being required.

5. The Commission shall issue guidelines for operators concerning the conditions for the application of this Article by 8 December 2023.

6. From 8 December 2023, producers as referred to in paragraph 1 may request an opinion from the Commission concerning the compatibility of agreements, decisions and concerted practices as referred to in paragraph 1 with this Article. The Commission shall send the applicant its opinion within four months of receipt of a complete request.

If the Commission finds at any time after issuing an opinion that the conditions referred to in paragraphs 1, 3 and 7 of this Article are no longer met, it shall declare that Article 101(1) TFEU shall apply in the future to the agreement, decision or concerted practice in question and inform the producers accordingly.

The Commission may change the content of an opinion at its own initiative or at the request of a Member State, in particular if the applicant has provided inaccurate information or misused the opinion.

7. The national competition authority as referred to in Article 5 of Regulation (EC) No 1/2003 may decide in individual cases that, in the future, one or more of the agreements, decisions and concerted practices referred to in paragraph 1 are to be modified, discontinued or not take place at all, if it considers that such a decision is necessary in order to prevent competition from being excluded or if it considers that the objectives set out in Article 39 TFEU are jeopardised.

For agreements, decisions and concerted practices covering more than one Member State, the decision referred to in the first subparagraph of this paragraph shall be taken by the Commission without applying the procedures referred to in Article 229(2) and (3).

When acting under the first subparagraph of this paragraph, the national competition authority shall inform the Commission in writing after initiating the first formal measure of the investigation and shall notify the Commission of any resulting decisions without delay after their adoption. The decisions referred to in this paragraph shall not apply earlier than the date of their notification to the undertakings concerned.

This new exemption for the agricultural sectors sets an incentive for going beyond legal requirements. The practical scope of the exemption remains to be seen but its scope of application seems extremely wide as soon as producers are involved: it covers horizontal and vertical agreements and a broad variety of sustainability goals as set out in para 3.[3] The provision has the potential to cover many sustainability initiatives in food production, or – put differently – to provide a cover for a less competitive structuring of the market. The exception is extremely far-reaching:

- The expected contribution to the attainment of sustainability goals is very low: it suffices to 'aim to apply a sustainability standard higher than mandated by Union or national law'. It suffices to pursue the aim. It is not necessary to document or prove effects or to evaluate the initiatives.
- There is no threshold of significance: the contribution can be minimal.
- The terms for the sustainability goals (e.g., animal welfare and animal health; environmental objectives) are vaguely formulated and can cover a wide range of practices.
- The assessment is in the hands of the companies involved; there is no obligation to notify, let alone an obligation to involve competition authorities for approval.

The competition price for this potentially low contribution to sustainability is a closer collaboration among different companies in the food value chain with effects that will lessen competition in the sector. According to its Guidelines, the Commission will follow the case law and administrative practice on Article 101(3) TFEU.[4] This means that price increases, long-term supply contracts or

---

[3]   Cf European Commission, 'Commission Guidelines on the application of the derogation from Article 101 TFEU for sustainability agreements of agricultural producers pursuant to Article 210(a) of Regulation (EU) 1308/2013' [2023] https://competition-policy.ec.europa.eu/document/download/52c6bf07-ed82-4ac1-a9ff -a37ed65a5861_en?filename=draft_sustainability_guidelines_in_agriculture_2023.zip accessed 28 June 2023.

[4]   Cf European Commission, 'Commission Guidelines on the application of the derogation from Article 101 TFEU for sustainability agreements of agricultural producers pursuant to Article 210(a) of Regulation (EU) 1308/2013' [2023] https://competition-policy.ec.europa.eu/document/download/52c6bf07-ed82-4ac1-a9ff

exclusivity obligations may also be enforced if it can be shown that it is indispensable for achieving the sustainability objective. The Commission will not be able to use the Guidelines or a very narrow definition of indispensability to provide more qualifications to the binding legal wording in Article 210a CMO.

On the national level, there can be further exceptions to different sectors. National exceptions to the prohibition of restrictive business practices have limited effect, since according to Article 3(2) of Regulation (EC) No 1/2003, European law takes precedence as soon as trade between member states is affected. In these cases, Article 101 TFEU prevails.

OPTION SC 1: NEW EXCEPTIONS

At the European level, the new rule in Article 210a of Regulation (EU) No 1308/2013 (CMO Regulation) in conjunction with the general provision in Article 39 TFEU grants a far-reaching privilege for sustainability agreements. This could possibly serve as a model for other sectors. It could be considered to create further areas of exemptions in order to exempt certain types of conduct from competition law.

Starting Points

There are three possible starting points for exceptions. The exceptions could be provided for certain industries; they could be linked to certain practices; and they could apply when certain sustainability goals are pursued. The model in Article 210a CMO is geared toward a sector and favours sustainability initiatives in this sector.

To identify sectors that are particularly relevant to sustainability is difficult in times when all initiatives count. However, if climate protection is seen as an aim that is claiming priority, the sectors singled out in European climate law may be of particular concern. Sector-specific EU climate initiatives are directed at energy, industrial processes and product use, agriculture, land use, land-use change and forestry, and waste.[5] Other definitions and sectoral specifications are conceivable.

One could distinguish different sustainability goals. If climate protection is seen as an urgent task that cannot be postponed, a climate protection excep-

---

-a37ed65a5861_en?filename=draft_sustainability_guidelines_in_agriculture_2023.zip accessed 28 June 2023.

[5]   Cf Commission Implementing Regulation (EU) 2020/1208 of 7 August 2020 on structure, format, submission processes and review of information reported by member states pursuant to Regulation (EU) 2018/1999 of the European Parliament and of the Council and repealing Commission Implementing Regulation (EU) No 749/2014.

tion could be justified. A paper from the Dutch antitrust authority takes this direction.[6] Business practices that demonstrably lead to a significant reduction in CO_2 emissions could then – without further ado – be exempted from competition law.

Sustainability requires a complex, comprehensive approach covering all aspects of the value chain and of the economy. That is true for climate protection, too. The European Union has pledged to reduce its greenhouse gas emissions across all sectors throughout Europe as part of the Paris Climate Agreement. Looking at other Sustainable Development Goals, it becomes clear that each sector must contribute to achieving the Sustainable Development Goals and that the Sustainable Development Goals interact closely with each other. Against this background, we see it as problematic to define specific competition law exceptions for some sectors (but not all) or for isolated sustainability targets.

Criteria for Exceptions

The areas of exemption could be designed more narrowly or more broadly by defining the requirements for competition aspects, sustainability targets, and the procedure to be followed more narrowly or more broadly in each case. A clear definition of the requirements is necessary not only to balance the interests, but also to ensure the necessary legal certainty.

In the case of Article 210a of the CMO, for example, the provision could have used a wording that is much narrower and more targeted, e.g., through more precise requirements for the standards to be achieved, a threshold for significance, an obligation to notify, stricter monitoring or the prohibition of certain hardcore restrictions. A monitoring of effects, both for competition and sustainability, seems vital for an evidence-based policy change.

ADVANTAGES AND DISADVANTAGES OF EXCEPTIONS

The advantages of reducing the scope of application of competition law are the simple applicability and the associated low regulatory costs. From the point of view of companies, such broad exemptions have the advantage that competition agencies cannot intervene. Even claims by private parties are ruled out

---

[6]   Autoriteit Consument & Markt, 'Sustainability Agreements, Draft' (7 September 2020) www.acm.nl/sites/default/files/documents/2020-07/sustainability-agreements %5B1%5D.pdf accessed 28 June 2023.

from the outset. This creates a high degree of legal certainty for sustainability initiatives, as they would no longer fall within the scope of scrutiny.

Their disadvantage is that they create little differentiated areas of exception and thus limit the protection of competition. It is no longer possible to seek a balance between competition and sustainability considerations in individual cases.

It is unclear how such exemptions could be analysed for their impact on market failures. It would be necessary – and very complex – to determine the (overall) societal benefits and to offset the resulting possible higher prices or other consequences of a lack of competition. Such an analysis would have to be carried out across the board for all or at least a large proportion of the agreements falling within the scope of the exemption. This is hardly possible. A general sectoral exemption does not allow for fine differentiation. This does not do justice to the complex relationship between competition and sustainability. General sustainability exemptions from competition unilaterally prioritise sustainability goals and forgo the use of competition as a factor for efficiency and innovation. Even in sectors with high relevance for sustainability, there is no evidence that competition law fundamentally stands in the way of important sustainability solutions on a wide scale. What would have to be proven is a market failure that can only be remedied by comprehensive competition-restricting measures and that cannot be cured by other legislative measures – be it a change in prohibited CO_2 emissions or farming. From an economic viewpoint, there is no reason to exempt entire industries from the principle of competition.

If one element in an industry can only be organised on a non-competition basis and when a government intervention is lacking or cannot prescribe the exact way, there may be room for a general exemption. For example, a recycling structure can function sufficiently cost-effectively if a sufficient number of market participants take part in it, so that horizontal and vertical agreements on participation in recycling can make sense. However, it is doubtful whether a legal exception upfront is necessarily required for this. The admissibility of a corresponding agreement under competition law could also stem from Article 101(3) TFEU.

From the point of view of competition, it should be insisted that exceptions be narrowly limited so as not to erode competition. From this perspective, Article 210a CMO cannot be regarded as exemplary.

Compatibility with higher-ranking law depends on the content and reference points in law in the multi-level system. At the European level, the areas for exceptions have to be based on conflicting Union objectives, such as in the case of the CMO Regulation on Articles 39, 43(3) TFEU. Objectives that are less clear or regulated on a different norm-hierarchical level may not serve as legitimate counterweights to Articles 101 et seq. TFEU. As seen above, national exceptions will often run into the problem of affecting trade between member states, and therefore being limited in value.

5. Prohibition of restrictive business practices

The discussion of sustainability considerations in competition law focuses on the prohibition of restrictive agreements.[1] In this chapter we look at Article 101(1) TFEU in relation to sustainability. The discussion revolves around initiatives by competitors that cooperate to achieve higher degrees of sustainability in various areas. While the sustainability effects may be welcome, such agreements may impair the competitive pressure between companies. Therefore, it is possible that some business practices by several parties fall under the prohibition of Article 101(1) TFEU or respective national rules. One way out of this is the ancillary restraints doctrine. There may also be the opposite case where an agreement harms sustainability and is also anti-competitive. In such cases competition law enforcement could be strengthened. We also look into standardisation agreements – a special case that is highly relevant.

COMPETITION LAW AS AN OBSTACLE TO SUSTAINABILITY INITIATIVES

There may be corporate initiatives that aim to achieve the Sustainable Development Goals but contain competition constraints. Until around the early 2000s, the European Commission had a quite generous practice in sustainability initiatives and exempted them. The current practice cannot be comprehensively mapped due to the self-assessment of companies: it is unclear how many companies have so far assumed that the exemption requirements have been met for their sustainability initiatives, as there is no obligation to provide

---

[1]   Cf Giorgio Monti, 'Article 81 EC and Public Policy' (2002) 39 CML Rev 1057; Christopher Townley, *Article 81 EC and Public Policy* (Hart Publishing 2009); Martin Gassler, 'Sustainability, the Green Deal and Art 101 TFEU: Where We Are and Where We Could Go' (2021) 12 JECLAP 430; Maarten Pieter Schinkel and Leonard Treuren, 'Green Antitrust: (More) Friendly Fire in the Fight against Climate Change' (2021) Amsterdam Law School Research Paper 7/2020 https:// papers .ssrn .com/sol3/papers.cfm?abstract_id=3749147 accessed 10 July 2023; Cento Veljanovski, 'Collusion as Environmental Protection – An economic assessment' (2022) 18 (3) *Journal of Competition Law & Economics* https://academic.oup.com/jcle/article/18/3/523/6389649 accessed 18 August 2023.

information in this respect. However, the criteria for exemptions under Article 101(3) TFEU are demanding and not well-tailored to sustainability initiatives. Attempts to incorporate the Sustainable Development Goals into case practice using economic tools, balancing effects, have proven difficult, as many Sustainable Development Goals defy clear measurement and offsetting with negative effects for competition.

This leaves companies with considerable legal uncertainty when designing sustainability initiatives. It must be taken into account that the exchange of information is often seen as a hardcore restriction of competition law so that even the exchange of information on sustainability and the preparation of a joint sustainability initiative is at risk of fines. A company that wants to be compliant with competition law will tend to shy away from exchanges with competitors.

Competition law does not have to stand in the way of sustainability initiatives.[2] At present, however, it is not particularly easy for companies to make a self-assessment of which cooperations are permitted under competition law. This also applies to the coordinated introduction of sustainability certificates, agreements on advertising or agreements on conditions. At present, the hurdles seem insurmountable if the agreements aimed at achieving higher Sustainable Development Goal targets come with higher prices or a reduction of offers.

If companies are seen as central players in sustainability, their options for action must 'grow' with them to a certain extent. In the following part we turn to the exemption under the ancillary restraints doctrine. At a later point (Chapter 6) we explore the options for exempting agreements under Article 101(3) TFEU.

THE ANCILLARY RESTRAINTS DOCTRINE AND SUSTAINABILITY

In competition law, some cases are excluded from the application of Article 101(1) TFEU when they are ancillary restraints to an agreement. Sustainability has become a topic of interest for the ancillary restraints doctrine. If an agreement between companies is aimed at achieving sustainability goals but contains restrictions of competition, the prohibition under competition law generally applies. However, this can be disregarded if an unwritten exemption under the ancillary restraints doctrine is granted. In this case, competition law does not stand in the way of the sustainability initiative. However, the

---

[2]   See Suzanne Kingston, 'Competition Law in an Environmental Crisis' (2019) 10 JECLAP 517 ff.

ancillary restraints doctrine has so far been available in only a small number of exceptional cases.

The background to this is the more formal approach of the European Court of Justice, which sees an unlawful restriction of competition in the fact that the freedom of action of a market participant is restricted.[3] To avoid the very difficult path of an exemption under Article 101(3) TFEU (in former times granted in a formal procedure by the European Commission) some constellations are identified as not even violating Article 101(1) TFEU – even though there is, technically, a restriction of the freedom of the undertakings concerned. This approach of excluding cases from Article 101(1) renders the examination under Article 101(3) superfluous. The ancillary restraints doctrine argues that some restraints of competition are part of a larger agreement that – in the end – fosters competition. This approach is to be distinguished from the so-called *Wouters* doctrine that we look at in the next part.

Legal Concept

The ECJ partially exempts agreements from the prohibition of Article 101(1) TFEU if the prohibition were to contradict the purpose of the ban on cartels.[4] It is argued that these cases do not even fit under the concept of a restriction of competition, if 'restriction of competition' is interpreted according to the spirit and purpose of the prohibition.[5] An agreement is not subject to the prohibition under Article 101(1) TFEU if it is merely a necessary ancillary agreement to a main agreement which is otherwise neutral or positive in terms of competition.[6] For this to be the case, the restriction must be 'necessary, proportionate, directly related to the main measure and not restrictive of competition as the main object of the agreement'.[7] If this is the case, there is no unlawful restriction of competition, and an exemption under Article 101(3) TFEU is then no longer relevant. The factual exception is made for reasons inherent in competition: without the restriction of competition (e.g., a non-competition

---

[3]   Cf Case 48/69 *ICI v Commission* ECLI:EU:C:1972:70, [1972] ECR 619, paras 104 ff; Case 40/73 *Suiker Unie v Commission* ECLI:EU:C:1975:174, [1975] ECR 1663, paras 172 ff; Case C-89/85 *Ahlström v Commission* ECLI:EU:C:1993:120, [1993] ECR I-1575, paras 59 ff.

[4]   Cf Richard Wish and David Bailey, *Competition Law* (10th edn, Oxford University Press 2021), 139.

[5]   Cf Case T-112/99 *M6 v Commission* ECLI:EU:T:2001:215, [2001] ECR II-2464, para 76.

[6]   Cf Case C-382/12 P *Mastercard v Commission* ECLI:EU:C:2014:2201, para 89; Case 161/84 *Pronuptia de Paris* ECLI:EU:C:1986:41, paras 15 to 17.

[7]   Case T-112/99 *M6 v Commission* ECLI:EU:T:2001:215, [2001] ECR II-2464, para 104.

clause for the seller in a company purchase agreement), the main agreement (the company purchase) would simply not take place.[8] The *Metro* case law on selective distribution[9] and cases where companies can only join the market because of their cooperation (e.g., when they jointly bid for a project that they could not pursue alone)[10] can also be seen as an expression of this reasoning.

In the European Commission's revised Horizontal Guidelines from 2023, the ancillary restraints doctrine is only mentioned in the general section of the guidelines, not in the chapter concerning sustainability agreements: restrictive agreements that are a necessary ancillary to an agreement, which has a positive or neutral effect on competition, are exempt from the antitrust prohibition.[11] The important point here is that there needs to be a 'main' agreement, which does not restrict competition. The Commission does not give an example or explain whether and how a sustainability agreement with restrictive elements can be separated into a competition-neutral 'main agreement' and a competition-restrictive ancillary agreement. Traditionally, the ancillary restraints doctrine, which – as has been noted – is unwritten in competition law applied only to those very specific cases where the courts saw such an ancillary restraint. These cases were usually obvious, like the one on market entry for smaller companies that join forces. It would therefore have been a mere formality to run the (more burdensome) full procedure under Article 101(3) TFEU. With this in mind, it is difficult to create a new exception under the ancillary restraints doctrine for a large number of sustainability initiatives. In particular, it would be essential to show the neutral or pro-competition effects of the main agreement. Nonetheless, we explore the option of such a restriction of Article 101(1) here.

Option RE 1: Competition Restraints in Sustainability Agreements as an Ancillary Restraint

Where sustainability initiatives fall into one of the established constellations of ancillary restraints (e.g., competition clauses in company purchases or where market entry is enabled) the doctrine applies. The question is whether this can be expanded to further cases. Is it an ancillary restraint if supermarkets jointly decide not to sell certain products anymore for reasons of animal welfare? Is it

---

[8]   Cf Richard Wish and David Bailey, *Competition Law* (10th edn, Oxford University Press 2021), 139.
[9]   Case 26/76 *Metro v Commission* [1977] ECR 1875, para 21.
[10] Case 56/65 *LTM v MBU* ECLI:EU:C:1966:38, [1966] OJ 304/1.
[11] European Commission, 'Guidelines on the applicability of Article 101 of the Treaty on the Functioning of the European Union to horizontal co-operation agreements' [2023] OJ C 259/1, para 34.

an ancillary restraint if insurance companies jointly decide not to offer insurance for certain CO_2-emitting factories anymore? The courts or the legislatures could extend the doctrine to such cases, establishing criteria for the necessity of the agreements. This is a policy option, but we do not think that most of the sustainability cases are fitting examples for the ancillary restraints doctrine. There is also no need for such an expansion if Article 101(3) is the better way to deal with such agreements or if the *Wouters* doctrine applies. Where sustainability initiatives raise prices or reduce the product range we find clear restrictions of competition, but no clear push for competition – unless competition is sharply defined as meaning that only sustainable products are on sale. That would be very far-reaching, though, even for advocates of a social-ecological market economy.

To fit into the pattern of ancillary restraints, there would have to be a contract in which a clear distinction could be drawn between a competition-neutral main agreement and a clearly defined subordinate restriction of competition.[12] If such a clear distinction is not possible, there is always the risk that the classification into main and subordinate agreements will be completely random depending on the interpretation. It does not seem obvious that the restriction of competition is of secondary importance, at least in those cases that are of particular interest. Typically, the restriction of competition is at the core of the sustainability initiative, be it that some products are no longer manufactured or the price for harmful products is raised. Such agreements directly relate to the market output and do not have a distinct aim (such as the transfer of a company from A to B). The cooperation agreements captured by the ancillary restraints doctrine typically enhance competition or are at least neutral. Pro-competition agreements are those that are an expression of the operation of competitive processes rather than their restriction. Sustainability cooperation initiatives, however, are designed to intervene in competition processes, i.e., precisely not to allow them to proceed undisturbed. Thus, there is no primarily competition-promoting effect that could justify permitting a comparatively insignificant restriction of competition. Thus, the whole idea of the ancillary restraints doctrine – except a small restriction of competition because of an overwhelming positive effect that needs some restriction – does not fit here.

It may be different when reporting standards for the phasing out of CO_2 emissions are harmonised. In this case, the main thrust of the agreement could be the reduction of environmental damage. The harmonisation of methodologies and standards leads to a certain loss in autonomy for companies that no longer set the standards themselves. Yet, this restriction of competition is necessary to

---

[12] Christoph Reymann, *Immanente Schranken des europäischen Kartellverbots* (Nomos 2004) 233 ff.

have comparable paths to CO_2 reduction and to be able to inform, monitor and compare the efforts. This approach, however, would best be dealt with under the rules for standardisation (to which we return later in this chapter).

The idea of joint market entry under the ancillary restraints doctrine (small companies join a market together) may be suitable for some problems that companies cite as an obstacle to more sustainable management.[13] This is the case when sustainability ambitions that would enhance competition expand the product range, lead to new offers, cannot be realised by one company alone, e.g., because it lacks the necessary financial resources, or because it cannot generate sufficient economies of scale. For example, switching to more sustainable packaging materials may not be possible because owing to insufficient demand suppliers do not want to offer such materials.[14] In these constellations, the idea of developing the market can be made fruitful: joint demand would enable the companies involved to enter a market for products with sustainable packaging in the first place. The companies need to prove the difficulties in achieving market entry on their own to profit from the ancillary restraints doctrine. The European Commission's guidelines could create more legal certainty for companies by providing better examples.

To sum up, the ancillary restraints doctrine as an unwritten element of EU competition law is not the master solution to take sustainability initiatives out of the reach of competition law. The standard constellation does not fit the idea of ancillary restraints. Some agreements however may fall into established categories of the ancillary restraints doctrine, e.g., when market entry is only possible by a joint initiative of companies. If they are able to offer more or new products that they were not able to offer on their own, a non-compete clause may be exempted. Where the range of offer or the demand is reduced, it is not a case for the ancillary restraints doctrine.

THE *WOUTERS* DOCTRINE AND SUSTAINABILITY

Another approach with a similar outcome as the ancillary restraints doctrine, namely an exemption from Article 101(1) TFEU, is the application of the so-called *Wouters* doctrine.[15] Although both approaches are discussed under

---

[13]   Cf Ella van Der Brink and Jordan Ellison, 'Article 101(3) TFEU: The Roadmap for Sustainable Cooperation' in Simon Holmes, Dirk Middelschulte and Martijn Snoep (eds), *Competition Law, Climate Change & Environmental Sustainability* (Concurrences 2021) 41.

[14]   Cf Christiane Dahlbender, 'Sustaining Both the Planet and Competition: A Call for more Guidance' (2021) WuW 392, 393 f.

[15]   Cf Giorgio Monti, 'Article 81 EC and Public Policy' (2002) 39 CML Rev 1057, 1088 f.

the heading of an exemption to Article 101(1) TFEU, the approach to be discussed here differs substantially from the ancillary restraints doctrine: the ancillary restraints doctrine rejects the existence of a prohibited restriction of competition within the meaning of Article 101(1) TFEU for reasons inherent to competition. Such a restriction thus remains within the competition logic of the Treaty. However, a legal rule can be subjected to a restriction not only for reasons inherent to it, but also for distinct considerations, external to the legal provision itself.[16] It is conceivable for a restrictive agreement to be allowed for non-competition reasons, namely in cases where the restriction of competition is necessary to achieve another legitimate objective which is considered to take priority over the protection of competition in the specific case.[17] It is assumed that European law does not give general priority to the protection of competition over all other legitimate objectives.[18] If there is a conflict of different objectives that are on the same level in the hierarchy of law, there must be a way to reconcile these objectives and to solve the conflict.

This concept can be applied to the pursuit of sustainability goals, especially those goals that have a normative foundation in EU primary law (TEU, TFEU and CFR) as objectives of the European Union. This amounts to a levelling of other objectives with the competition agenda of the EU (*levelling approach*). Historically, the protection of competition was a key pillar of the European project, and there were no non-economic objectives pursued in the European project. This led to the assumption in competition law circles that the protection of competition always takes priority. With the more recent developments in the European Union – the expansion of political aims, the introduction of a Charter of Fundamental Rights, ever more competences in fields unrelated to the internal market – the supremacy of the competition principle is challenged. This is all the more so when sustainability is seen as an integral part of a social-ecological market economy.

The objective of the sustainable development of Europe, a strong social market economy and a high level of environmental protection and quality, as set out in Article 3(3) sentence 2 TEU, can be mentioned here. Pursuant to Article 3(5) sentence 2 TEU, the European Union shall also contribute to global sustainable development. Since the Treaty of Lisbon, the protection of competition is no longer listed as an independent objective in Article 3 TEU,

---

[16] Ludger Breuer, *Das EU-Kartellrecht im Kraftfeld der Unionsziele* (Nomos 2012) 629.

[17] Ludger Breuer, *Das EU-Kartellrecht im Kraftfeld der Unionsziele* (Nomos 2012) 629.

[18] Cf Ludger Breuer, *Das EU-Kartellrecht im Kraftfeld der Unionsziele* (Nomos 2012) 629.

but has been moved to a protocol,[19] which is nevertheless part of primary law according to Article 51 TEU. Still, it is obvious that there is room for some coordination of the different objectives.

Starting Point in Case Law: *Albany* and *Wouters*

The starting points for the consideration of other legitimate objectives are the ECJ decisions in *Albany*[20] and *Wouters*.[21] The ECJ later referred to the principles of *Albany* and *Wouters* in a number of other cases and expanded and defined what is now usually called the *Wouters* doctrine.[22]

The subject of *Wouters* is the relationship between the protection of competition and the objective of an orderly administration of justice.[23] The professional code of conduct of the Dutch Bar Association provided for a ban on the formation of mixed partnerships of lawyers and auditors.[24] The reason for the prohibition was the professional secrecy of lawyers in the interest of their clients, which did not exist in a comparable form for auditors.

The ECJ found that in applying the competition rules in a particular case:

> account must first of all be taken of the overall context in which the decision of the association of undertakings was taken or produces its effects. More particularly, account must be taken of its objectives, which are here connected with the need to make rules relating to organisation, qualifications, professional ethics, supervision and liability, in order to ensure that the ultimate consumers of legal services and the sound administration of justice are provided with the necessary guarantees in relation to integrity and experience.[25]

The ECJ therefore did not consider the professional code of conduct to be a violation of the prohibition of agreements restricting competition. By setting the framework for the profession of lawyer, the disputed provision served the goal of enabling a trusting relationship between lawyer and client and

---

[19]   Protocol (No 27) on the internal market and competition [2008] OJ C 115/309.
[20]   Case C-67/96 *Albany* ECLI:EU:C:1999:430, [1999] ECR I-5863.
[21]   Case C-309/99 *Wouters* ECLI:EU:C:2002:98, [2002] ECR I-1653.
[22]   Case C-180/98 *Pavlov* ECLI:EU:C:2000:428, [2000] ECR I-6497; Case C-222/98 *van der Woude* ECLI:EU:C:2000:475, [2000] ECR I-7129; Case C-184/13 et al *API and Others* ECLI:EU:C:2014:2147, [2014]; Case C-1/12 *OTOC* ECLI:EU:C:2013:127 [2013]; Case C-136/12 *Consiglio nazionale dei geologi* ECLI:EU:C:2013:489 [2013]; Case T-93/18 *ISU* ECLI:EU:T:2020:610 [2020] para 71.
[23]   Case C-309/99 *Wouters* ECLI:EU:C:2002:98, [2002] ECR I-1653.
[24]   Case C-309/99 *Wouters* ECLI:EU:C:2002:98, [2002] ECR I-1653.
[25]   Case C-309/99 *Wouters* ECLI:EU:C:2002:98 [2002] ECR I-1653, para 97.

the orderly administration of justice.[26] This is an important objective, and the provision is also objectively necessary to achieve this objective.[27]

In *Albany,* the exception was explicitly based on the pursuit of a Union objective.[28] In addition to the protection of competition, the European Treaties also pursue social policy objectives (Articles 153–155 TFEU). These objectives must be reconciled.[29] Insofar as the application of the competition rules would seriously jeopardise the objectives of social policy, the facts must be interpreted restrictively in the opinion of the ECJ.[30]

The subject of the proceedings was compulsory membership in a company pension fund designed to secure a certain pension level and working conditions. The core issue was the permissibility of restrictions on competition in collective agreements.[31] The responsible Dutch minister declared the obligation contained in a collective agreement to compulsorily join an occupational pension fund to be binding.[32] The ECJ held that, despite the intrinsically restrictive effect of the measure, the facts did not meet Article 101(1) TFEU.[33] If the ban on cartels were to have full effect, the objectives of European social policy as laid down in the Treaties would be seriously harmed.[34] There is therefore no illegal restriction of competition if agreements are made in collective agreements to improve employment and working conditions.[35]

This case also illustrates the tension between competition and the public interest, in this case social policy.[36] Unlike in *Wouters*, the ECJ in *Albany* explicitly relies on the Union objectives standardised in the Treaties. What both cases have in common is that the prohibition under Article 101(1) TFEU was declared inapplicable with regard to objectives other than the protection of competition.

---

[26] Case C-309/99 *Wouters* ECLI:EU:C:2002:98 [2002] ECR I-1653, paras 107 ff.
[27] Case C-309/99 *Wouters* ECLI:EU:C:2002:98, [2002] ECR I-1653, paras 107 ff.
[28] Case C-67/96 *Albany* ECLI:EU:C:1999:430 [1999] ECR I-5863.
[29] Cf Case C-67/96 *Albany* ECLI:EU:C:1999:430 [1999] ECR I-5863, para 54.
[30] Case C-67/96 *Albany* ECLI:EU:C:1999:430 [1999] ECR I-5863, paras 59 f.
[31] Case C-67/96 *Albany* ECLI:EU:C:1999:430 [1999] ECR I-5863, paras 63 f.
[32] Case C-67/96 *Albany* ECLI:EU:C:1999:430 [1999] ECR I-5863, para 25.
[33] Case C-67/96 *Albany* ECLI:EU:C:1999:430 [1999] ECR I-5863, paras 60, 64.
[34] Case C-67/96 *Albany* ECLI:EU:C:1999:430 [1999] ECR I-5863, paras 59 f.
[35] Case C-67/96 *Albany* ECLI:EU:C:1999:430 [1999] ECR I-5863, para 59.
[36] Clemens Latzel and Stephan Serr, 'Kartellkontrollprivileg für Tarifverträge als formeller Rahmen eines Unionstarifrechts' (2014) EuZW 410, 411.

Special Constellation or General Rule?

The ECJ has not yet applied the *Wouters* doctrine in favour of environmental protection or other sustainability goals in any proceedings, but it has not yet been involved in such a case.

As a preliminary consideration for whether the idea of the decisions can be applied to sustainability initiatives, it is important to discuss how *Wouters* and *Albany* should be understood. Their interpretation is still disputed two decades after their pronouncement, despite some follow-up decisions. Common to both decisions is that the ECJ denied a violation of Article 101(1) TFEU despite the existence of a formal restriction of competition. What is disputed is the legal reasoning on which the exception is granted.

According to some scholars, the ECJ has created a system with which conflicts between the protection of competition and other legitimate objectives can be resolved. The pursuit of an important general interest or Union objective is sufficient to justify the restriction of competition, so that the decisions can be applied to other cases involving public interests.[37]

According to this view, the ECJ approximates competition law to the case law on the fundamental freedoms under Articles 34 et seq. TFEU, where state intervention in the internal market is ultimately also allowed for reasons of public interest.[38] This is supported in particular by the fact that the ECJ in *Wouters* refers to its decision *Reisebüro Broede*[39] on the freedom to provide services (Article 56 TFEU).[40] While the fundamental freedoms protect the internal market from interference by the state, Articles 101, 102 TFEU are intended to protect the internal market from harmful conduct by private parties.[41] If the fundamental freedoms can be restricted for various reasons, this

---

[37]   In this sense Giorgio Monti, 'Article 81 EC and Public Policy' (2002) 39 CML Rev 1057, 1088 f; Maurits Dolmans, 'Sustainable Competition Policy and the "Polluter Pays" Principle' in Simon Holmes, Dirk Middelschulte and Martijn Snoep (eds), *Competition Law, Climate Change & Environmental Sustainability* (Concurrences 2021) 28 ff; Roman Inderst and Stefan Thomas, 'Legal Design in Sustainable Antitrust' (*SSRN*, 2022), 7 https:// papers .ssrn .com/ sol3/ papers .cfm ?abstract _id = 4058367 accessed 24 July 2023.

[38]   Giorgio Monti, 'Article 81 EC and Public Policy' (2002) 39 CML Rev 1057, 1088 f; Assimakis P Komninos, 'Non-competition Concerns: Resolution of Conflicts in the Integrated Article 81 EC' (2005) The University of Oxford Centre for Competition Law and Policy Working Paper 8/2005, 13 www .law .ox .ac .uk/ sites/ default/ files/ migrated/cclp_l_08-05.pdf accessed 15 August 2023.

[39]   Case C-3/95 *Reisebüro Broede* ECLI:EU:C:1996:487, [1996] ECR I-6529.

[40]   Giorgio Monti, 'Article 81 EC and Public Policy' (2002) 39 CML Rev 1057, 1087.

[41]   Anna Gerbrandy, Willem Janssen and Lyndsey Thomsin, 'Shaping the Social Market Economy After the Lisbon Treaty: How "Social" is Public Economic Law?' (2019) *Utrecht Law Review* 32, 36.

argues in favour of also viewing the competition provisions as being open to a balancing with other objectives. According to this reading of *Wouters*, the justification test in the *Cassis de Dijon*[42] style was therefore transferred by the ECJ to Article 101(1) TFEU in order to avoid contradictory results.[43]

Moreover, so it is argued, the *Wouters* case law is not limited to cases in which original state legislative tasks are delegated to private self-regulatory organisations.[44] This is supported in particular by the follow-up decision in *Meca-Medina*:[45] The subject of this case was the admissibility under competition law of anti-doping regulations in the rules and regulations of sports associations. The ECJ found no violation of Article 101(1) TFEU despite the formal anti-competitive nature of the anti-doping rules and corresponding sanctions, as the rules were necessary and proportionate for the functioning of a sporting competition. For this reasoning, the ECJ referred to *Wouters*.[46]

Other voices see non-generalisable special constellations in the decisions for a variety of reasons.[47]

Some argue that the prohibition of mixed partnerships of lawyers and auditors at issue in *Wouters,* just as in the decisions *API*,[48] *OTOC*[49] and *Consiglio nazionale di geologi*[50] referring to it, is about the delegation of typical state legislative powers to specially recognised professional organisations.[51] This is supported by the fact that the ECJ repeatedly refers to the public law structure of the professional code of conduct in the Netherlands.[52] The *Meca-Medina*

---

[42] Case C-120/78 *Cassis-de-Dijon* ECLI:EU:C:1979:42 [1979] ECR 649.

[43] Giorgio Monti, 'Article 81 EC and Public Policy' (2002) 39 CML Rev, 1088.

[44] Cf Ludger Breuer, *Das EU-Kartellrecht im Kraftfeld der Unionsziele* (Nomos 2012) 566.

[45] Case C-519/04 *Meca-Medina* ECLI:EU:C:2006:492 [2006] ECR I-7006.

[46] Case C-519/04 *Meca-Medina* ECLI:EU:C:2006:492 [2006] ECR I-7006, para 42.

[47] Edith Loozen, 'Strict Competition Enforcement and Welfare: A Constitutional Perspective Based on Article 101 TFEU and Sustainability' (2019) 56 CML Rev 1256, 1290; Ella van den Brink and Jordan Ellison, 'Article 101(3) TFEU: the Roadmap for Sustainable Cooperation' in Simon Holmes, Dirk Middelschulte and Martijn Snoep (eds), *Competition Law, Climate Change & Environmental Sustainability* (Concurrences 2021) 42; see also Edith Loozen, 'Professional Ethics and Restraints of Competition' (2006) 31 EL Rev 28, 47.

[48] Case C-184/13 et al *API and Others* ECLI:EU:C:2014:2147 [2014].

[49] Case C-1/12 *OTOC* ECLI:EU:C:2013:127 [2013].

[50] Case C-136/12 *Consiglio nazionale dei geologi* ECLI:EU:C:2013:489 [2013].

[51] Cf Christoph U Schmid, 'Diagonal Competence Conflicts between European Competition Law and National Regulation – A Conflict of Laws Reconstruction of the Dispute on Book Price Fixing' (2000) 8 *European Review of Private Law* 155, 166 f, who requires the assumption of a sovereign activity by private parties.

[52] Edith Loozen, 'Strict Competition Enforcement and Welfare: A Constitutional Perspective Based on Article 101 TFEU and Sustainability' (2019) 56 CML Rev 1256,

proceedings can be interpreted similarly,[53] even if at first glance there is no delegation of legislative powers. Some argue that although the ECJ referred to the *Wouters* criteria, it actually used an argument comparable to the ancillary restraints doctrine.[54] The justification for the admissibility of anti-doping regulations in professional sports was not the pursuit of a reasonable cause in itself, but that such regulations were necessary for the functioning of the sports market – or immanent to it.[55] The fact that the ECJ referred to the *Wouters* case law was therefore superfluous and an error that invited misinterpretation.[56]

Other voices see the essential point of *Wouters* not in a delegation of state law-making powers, but generally in an exceptionally permissible private self-regulation. According to this view, *Meca-Medina* fits in with the *Wouters* doctrine, since in both cases there is a permissible self-regulation of sports associations on the basis of their fundamental rights (Article 11 para 1 ECHR, Article 12 CFR).[57] This is also supported, for example, by the frequent use of terms such as 'rules and regulations', which are typical for self-regulating organisations. In the *ISU* proceedings from 2020, the court also referred very clearly to the regulatory power of a sports federation.[58] Still, others see the reason for the exception in the correction of a market failure.[59] This cannot be applied to every agreement between competitors that are pursuing a supposedly legitimate goal.[60]

1290. See also Charlotte Janssen and Erik Kloosterhuis, 'The Wouters Case Law, Special for a Different Reason?' (2016) 37 ECLR 335, 338.

[53]   Case C-519/04 *Meca-Medina* ECLI:EU:C:2006:492 [2006] ECR I-7006.

[54]   Heike Schweitzer, 'Die Bedeutung nicht-wettbewerblicher Aspekte für die Auslegung von Art. 101 AEUV im Lichte der Querschnittsklauseln' in Monopolkommission (ed), *Politischer Einfluss auf Wettbewerbsentscheidungen* (Nomos 2015) 36.

[55]   Edith Loozen, 'Strict Competition Enforcement and Welfare: A Constitutional Perspective Based on Article 101 TFEU and Sustainability' (2019) 56 CML Rev 1256, 1292.

[56]   Edith Loozen, 'Strict Competition Enforcement and Welfare: A Constitutional Perspective Based on Article 101 TFEU and Sustainability' (2019) 56 CML Rev 1256, 1292 ff.

[57]   Cf Richard Wish and David Bailey, *Competition Law* (10th edn, Oxford University Press 2021), 142.

[58]   Case T-93/18 *ISU* ECLI:EU:T:2020:610 [2020] para 71.

[59]   Charlotte Janssen and Erik Kloosterhuis, 'The Wouters Case Law, Special for a Different Reason?' (2016) 37 ECLR 335, 336 f.

[60]   Cf Heike Schweitzer, 'Die Bedeutung nicht-wettbewerblicher Aspekte für die Auslegung von Art. 101 AEUV im Lichte der Querschnittsklauseln' in Monopolkommission (ed), *Politischer Einfluss auf Wettbewerbsentscheidungen* (Nomos 2015) 33.

Similar concerns are also raised with *Albany*. It is not sufficient for the exception that the agreement serves a Union objective. It is a non-negligible prerequisite that the European treaties leave the responsibility for determining working conditions to the parties to collective agreements.[61] In other words, a restriction in the sense of the *Albany* decision requires that European primary law expressly approves an act of private parties (in the case of *Albany*: conclusion of collective agreements on certain contractual conditions).[62] This is also made clear in the *Pavlov* decision.[63] The ECJ stated that a restriction of competition rules cannot be considered because primary law does not approve of collective agreements by members of the liberal professions.

Overall, so the proponents of a narrow reading of *Wouters* say, it cannot be assumed that the ECJ was generally prepared to open up the ban on restrictive business agreements for balancing with all sorts of other objectives. The sole purpose of the competition law is to protect competition – all overriding objectives need a much better legitimacy.[64]

The case law of the ECJ in *Albany* and *Wouters* is unclear. Apart from the constellations already specifically decided, it does not provide any certainty with regard to the pursuit of non-competition objectives through agreements restricting competition.[65]

To clarify these issues, the ECJ would have to rule on agreements between competitors which have the objective of promoting sustainability concerns. For this, the European Commission would have to conduct proceedings against companies involved in sustainability cooperation or civil law actions would have to be brought against sustainability cooperation. This would clarify which other legitimate objectives can justify an exception to Article 101(1)

---

[61] Heike Schweitzer, 'Die Bedeutung nicht-wettbewerblicher Aspekte für die Auslegung von Art. 101 AEUV im Lichte der Querschnittsklauseln' in Monopolkommission (ed), *Politischer Einfluss auf Wettbewerbsentscheidungen* (Nomos 2015) 33.

[62] Roman Inderst and Stefan Thomas, 'Legal Design in Sustainable Antitrust' (*SSRN*, 2022) https://papers.ssrn.com/sol3/papers.cfm?abstract_id=4058367 accessed 24 July 2023.

[63] Case C-180/98 *Pavlov* ECLI:EU:C:2000:428 [2000] ECR I-6497, para 69.

[64] Edith Loozen, 'Professional Ethics and Restraints of Competition' (2006) 31 EL Rev 28, 46.

[65] Charlotte Janssen and Erik Kloosterhuis, 'The Wouters Case Law, Special for a Different Reason?' (2016) 37 ECLR 335; Giorgio Monti and Jotte Mulder, 'Escaping the Clutches of EU Competition Law: Pathways to Assess Private Sustainability Initiatives' (2017) 42 EL Rev 635, 646; Ella van den Brink and Jordan Ellison, 'Article 101(3) TFEU: The Roadmap for Sustainable Cooperation' in Simon Holmes, Dirk Middelschulte and Martijn Snoep (eds), *Competition Law, Climate Change & Environmental Sustainability* (Concurrences 2021) 43; see also Constanze Semmelmann, *Social Policy Goals in the Interpretation of Article 81 EC* (Nomos 2008) 106.

TFEU. In particular, the court would have to spell out what legal quality such objectives must have. There may also be further requirements beyond the pursuit of a legitimate objective and the necessity and proportionality to achieve the objective. Necessity and proportionality would have to be defined in the context of sustainability agreements, including a yardstick for balancing the restraint of competition with the attainment of other goals. Where the whole functioning of another sub-system that is recognised by European law, e.g., trade unions that enter into collective agreements, or sporting events that want to abolish doping, is at stake, it is conceivable to have another *Wouters* style exception. It is not so clear where sustainability concerns reach a similar degree of organisation.

Horizontal Guidelines 2023

In the European Commission's revised horizontal guidelines from 2023 exemptions for non-competition reasons are only touched upon once. In the section devoted to sustainability initiatives, it says that a restrictive agreement cannot escape the prohibition in Article 101(1) simply by referring to a sustainability objective.[66] In a footnote, there is a reference to the *Wouters* and *Meca-Medina* decisions. The cases are summarised by saying that restrictive agreements may fall outside the scope of Article 101(1) if they are inherent to the pursuit of a legitimate objective and proportionate thereto.[67] In principle, this opens the door to the application of this case law to sustainability agreements, especially since in the draft version of the revised horizontal guidelines, the Commission was a bit more restrictive. In the draft guidelines, the Commission had stressed that these cases deal with agreements concerning the practice of certain professions. The new wording seems to be more open in this regard. However, an application of this line of case law to sustainability goals is not discussed further in the Guidance.

Option RE 2: General Exception Under the *Wouters* Doctrine in Favour of Sustainability

An exception for sustainability agreements in the sense of the *Albany* and *Wouters* decisions is one of the main approaches discussed when the integra-

---

[66] European Commission, 'Guidelines on the applicability of Article 101 of the Treaty on the Functioning of the European Union to horizontal co-operation agreements' [2023] OJ C 259/1, para 521.
[67] European Commission, 'Guidelines on the applicability of Article 101 of the Treaty on the Functioning of the European Union to horizontal co-operation agreements' [2023] OJ C 259/1, para 521.

tion of Sustainable Development Goals is at stake in competition law.[68] This approach is advocated, for example, by the Hellenic Competition Authority.[69]

In evaluating this option, a distinction must be drawn between *Albany* and *Wouters* due to the differences highlighted above. In our view, the *Albany* decision cannot be applied to sustainability initiatives.[70] The exception accepted there does not merely presuppose that the parties are pursuing a legitimate goal with the improvement of working and employment conditions. The exception is based on the European primary law that concretely places value on collective agreements.[71] Article 101(1) TFEU cannot prohibit conduct which primary law elsewhere approves and even supports. There is no indication in primary law that environmental protection or other sustainability goals are to be achieved precisely through the cooperation of undertakings. This is different for collective agreements like in *Albany*.

In contrast, the *Wouters* doctrine is a viable way to better take into account sustainability aspects in the prohibition of restrictive business practices under Article 101(1) TFEU.

Concept

Making an exemption as in *Wouters* for sustainability initiatives means that restrictive agreements between undertakings are exempt from the ban under Article 101(1) TFEU, provided that two criteria are cumulatively met: the agreement must serve a legitimate purpose and be necessary or indispensable to the achievement of that purpose. Proving the necessity of the restriction of competition for achieving the objective is the bottleneck of this solution.

If these conditions are met, the approach offers a relatively clear solution that provides legal certainty to businesses. It avoids the complexity of exemptions under Article 101(3) TFEU and does not undermine the competition law approach within Article 101 TFEU. Necessity (as in this exception) is less

---

[68] Thus Giorgio Monti, 'Article 81 EC and Public Policy' (2002) 39 CML Rev 1057, 1090; Simon Holmes, 'Climate Change, Sustainability, and Competition Law' (2020) 8 *Journal of Antitrust Enforcement* 354, 371; Giorgio Monti and Jotte Mulder, 'Escaping the Clutches of EU Competition Law: Pathways to Assess Private Sustainability Initiatives' (2017) 42 EL Rev 635, 646.

[69] Hellenic Competition Authority, 'Draft Staff Discussion Paper on Sustainability Issues and Competition Law' (2020) paras 56 f. In its draft guidelines for sustainability cooperation, the Austrian Competition Authority is cautious about the application of the *Wouters criteria* and merely states that a case-by-case assessment is necessary.

[70] Martin Gassler, 'Sustainability, the Green Deal and Art 101 TFEU: Where We Are and Where We Could Go' (2021) 12 JECLAP 430, 433.

[71] Roman Inderst and Stefan Thomas, 'Legal Design in Sustainable Antitrust' (*SSRN*, 2022), 8 https:// papers .ssrn .com/ sol3/ papers .cfm ?abstract _id = 4058367 accessed 24 July 2023.

loaded with economic evidence and complex calculations than the balancing of positive and negative effects under Article 101(3) TFEU – it is much more driven by normative determinations.

On substance, a public interest is given priority over the protection of competition.[72] This is the key difference from the balancing process presented below as Option EX3. However, the public interest objectives that can be considered under this doctrine are predefined by law. While competition law loses its supremacy, the solution is very much in line with the rule of law and democratic values. Usually, the legislature could force undertakings to fulfil certain standards or to cooperate. If it so decided, competition would also need to take a back seat. It therefore seems appropriate to allow other objectives to take precedence over competition if there is a legislative specification and the agreement is necessary to achieve this objective.

A limitation of the approach arises for sustainability goals for which there is no specific and concrete legislative anchor. Sustainability cooperation on such objectives could not rely on the *Wouters* doctrine and would continue to fall under the exemption under Article 101(3) TFEU.

The comparison with the approach to the fundamental freedoms highlights a difference that may be taken into account. Although the *Wouters* criteria are reminiscent of the *Cassis de Dijon* case law on the restriction of European fundamental freedoms, state restrictions of the internal market are democratically decided upon and are not just a vague possibility of action (as in the cases at hand).[73] In the *Cassis* line of cases, government intervention is aligned with EU rules. In *Wouters*, the actions of private companies are at stake – undertakings cannot be granted that same power to interfere with the internal market or competition, even if the legislature could order them to do so. It has not done so, that is why the problem arises in the first place. The legitimacy has a different origin.[74] In order to pursue this approach, the legitimate objectives need to be clearly defined and limited. Competition law cannot forego its regulatory power to undertakings.

---

[72] Critically also Christoph U Schmid, 'Diagonal Competence Conflicts between European Competition Law and National Regulation – A Conflict of Laws Reconstruction of the Dispute on Book Price Fixing' (2000) *European Review of Private Law* 155, 167.

[73] Cf Christoph U Schmid, 'Diagonal Competence Conflicts between European Competition Law and National Regulation – A Conflict of Laws Reconstruction of the Dispute on Book Price Fixing' (2000) *European Review of Private Law* 155, 166.

[74] Cf Christoph U Schmid, 'Diagonal Competence Conflicts between European Competition Law and National Regulation – A Conflict of Laws Reconstruction of the Dispute on Book Price Fixing' (2000) *European Review of Private Law* 155, 166 f.

It has been argued that a key difference to *Wouters* and *Meca-Medina* is that the associations (the Dutch bar organisation, sports federations) in these cases have some specific regulatory privilege granted by the state that is missing in sustainability initiatives. This makes a difference and speaks at least for a much more thorough investigation of necessity.

The proposals by *Roman Inderst* and *Stefan Thomas* address some of these concerns in a sensible way.

Proposal by *Inderst/Thomas*

Inderst and *Thomas* have presented a concept for restrictions in favour of sustainability initiatives.[75] For reasons of simplification, they refer to the application of the ancillary restraints doctrine, but essentially apply the *Wouters* line of jurisprudence. As a common element of both doctrines, it is emphasised that no balancing between anti-competition effects on the one hand and positive effects for other objectives is to be carried out. This is supposed to be the advantage of this approach compared to solutions under Article 101(3) TFEU, where a case-by-case examination of the concrete and measurable effects is always required.[76]

The authors highlight two criteria for an exception to the ban on cartels under Article 101(1) TFEU: the agreement must pursue a legitimate objective and the agreement must be necessary or indispensable to the achievement of this objective.[77] The fact that this is a legitimate objective must result from European law itself and cannot be determined by the companies involved.[78] In particular, the objectives of the Union (Article 3 TEU) and the horizontal clauses (Articles 7 et seq. TFEU) can be used here.[79]

However, for *Inderst* and *Thomas* it is not sufficient that the objective of an agreement restricting competition can be subsumed under the broadly for-

---

[75] Roman Inderst and Stefan Thomas, 'Legal Design in Sustainable Antitrust' (*SSRN*, 2022) https://papers.ssrn.com/sol3/papers.cfm?abstract_id=4058367 accessed 24 July 2023.

[76] Roman Inderst and Stefan Thomas, 'Legal Design in Sustainable Antitrust' (*SSRN*, 2022), 4 f https:// papers .ssrn .com/ sol3/ papers .cfm ?abstract _id = 4058367 accessed 24 July 2023.

[77] Roman Inderst and Stefan Thomas, 'Legal Design in Sustainable Antitrust' (*SSRN,* 2022), 9 https:// papers .ssrn .com/ sol3/ papers .cfm ?abstract _id = 4058367 accessed 24 July 2023.

[78] Roman Inderst and Stefan Thomas, 'Legal Design in Sustainable Antitrust' (*SSRN*, 2022), 10 https:// papers .ssrn .com/ sol3/ papers .cfm ?abstract _id = 4058367 accessed 24 July 2023.

[79] Roman Inderst and Stefan Thomas, 'Legal Design in Sustainable Antitrust' (*SSRN*, 2022), 14 ff https:// papers .ssrn .com/ sol3/ papers .cfm ?abstract _id=4058367 accessed 24 July 2023.

mulated objectives of the European Union. Rather, it is additionally required that the respective national legislator concretise these legitimate objectives.[80] Thus, it would not be sufficient for an agreement to abstractly serve environmental protection. What this specification could mean is shown by *Inderst* and *Thomas* in three groups of cases:

- The first type of specification relates to sustainability goals that national legislators have set out in concrete regulation. For example, if a national legislator provides for due diligence obligations in supply chains this would serve as a specification of the abstract EU objective of complying with human rights. Compliance with human rights in the concrete form of the national supply chain act can be regarded as a legitimate objective within the meaning of the *Wouters* case law.[81] This opens the way to legal agreements, provided that they are indispensable for the compliance with the objective.[82] This could be the case, for example, if companies develop joint standards for compliance with due diligence obligations in order to minimise the risk of violations.[83]
- The second group of cases involves sovereign mandates for the development of common standards. For example, the legislator could set a target stating that 80 per cent of slaughtered animals must meet certain animal welfare criteria but leave the specific design how to reach that target to the industry. It is conceivable that a uniform specification by the industry could lead to more cost-effective solutions. In such a case, agreements

---

[80] Roman Inderst and Stefan Thomas, 'Legal Design in Sustainable Antitrust' (*SSRN*, 2022), 17 https:// papers .ssrn .com/ sol3/ papers .cfm ?abstract _id = 4058367 accessed 24 July 2023. In this sense also Charlotte Janssen and Erik Kloosterhuis, 'The Wouters Case Law, Special for a Different Reason?' (2016) 37 ECLR 335, 338; Hellenic Competition Commission, 'Draft Staff Discussion Paper on Sustainability Issues and Competition Law' (2020) para 57 www.epant.gr/ files/ 2020/ Staff_Discussion_paper .pdf accessed 17 August 2023.

[81] Cf Roman Inderst and Stefan Thomas, 'Legal Design in Sustainable Antitrust' (*SSRN*, 2022), 18 ff https:// papers .ssrn .com/ sol3/ papers .cfm ?abstract_id=4058367 accessed 24 July 2023.

[82] Cf Roman Inderst and Stefan Thomas, 'Legal Design in Sustainable Antitrust' (*SSRN*, 2022), 19 f https:// papers .ssrn .com/ sol3/ papers .cfm ?abstract _id = 4058367 accessed 24 July 2023.

[83] Roman Inderst and Stefan Thomas, 'Legal Design in Sustainable Antitrust' (*SSRN*, 2022), 19 https:// papers .ssrn .com/ sol3/ papers .cfm ?abstract _id = 4058367 accessed 24 July 2023.

could be justified, since a specific form of joint action by undertakings has been mandated by law.[84] This is closer to the *Albany* jurisprudence.[85]

• The third group of cases concerns sustainability targets which the legislator has not specified in concrete terms by imposing obligations on specific companies, as in the first group of cases, but by setting national, more abstract targets. Obviously, this relates to the reduction of CO_2 emissions, to which the member states of the EU have committed themselves through international, EU and national law.[86] The specification may be concrete enough to lead to a permissible cooperation under the *Wouters* criteria.[87]

The latter approach is similarly advocated by the Dutch ACM in its draft guidelines, there relating to an exemption under Article 101(3) TFEU.[88] Companies cannot rely on any legitimate objectives arising from the European or national legal systems, but only those that have undergone a concretisation by the national (or the European) legislator. The legislator must have already imposed concrete obligations on the companies involved to achieve a legitimate objective (e.g., environmental protection), where the companies can then prove that only joint realisation is possible. Even without concrete obligations on the part of individual companies, legislative concretisation can also be achieved by specifying national targets. The necessity of the joint agreement should not be understood in the sense that it would not be possible to achieve the objective in another way.[89] After all, other ways are always possible for such objectives. In this case, it should only be considered whether the specific reduction of CO_2 sought (e.g., through the installation of better filter systems)

---

[84] Roman Inderst and Stefan Thomas, 'Legal Design in Sustainable Antitrust' (*SSRN*, 2022), 20 f https://papers.ssrn.com/sol3/papers.cfm?abstract_id=4058367 accessed 24 July 2023.

[85] Cf Roman Inderst and Stefan Thomas, 'Legal Design in Sustainable Antitrust' (*SSRN*, 2022), 10 f https://papers.ssrn.com/sol3/papers.cfm?abstract_id=4058367 accessed 24 July 2023.

[86] Roman Inderst and Stefan Thomas, 'Legal Design in Sustainable Antitrust' (*SSRN*, 2022), 21 ff https://papers.ssrn.com/sol3/papers.cfm?abstract_id=4058367 accessed 24 July 2023.

[87] Roman Inderst and Stefan Thomas, 'Legal Design in Sustainable Antitrust' (*SSRN*, 2022), 22 https://papers.ssrn.com/sol3/papers.cfm?abstract_id=4058367 accessed 24 July 2023.

[88] Autoriteit Consument & Markt, 'Second draft version: Guidelines on Sustainability Agreements – Opportunities within competition law' (26 January 2021) para 38 www.acm.nl/en/publications/second-draft-version-guidelines-sustainability-agreements-opportunities-within-competition-law accessed 22 June 2023.

[89] Cf Roman Inderst and Stefan Thomas, 'Legal Design in Sustainable Antitrust' (*SSRN*, 2022), 23 f https://papers.ssrn.com/sol3/papers.cfm?abstract_id=4058367 accessed 24 July 2023.

could also be achieved without an agreement.[90] In addition, the requirements for concretisation should not be too strict, otherwise the boundary to regulation would be blurred.

Advantages of this option

The approach of *Inderst* and *Thomas* has several merits. The authors clear up the ambiguities of the *Wouters* line of jurisprudence, in particular through opening the way for a better specification of the more general objectives in EU law. Without such specification there may be a lack of sufficient legitimacy for private intervention in the market mechanism.[91] However, it is unclear whether the ECJ actually considers a concretisation by the legislator to be necessary. While *Wouters* can be interpreted in this way, *Meca-Medina* does not indicate that this is the case.[92]

The requirement of legislative concretisation offers the advantage that the objectives are more limited and better legitimised. This is more elegant than seeking a difficult balancing exercise in agencies or courts, trying to calculate the trade-offs of anti-competition activities and pro-sustainable efforts.

Procedural dimension

The option explored here – expanding the *Wouters* doctrine to certain sustainability agreements – does not require changes in procedure. Once national or European legislators have given the objectives a specification that makes them more concrete, it is for the companies (in self-assessment) or the competition agencies (in case of doubt) to assess whether the agreements are necessary to achieve the aims. This is where the individual assessment of the case kicks in. The European Commission could increasingly make use of the non-applicability decision pursuant to Article 10 of Regulation (EC) 1/2003, whereby the Commission can determine by decision that there is no violation of Article 101 TFEU. This provides more guidance.

---

[90]　Cf Roman Inderst and Stefan Thomas, 'Legal Design in Sustainable Antitrust' (*SSRN*, 2022), 22 f https://papers.ssrn.com/sol3/papers.cfm?abstract_id=4058367 accessed 24 July 2023; see also on the exemption Theon van Dijk, 'A New Approach to Assess Certain Sustainability Agreements under Competition Law' in Simon Holmes, Dirk Middelschulte and Martijn Snoep (eds), *Competition Law, Climate Change & Environmental Sustainability* (Concurrences 2021) 61.

[91]　Cf Constanze Semmelmann, *Social Policy Goals in the Interpretation of Article 81 EC* (Nomos 2008) 107 f; Charlotte Janssen and Erik Kloosterhuis, 'The Wouters Case Law, Special for a Different Reason?' (2016) 37 ECLR 335, 339.

[92]　Constanze Semmelmann, *Social Policy Goals in the Interpretation of Article 81 EC* (Nomos 2008) 106.

RESTRICTIONS OF COMPETITION HARMING SUSTAINABILITY

If companies collude and as a result of the collusion sustainability is weakened, the question arises of whether Article 101 TFEU or respective national rules are applicable to the case. The answer may be yes is if there is a restriction of competition.

A restriction of competition relevant to sustainability occurs when companies agree on competition parameters and thereby harm the environment or disregard other sustainability goals. This could be the case, for example, if companies jointly decide not to use environmentally friendly packaging, to continue using certain toxic ingredients, or if they jointly decide against human rights improvements for suppliers in other countries.

Case Study: *Car Emissions*

A prominent antitrust case with a sustainability connection is the European Commission's '*Car Emissions*' case involving leading German car manufacturers.[93] The Commission ruled that agreements restricting competition for innovation are subject to the prohibition of cartels. Over a period of five years, the manufacturers agreed not to compete in the area of cleaning the exhaust gas stream. They decided not to over-fulfil legal requirements, i.e. to compete on cleaning better than required by the law.[94] These agreements led to the elimination of uncertainty about future market behaviour. The Commission imposed fines of €875,189,000.

The European Commission took a similar decision in 2011 in the *Consumer Detergents case*.[95] The proceedings were based on agreements between detergent manufacturers who initially lawfully agreed on certain environmental standards as part of an environmental protection initiative. However, as part of this initiative, the companies also agreed not to use the initiative to outdo each other in competition and that market conditions should remain unaffected by

---

[93] *Car Emissions* (Case AT.40178) Commission Decision C 458/11 [2021] 4955 final.

[94] *Car Emissions* (Case AT.40178) Commission Decision C 458/11 [2021] 4955 final, paras 103 ff.

[95] *Consumer Detergents* (Case COMP/39.579) Commission Decision 2011/C 193/06 [2011] OJ C 193/14.

the initiative.[96] In addition, they agreed not to pass on potential cost savings to consumers.[97] The Commission imposed fines of €315,200,000.

As these decisions show, the ban on cartels can be used against agreements that restrict competition for sustainable solutions.[98] In this respect, competition law acts as a 'sword' against practices that are harmful to sustainability.

Restrictions on Innovation

If one generalises the 'theory of harm' from *Car Emissions*, it becomes clear that the obstruction of innovations can be harmful to sustainability – especially if one regards technological solutions as an essential element in combating the climate catastrophe. So far, however, pure restrictions on innovation had not been identified as hardcore restrictions. In *Consumer Detergents*, there had still been pricing elements and a tangible monetary loss for consumers, so that the case still falls into the more established categories of restrictions on price. This changed with *Car Emissions* in 2021 when, for the first time, there was no pricing element and no direct loss for consumers was involved. Competition law can promote the achievement of sustainability goals by eliminating restrictions on competition that limit competition for sustainable solutions. The example of *Car Emissions* is proof of this.

Similarly, agreements could be prohibited that foreclose access to markets that are particularly relevant to sustainability for innovative suppliers or suppliers that operate in a particularly sustainable manner.

However, innovations do not necessarily promote sustainability. For example, an innovation could be that a product becomes more convenient for consumers to use but requires more energy input. If companies collude to stop innovations that are detrimental to sustainability, this is a case where competition law could be an obstacle to greater sustainability – we go into more detail below.

If innovation competition is generally restricted without the outcome being certain, this can be qualified as detrimental to sustainability. Admittedly, keeping innovation paths open does not yet indicate whether an innovation is sustainable or not. On the other hand, pressing problems require disruptive innovations, so that any curtailment of inventiveness cuts off this potential.

---

[96]   *Consumer Detergents* (Case COMP/39.579) Commission Decision 2011/C 193/06 [2011] OJ C 193/14, paras 22 ff.
[97]   *Consumer Detergents* (Case COMP/39.579) Commission Decision 2011/C 193/06 [2011] OJ C 193/14, para 25.
[98]   Julian Nowag, 'Competition Law's Sustainability Gap? Tools for an Examination and a Brief Overview' (2022) 5(1) *Nordic Journal of European Law* 9 https://journals .lub.lu.se/njel/article/view/24504 accessed 18 August 2023.

Second, regulation and financing instruments today largely ensure that innovation paths tend to be designed sustainably. Agreements that hinder innovation should therefore continue to be prohibited by competition law on the basis of the precedent set in *Car Emissions*.

Other Restrictions on Competition

In addition to restrictions on innovation, there may be other agreements that can have an impact on the achievement of the Sustainable Development Goals. It is conceivable, for example, that agreements are made with suppliers that in turn promote the violation of social Sustainable Development Goals – for example, by increasing the joint cost pressure on suppliers. Companies can also discriminate against other companies in a coordinated manner, e.g., if labour rights are better enforced in a supplier company. In such cases, too, strict enforcement of competition law benefits the achievement of sustainability goals.

Competition incentivises lower costs and better performance. When achieving Sustainable Development Goals results in lower costs, e.g., by using fewer resources, avoiding pollution penalties, or when there is demand for more sustainable products or services, a consistent application of the competition law prohibition helps maintain competition and thus promotes the best and most efficient way to achieve these goals.

Option RE 3: Better Visibility for Agreements on Sustainability-relevant Competition Parameters

In future it could be better documented and made more visible how anti-competitive agreements also harm sustainability. To this end, it would make sense to identify relevant groups of cases in guidelines on Article 101(1) TFEU. Clarification would also lead to more frequent recognition of such agreements. The cases *Car Emissions* and *Consumer Detergents* are good examples: for competition lawyers, both cases have anti-competitive elements that are clearly set out in the decisions and form the theory of harm. It is less obvious, at least in the competition community, that both cases also have a negative impact for sustainability. A better visibility of these effects would not deviate from the classic competition law framework, but it would make it easy to identify the overlaps of competition and sustainability and record the contribution of competition law to achieving sustainability.

Up to now, the sustainability objective has always been protected only as a by-product of the protection of competition. The restriction of competition was not pursued due to a lack of sustainability, but because of the restriction of competition. The coordinating element and the competition relevance of the agreed parameters is therefore dominant in reporting and reasoning of the case. With the increasing importance of sustainability for economic activity, a link of both fields will occur more often. Yet, the classification depends on the concept of restraint of competition. Two fundamental directions can be distinguished here:

According to one view, a restriction of competition already exists if companies limit their economic freedom of action by coordinating with other companies. According to another view, the market effects must also be taken into account with consumer welfare as the yardstick. While the European Commission tends to embrace parts of the effects-based approach, the Court of Justice seems to cling to the first position. This debate on the 'more economic approach' also affects the visibility of harm to sustainability: numerous sustainability problems arise at the production stage, i.e., before consumers are directly affected. This applies, for example, to production methods, ingredients or responsibility in the supply chain. If a narrow approach is taken that takes monetary consumer welfare as the yardstick, it may be more difficult to prove a restriction of competition, for example if companies agree on production methods without this becoming tangible in the end product or in the price.[99]

The concept of consumer welfare may also be understood in a broader sense. In recent times, consumer choice has increasingly been regarded as relevant to competition. The possibility for consumers to choose between products or services according to sustainability impact would then possibly suffice as a harmful effect.

Consumer welfare would be safeguarded all the more if the resulting benefits (e.g., better climate protection, higher animal welfare, better pay for banana workers) were regarded as part of consumer welfare. This would, of course, require a very broad concept of consumer welfare, or a reorientation toward a competition model according to which only ecologically and socially sustainable competition can be protected.

It should be noted that market failures can be addressed in this way. Environmentally harmful agreements can, for example, increase negative external effects if there is no longer any competition to reduce them. A change in the concept of competition can also translate these considerations into competition law. This would mean that sustainability effects would be taken into account within the antitrust review, since competition should also promote the achievement of sustainability goals. If harmful environmental effects did not occur under competition conditions and only arose in the aftermath of agreements, this objective would be impaired by the agreement, regardless of

---

    99   Reject *Car Emissions* (Case AT.40178) Commission Decision C 458/11 [2021] 4955 final, para 119.

whether the purely competition effects were appreciable. However, this would also require a clear standard as to what is meant by impairment of sustainability goals. If the legislator has not (yet) defined this in a binding manner, this determination will be difficult for the competition authorities and the courts. They would then be confronted with the 'legitimacy problem'[100] (see Chapter 13).

Option RE 4: Appreciable Effect Due to Harm to Sustainability

In its De-minimis Notice, the European Commission states that some agreements that have as their effect the prevention, restriction or distortion of competition do not constitute an appreciable restriction of competition under Article 101 TFEU since they are seen as being unappreciable.[101] This is defined according to market share thresholds (10 per cent for agreements of competitors, 15 per cent for agreements between non-competitors). Appreciability is an unwritten element of Article 101 TFEU. It privileges some anti-competition agreements.

The Commission's notice could be amended so that anti-competition agreements that harm sustainability are always seen as appreciable, independent of the market share thresholds. If, for example, two smaller companies agree to jointly limit their monitoring efforts in the supply chain or to stick to certain unhealthy ways of production, this may not affect markets too adversely, but the sustainability effect may nonetheless make it appreciable. Such an approach is particularly convincing for proponents of a concept of competition that encompasses sustainability (as in the 'Sustainable Competition' model). Yet, the courts have already taken other legal aspects but competition into account when examining appreciability.[102] It would nonetheless be important to amend the Notice in this way.

DEALING WITH STANDARDS AND NORMS

Sustainability targets are often the subject of industry agreements, standards, and norms. These often have no binding legal quality as official rules, but they do have a considerable practical impact. They are of particular importance for competition because they are often decided by the coordination of market par-

---

[100] Chapter 13.

[101] European Commission, 'Notice on agreements of minor importance which do not appreciably restrict competition under Article 101(1) of the Treaty on the Functioning of the European Union (De Minimis Notice)' [2014] OJ C 291/1.

[102] Cf Rainer Bechtold, Wolfgang Bosch and Ingo Brinker (eds), *EU-Kartellrecht* (3rd edn, C.H.Beck 2014) Art. 101 TFEU para 109.

ticipants, e.g., in associations or expert committees. On the one hand, standards can open up or expand competition. On the other hand, they can exclude innovations and individual market participants. The ambivalent role of standards and norms for competition has been described many times.[103] It is reflected in the Commission's Horizontal Guidelines.[104]

Similar problems arise with labels and certificates that are awarded in certain industries. While standards usually involve a technological shift, labels and certificates overcome information asymmetries and give guidance to customers or business partners. In practice, they may also lead to the adherence to common standards. Labels and certificates are very common in the sustainability debate. For instance, supermarkets can award labels to products that show how animals were treated in the production process. If companies advertise that products are climate neutral, this is usually proven with standards and certificates. Sustainability standards and labels are common in all industries. The definition of 'climate neutral' or similar claims referring to emissions may serve as a good example. To assess this, it will be necessary to define what emissions are looked at (e.g., scope 1, scope 2 or scope 3 emissions), how compensation is measured (e.g., when CO_2 emissions shall be offset with reforestation programmes), or what reduction paths are followed. As soon as definitions are found by joint efforts, i.e. by cooperation within a trade (e.g., in a standard-setting organisation of the industry) competition law issues may arise.

Status Quo for Standardisation Agreements

According to the 2023 revised Horizontal Guidelines of the European Commission, under certain conditions there is no infringement of Article 101(1) TFEU if companies reach an agreement on standards (which are mostly of a technical nature).[105] For sustainability standards, the Commission

---

[103]   See, for example, Robert L Steiner, 'The Nature and Benefits of National Brand/Private Label Competition' (2004) *Review of Industrial Organization* 105; Amitav Chakravarti and Jinhong Xie, 'The Impact of Standards Competition on Consumers: Effectiveness of Product Information and Advertising Formats' (2006) *Journal of Marketing Research* 224.

[104]   European Commission, 'Guidelines on the applicability of Article 101 of the Treaty on the Functioning of the European Union to horizontal co-operation agreements' [2023] OJ C 259/1, paras 538 ff.

[105]   European Commission, 'Guidelines on the applicability of Article 101 of the Treaty on the Functioning of the European Union to horizontal co-operation agreements' [2023] OJ C 259/1, paras 436 ff.

included a 'safe harbour' for standardisation agreements in a separate section.[106] Agreements on certain standards/norms do not constitute an infringement of Article 101(1) TFEU if the following conditions are met:[107]

- the process for developing the standard is transparent and open to all interested competitors;
- the standard must not directly or indirectly force uninvolved companies to also comply with the standard against their will;
- companies are free to achieve a level of sustainability above the agreed standard;
- the companies involved must not exchange information that is not essential for the development or implementation of the standard;
- all interested companies must have access to the standard on reasonable terms even after the development process has been completed;
- one of the following two conditions is met: (1) the standard must not lead to a significant price increase or a significant reduction in the quality of the products concerned or (2) the combined market share of the participating undertakings must not exceed 20 per cent on any relevant market affected by the standard.

These are clear criteria for sustainability cooperations aimed at introducing a specific standard or label. This provides some legal certainty for such types of cooperation. If methodologies and targets for sustainability can be standardised from industry to industry, this will usually make it easier to compare and to inform, incentivise companies to do more and allow for a better competition on the merits. Competition is opened up by creating similar competition conditions for a large number of market participants.

Some issues remain, however. Standardisation is considered problematic if compliance is binding for the companies concerned, i.e., they are no longer allowed to manufacture products that do not comply with the standard.[108] Some sustainability initiatives try to establish exactly this so as to have an impact on the industry as a whole and to avoid free-riding by environmental sinners. (There may be exceptions if the agreement concerns only a subordinate part

---

[106] European Commission, 'Guidelines on the applicability of Article 101 of the Treaty on the Functioning of the European Union to horizontal co-operation agreements' [2023] OJ C 259/1, paras 537 ff.

[107] European Commission, 'Guidelines on the applicability of Article 101 of the Treaty on the Functioning of the European Union to horizontal co-operation agreements' [2023] OJ C 259/1, para 549.

[108] European Commission, 'Guidelines on the applicability of Article 101 of the Treaty on the Functioning of the European Union to horizontal co-operation agreements' [2023] OJ C 259/1, para 464.

of a larger product.)[109] The safe harbour also does not apply when an agreement concerns a limitation of output.[110] This is a severe limitation to the safe harbour since this prevents the establishment of a standard designed to phase out certain unsustainable product variants.

Option RE 5: Extended Exception for Sustainability Standards

One option for an even better consideration of sustainability aspects in competition law could be an expansion of the guidelines on standardisation agreements. In particular, the catalogue of criteria for environmental and social standard setting could be further enhanced, possibly including requirements regarding the significance and substance of the standard, so that standard-setting organisations have an incentive to aim high.

Sustainability agreements that go beyond the creation of a standard or have a significant impact on product variety or prices are not covered by the safe harbour. However, it is precisely such changes in the market that may be necessary for effective progress on sustainability. It is understandable that the Commission wants to draw rather narrow boundaries for a 'safe harbour': once the standard setters have reached that harbour, their activities can no longer be assessed on a case-by-case-basis.

What remains problematic in this context and elsewhere is the Commission's rigid practice on information exchange, which can become a burden for companies as antitrust concerns with sustainability issues increase. They may be less free to discuss regulatory issues, standards and methodologies if they can be seen to be exchanging information along the lines of the *Car Emissions* decision. At the same time, such exchanges become more important for industry initiatives and standardisation agreements.

The safe harbour for standardisation agreements could become even more meaningful: the Commission could add a requirement of substantive significance so that there is real progress on sustainability, and not merely some kind of 'greenwashing'. At the same time, the Commission could become more lenient by allowing some more information exchange and more practical effects on products.

---

[109] European Commission, 'Guidelines on the applicability of Article 101 of the Treaty on the Functioning of the European Union to horizontal co-operation agreements' [2023] OJ C 259/1, para 464.
[110] European Commission, 'Guidelines on the applicability of Article 101 of the Treaty on the Functioning of the European Union to horizontal co-operation agreements' [2023] OJ C 259/1, para 539.

6. Exemption

Philipp Offergeld

The current discussion on the consideration of sustainability objectives mainly revolves around the exemption of restrictive agreements under Article 101(3) TFEU.

EFFICIENCY BENEFITS AND FAIR SHARE FOR CONSUMERS

According to Article 101(3) TFEU, the exemption requires that the restrictive agreement contributes to 'improving the production or distribution of goods or to promoting technical or economic progress, while allowing consumers a fair share of the resulting benefit'. Also, the agreement must not impose restrictions which are not indispensable to the attainment of the objectives or eliminate competition to a substantial degree.

In essence, the rule enables a balancing of pro- and anti-competition effects.

Basics

The legal terms are interpreted in an economic way by the European Commission in its 2004 guidelines on the application of the exemption.[1] Although qualitative efficiency gains are also recognised, improvements in the sense of increased sustainability are not seen as improvements on their own in the 2004 guidelines where these improvements are defined as 'efficiency gains'.[2] However, neither the Commission nor the European courts have always interpreted improvements as 'efficiency gains' in a narrowly understood economic sense as we see from the decision-making practice below.

---

[1]   European Commission, 'Guidelines on the application of Article 81(3) of the Treaty' [2004] OJ C 101/97, paras 48 ff.

[2]   European Commission, 'Guidelines on the application of Article 81(3) of the Treaty' [2004] OJ C 101/97, para 33.

The term 'consumer' is to be understood broadly and includes every purchaser of the respective good or service.[3] However, the focus is not on individuals, but on the group. There may also be a certain period of time between the negative effects and the realisation of the efficiencies.[4] According to the Commission's guidelines, the benefits passed on to consumers must at least offset the negative effects.[5] In principle, at least according to the 2004 guidelines, the benefits must accrue to the same consumers as the negative effects of the restriction of competition.[6] The question of whether efficiencies can also be taken into account if they affect consumers outside the relevant market ('out-of-market efficiencies') is a controversial topic.[7] The sometimes contradictory case practice of the Commission and national competition agencies is discussed below.

Where the interpretation of efficiency gains and fair share for consumers or the balancing process of pros and cons remains close to a narrowly defined economic, quantifiable concept of consumer welfare it will be difficult to integrate sustainability concerns in a meaningful way. A more sustainable approach will likely be a less economic one; and it may open up competition law and its institutions for a wider arena of issues. Whether that is a chance or a danger, lies in the eye of the beholder.

These principles and issues apply *mutatis mutandis* to respective national exemptions. It needs to be pointed out that national specifics in the EU can only play a role when the agreement in question does not fall under EU law, i.e., does not have an appreciable effect for trade between member states.

The Insurers' Case

In 2023, an exemplary case made headlines that perfectly illustrated the difficulties of sustainability initiatives with an impact.[8]

---

[3]   European Commission, 'Guidelines on the application of Article 81(3) of the Treaty' [2004] OJ C 101/97, para 84.

[4]   European Commission, 'Guidelines on the application of Article 81(3) of the Treaty' [2004] OJ C 101/97, para 86.

[5]   European Commission, 'Guidelines on the application of Article 81(3) of the Treaty' [2004] OJ C 101/97, para 85.

[6]   European Commission, 'Guidelines on the application of Article 81(3) of the Treaty' [2004] OJ C 101/97, para 86.

[7]   See, e.g., Giorgio Monti, 'Four Options for a Greener Competition Law' (2020) 11 JECLAP 124, 129.

[8]   The following information on the two initiatives follows from the documents released by NZIA and NZAOA: see UN environment programme, 'Net-Zero Insurance Alliance' (5 July 2023) www.unepfi.org/net-zero-insurance/ accessed 10 August 2023

Twenty-nine leading insurance and reinsurance companies from all over the world came together in 2021 under the auspices of the United Nations Environmental Programme (UNEP) to build the Net Zero Insurance Alliance (NZIA). They took a joint obligation to reduce their insurance portfolio to net zero greenhouse gas emissions by 2050 (with a dedicated path, sectoral targets and common parameters for the methodology). Additionally, an insurance of the transformation (opportunities) was part of this. There was a yearly reporting prescribed. Yet, the reduction and targets were to be reached autonomously, based on individual non-disclosed decisions of the undertakings. Targets in that joint effort were to be disclosed for the first time in July 2023.

This never happened.

The insurers were also the drivers of the Net Zero Asset Owner Alliance (NZAOA), another initiative with UNEP support. Here, 85 institutional investors (insurance companies, pension funds and others) with US\$ 11 billion under management agreed to get their investment portfolio climate-neutral (net zero) by 2050. Again, sectoral targets were defined with common parameters that were to be reached autonomously. The parties to the NZAOA aim for a 40–60 per cent reduction of CO_2 in their portfolios by 2030.

For high-emitting sectors, e.g., fossil energy, there was a positioning statement saying that there should be no financing of new coal-based assets and new oil and gas fields; no investment or financing of the expansion of coal, oil or gas production; and a decrease of investments in fossil energy according to certain scenarios with commonly agreed metrics for sector-specific targets.

Arguably, the two alliances could have enormous leverage and impact for climate change – if insurance companies drop out of the business and no longer insure certain high-emitting facilities, the business could soon become too risky and costly. Also, finance and investment would be re-directed to a large degree to more climate-friendly technologies.

Having said that, the two alliances can also be viewed as restrictions of competition. In the case of the NZIA, it may even be considered a hardcore restriction when horizontal competitors decide collectively to take certain products off the shelf (in this case: insurance services). If companies decide on this autonomously, there is no issue with competition law, but as a joint action of competitors, it is a matter for antitrust investigation. The 'first mover' that decarbonises the portfolio runs the risk of foregoing profits to a considerable extent. Thus, companies seek the comfort of their competitors. For the investment case of the NZAOA, one would have to see whether the initiative is

---

and UN environment programme, 'UN-convened Net-Zero Asset Owner Alliance' www.unepfi.org/net-zero-alliance/ accessed 10 August 2023.

appreciable in the market – even the joint portfolios of the members here may not constitute more than a negligible quantity.

At the same time, the joint initiatives, in particular the NZIA, have the big asset of having an impact: if only one of the companies drops out of the non-insurance-pledge, there will be enough undertakings in the market to pursue the 'dirty business'. The political effort of bringing the companies together, creating a spirit, with some moral impetus added, helps to move forward. From a sustainability perspective, the example shows that there is some value in cooperation.

With a more radical view one could argue that the competition of insuring CO_2 emissions or other unsustainable business practices is not part of 'sustainable competition' and risks market failures in the long run. If the concept of competition encompasses such value judgements, one could even argue that this cannot be an infringement of competition rules.

With more traditional views, one could consider the ancillary restraints doctrine or the *Wouters* doctrine for help. Both have their weaknesses and do not seem to be helpful. Thus, the question is whether an individual exemption under Article 101(3) TFEU could be of help here. Does the agreement lead to improvements or efficiency gains with a fair share of consumers? Is the restriction indispensable and is competition not eliminated?

In Europe, the cases have not yet come under scrutiny. Yet, in the United States there were concerns that these two agreements will be struck down, potentially with hefty fines, by state attorney generals for antitrust who are not so convinced that climate change needs urgent action. In 2023, the NZIA essentially collapsed with companies leaving the initiative.[9]

Decisions

Before the turn of the millennium, the European Commission explicitly used sustainability considerations in several cases, particularly in the area of environmental protection, although sustainability considerations were often only a secondary aspect of the decisions and the outcome might have been

---

[9]   See Tommy Wilker, Alexander Hübner and Tom Slims, 'Insurers flee climate alliance after ESG backlash in the US' (*Reuters*, 26 May 2023) www.reuters.com/business/allianz-decides-leave-net-zero-insurance-alliance-2023-05-25/ accessed 11 August 2023 or Dominic Webb, 'NZIA says US attorneys general concerns based on "mistaken interpretation" of its activities' (*responsible investor*, 4 July 20223) www.responsible-investor.com/nzia-says-us-attorneys-general-concerns-based-on-mistaken-interpretation-of-its-activities/ accessed 11 August 2023.

the same without them.[10] Since the adoption of Regulation (EC) 1/2003 and the abolition of the Commission's exemption monopoly, no such cases have become known at the European level. It is only in recent years that the issue has regained importance, among other things through decisions by the Dutch competition authority.

CECED

In the exemption decision in the *CECED* case in 1999, the Commission considered benefits to society as a whole in the context of the exemption.[11] Accordingly, the overall societal benefits of sustainability initiatives may be sufficient to offset the effects of the restriction of competition without the efficiency benefits directly benefiting the negatively affected consumers.[12] The Commission exempted the agreement of washing machine manufacturers to no longer manufacture or import certain washing machines that were particularly inefficient in terms of energy consumption. The Commission stated that lower energy consumption and emissions would mean that society as a whole saves more than the higher purchase costs that have to be borne by the buyer.[13] No benefits would have to accrue directly to the consumers who bought the washing machines; benefits to society would suffice to compensate for the restriction of competition.[14] In *CECED*, the Commission quantified the tons of CO_2 saved and the overall societal costs avoided as a result.[15]

The 1999 decision is an example of the extent to which the Commission's earlier practice of taking into account benefits for society in the context of the exemption. Although the Commission states in the 2011 Horizontal Guidelines that it still considers the agreement permissible, it no longer bases this on these

---

[10] Suzanne Kingston, Sustainability and Competition Policy (2023) N° 1 Concurrences 4.

[11] *CECED* (Case IV.F.1/36.718.) Commission Decision 2000/475/EC [2000] OJ L 187/47.

[12] *CECED* (Case IV.F.1/36.718.) Commission Decision 2000/475/EC [2000] OJ L 187/47, para 48.

[13] *CECED* (Case IV.F.1/36.718.) Commission Decision 2000/475/EC [2000] OJ L 187/47, para 56; Maurits Dolmans, 'Sustainability Agreements and Antitrust – Three Criteria to Distinguish Beneficial Cooperation from Greenwashing' (*SSRN* 2021) https:// papers .ssrn .com/ sol3/ papers .cfm ?abstract_id = 3920369 accessed 17 August 2023.

[14] *CECED* (Case IV.F.1/36.718.) Commission Decision 2000/475/EC [2000] OJ L 187/47, para 56; Gaetano Lapenta and Matteo Giangaspero, 'Greening Antitrust: Lessons from the ACCC's Authorisation of a Recycling Co-Operation Agreement' (2021) 12 JECLAP 758, 763; Giorgio Monti, 'Four Options for a Greener Competition Law' (2020) 11 JECLAP 124, 125.

[15] *CECED* (Case IV.F.1/36.718.) Commission Decision 2000/475/EC [2000] OJ L 187/47, para 56.

so-called out-of-market efficiencies,[16] but essentially on the lower operating costs of newer machines.[17]

In the *Mastercard*[18] case in 2014, the ECJ took a narrow view, which the Commission endorsed: the efficiency gains must at least also occur in the affected market, i.e., among the consumers directly affected.[19]

DSD

A prominent Commission decision from 2001 concerns waste management in Germany, *Duales System Deutschland* (DSD).[20] The Commission held that an agreement, with the help of which statutory regulations on environmental protection are implemented, can bring about an improvement in the production and distribution of goods.[21]

Duales System Deutschland (DSD) is a joint venture operating throughout Germany in the field of the collection and recovery of used sales packaging.[22] The Commission exempted the cooperation of the joint venture's shareholders, as it serves to implement German and European regulations. According to the Commission, consumers benefit from an increase in 'environmental quality' as less waste remains in circulation.[23] Waste disposal becomes plannable and gains positive network effects that justify an exclusive tie to DSD's services.[24] Competitors' access to collection facilities is secured by commitments and obligations.[25]

---

[16] Jacques Buhart and David Henry, 'Think Green Before You Apply: EU Competition Law and Climate Change Abatement' (2021) 46 *World Competition* 147, 153.

[17] European Commission, 'Guidelines on the applicability of Article 101 of the Treaty on the Functioning of the European Union to horizontal co-operation agreements' [2011] OJ C 11/1, para 329.

[18] Case C-382/12 P *Mastercard* ECLI:EU:C:2014:2201 [2014].

[19] Case C-382/12 P *Mastercard* ECLI:EU:C:2014:2201 [2014], paras 242 f.

[20] *DSD* (Cases COMP/34493 et al) Commission Decision 2001/837/EC [2001] OJ L 319/1.

[21] *DSD* (Cases COMP/34493 et al) Commission Decision 2001/837/EC [2001] OJ L 319/1, para 143.

[22] *DSD* (Cases COMP/34493 et al) Commission Decision 2001/837/EC [2001] OJ L 319/1, para 1.

[23] *DSD* (Cases COMP/34493 et al) Commission Decision 2001/837/EC [2001] OJ L 319/1, para 148.

[24] *DSD* (Cases COMP/34493 et al) Commission Decision 2001/837/EC [2001] OJ L 319/1, para 145.

[25] *DSD* (Cases COMP/34493 et al) Commission Decision 2001/837/EC [2001] OJ L 319/1, paras 69 ff, 164 ff; an action before the European Court of Justice against the conditions remained unsuccessful, Case T-289/01 *Duales System Deutschland v Commission* ECLI:EU:T:2007:155 [2007] ECR II-1694.

The *DSD* decision is characterised by the fact that better environmental performance is seen as an efficiency that is relevant to consumers, even if it is not accompanied by concrete cost benefits. The assessment was made without gathering data on the actual preferences of consumers.

Philips/Osram

In the *Philips/Osram* case, reduced air pollution was considered one of several efficiency benefits.[26]

The decision concerns the establishment of a joint venture by lighting manufacturers Philips and Osram. Lead glasses were to be produced for both companies in a joint facility. In addition to a non-competition clause, the parties agreed that they had to purchase at least 80 per cent of their lead glass needs from the joint venture. Although finding this agreement restricted competition, the Commission granted the requested exemption, among other things, regarding cleaner air as an efficiency that would benefit consumers.

SER Energy chord

In the decision of the Dutch competition authority ACM in the *SER Energieakkoord* case (2013), lower emissions were regarded as quantifiable efficiency benefits.[27] The emissions were to be quantified on the basis of the overall societal savings from the lower emissions or the overall societal damage avoided.[28]

The agreement concerned the early decommissioning of five coal-fired power plants of various energy companies in the Netherlands in the period 2016–2017. The agreement was declared illegal under antitrust law. Although the closure was welcome from an environmental perspective, it would in all likelihood merely result in the released CO_2 certificates being purchased by other companies, so that almost no CO_2 would be saved overall. Therefore, only the lower emissions of nitrogen, sulfur oxide, and particulates were taken

---

[26] *Philips-Osram* (Case IV/34.252) Commission Decision 94/986/EC [1994] OJ L 378/37, para 27.

[27] Autoriteit Consument & Markt, 'ACM analysis of closing down 5 coal power plants as part of SER Energieakkoord' (press release, 26 September 2013) 4 www.acm .nl/en/publications/publication/12082/ACM-analysis-of-closing-down-5-coal-power -plants-as-part-of-SER-Energieakkoord accessed 11 August 2023; Maurits Dolmans, 'Sustainability Agreements and Antitrust – Three Criteria to Distinguish Beneficial Cooperation from Greenwashing' (*SSRN* 2021) https://papers.ssrn.com/sol3/papers .cfm?abstract_id=3920369 accessed 17 August 2023.

[28] Autoriteit Consument & Markt, 'ACM analysis of closing down 5 coal power plants as part of SER Energieakkoord' (press release, 26 September 2013) 4 f www .acm.nl/en/publications/publication/12082/ACM-analysis-of-closing-down-5-coal -power-plants-as-part-of-SER-Energieakkoord accessed 11 August 2023.

into account by the agency as efficiency benefits, which were determined at €180 million in the relevant period.[29] However, since the shutdowns led to higher electricity costs of about €450 million, the agreement was not exempt.[30]

The Dutch competition authority, like the European Commission in *CECED*, quantified lower emissions and saw them as a consumer benefit, even though the benefits would not accrue to the consumers specifically affected but to society as a whole (out-of-market-efficiencies).

Chicken of Tomorrow

In 2015, the Dutch ACM continued its efforts to quantify sustainability aspects. The ACM had to deal with a cooperation of supermarkets for the purchase of poultry meat. With their joint initiative, called *Chicken of Tomorrow*, the supermarkets aimed at more species-friendly poultry husbandry. The increase in animal welfare was recognised as an efficiency benefit, insofar as consumers attached an economic value to it.[31] This was to be determined by their willingness to pay for better conditions for the animals. The willingness to pay was to be established by means of consumer surveys. The amount consumers were willing to pay more for increased animal welfare was contrasted with expected price increases.[32] According to the concept of the Dutch agency, an exemption was merited if consumer interest in animal welfare, quantified in monetary terms, exceeded the increased costs.[33]

The Dutch competition authority determined that increased animal welfare was worth €0.68 per kilo to consumers, while prices increased by €1.46 per kilo. Therefore, the agreement was not exempted from the cartel prohibition.

---

[29]   Autoriteit Consument & Markt, 'ACM analysis of closing down 5 coal power plants as part of SER Energieakkoord' (press release, 26 September 2013) 4 f www .acm .nl/ en/ publications/ publication/ 12082/ ACM -analysis -of -closing -down -5 -coal -power-plants-as-part-of-SER-Energieakkoord accessed 11 August 2023.

[30]   Autoriteit Consument & Markt, 'ACM analysis of closing down 5 coal power plants as part of SER Energieakkoord' (press release, 29 September 2013) 5 www.acm .nl/en/publications/publication/12082/ACM-analysis-of-closing-down-5-coal-power -plants-as-part-of-SER-Energieakkoord accessed 11 August 2023.

[31]   Autoriteit Consument & Markt, 'ACM's analysis of the sustainability arrangements concerning the "Chicken of Tomorrow"' (press release 26 January 2015) 5 www.acm.nl/en/publications/publication/13789/ACMs-analysis-of-the-sustainability -arrangements-concerning-the-Chicken-of-Tomorrow accessed 17 August 2023.

[32]   Cf Roman Inderst and Stefan Thomas, 'Measuring Consumer Sustainability Benefits' (*SSRN*, 2021) https://papers.ssrn.com/sol3/papers.cfm?abstract_id=3916070 accessed 28 July 2023.

[33]   Autoriteit Consument & Markt, 'ACM's analysis of the sustainability arrangements concerning the "Chicken of Tomorrow"' (press release 26 January 2015) 5 www.acm.nl/en/publications/publication/13789/ACMs-analysis-of-the-sustainability -arrangements-concerning-the-Chicken-of-Tomorrow accessed 17 August 2023.

Chicken of Tomorrow is significant as an attempt to quantify even those sustainability goals that do not have a direct market price. In its quantification effort, the decision is wedded to a narrow understanding of the so-called 'more economic approach' in competition law and its goal of analysing impacts for consumer welfare. Again, the limitations of this approach become clear in the case of sustainability goals.[34] One major problem with this type of survey is that, among other things, consumers are only surveyed, and actual behaviour is not observed. Various biases can lead to incorrect results under these conditions (see Chapter 12 for an in-depth analysis of methods of quantifying sustainability effects). This is, for example, the social desirability bias, under which consumers indicate they are willing to spend more money on better husbandry conditions because this is seen as socially desirable. However, this type of survey cannot show whether consumers are actually willing to pay more for increased animal welfare. Further biases may arise from the hypothetical situation, wishful thinking, or experience.[35] Accordingly, the surveys can only reflect claimed or hypothetical behaviour. Another problem is the selection problem. Consumers interested in chicken having better living conditions are partly not consumers of chicken meat at all. The decision also shows the deficits of this approach in the result: the ecologically desired sustainability goal fails due to the consumers' unwillingness to pay for ecologically meaningful projects.

The result in *Chicken of Tomorrow* looked like a master class in heartless capitalism and economic competition theory. It sparked so much outrage that the debate was considerably moved further, not least by the Dutch authority.

Other decisions
In addition to these landmark decisions, there are others in which sustainability aspects were taken into account in the context of efficiency benefits and the question of a fair share for consumers. Table 6.1 provides an overview of the most important decisions on the European level and their key messages.

The decisions presented show that the benchmarks for pursuing sustainability aspects as a reason for exemption are currently unclear. The 2004 Guidelines on Article 101(3) TFEU do not adequately address the issue. The broad recognition that sustainability considerations and similar overall societal benefits received in *CECED* in 1999 has been rolled back. More recently, in

---

[34] Cf Edith Loozen, 'Strict Competition Enforcement and Welfare: A Constitutional Perspective Based on Article 101 TFEU and Sustainability' (2019) 56 CML Rev 1265, 1281 ff.
[35] Erasmo Lopez-Beccerra and Francisco Alcon, 'Social Desirability Bias in the Environmental Economic Valuation: An Inferred Valuation Approach' (2021) *Ecological Economics* 3.

Table 6.1   *Other decisions on sustainability*

Name	Reference	Core statement
Carbon Gas Technology	COM, 8.12.1983, 83/669/ EEC	Stable energy supply in view of the political desire for more independence of European energy companies as an efficiency benefit (p. 19 f.)
ANSAC	COM, 15.6.1991, 91/301/ EEC	Lower environmental impact conceivable as an efficiency benefit (para 23)
Ford/Volkswagen	COM, 28.1.1993, 93/49/ EEC	Lower emissions, lower fuel consumption, and less harmful production materials as efficiency benefits (para 26)
Matra Hachette	ECJ, 15.7.1994, Case T-17/93, ECLI:EU:T:1994:89	Preservation of jobs as economic/technical progress (para 96), although not examined by the court (para 107)
ARGEV, ARO	COM, 16.10.2003, 2004/208/EC	Fulfilment of the requirements of a directive/ national laws on environmental protection can justify a restriction of competition as promotion of technical and economic progress (paras 220 ff.)
Montecatini	ECJ, 8.7.1999, Case 235/92 P, ECLI:EU:C:1999:362	Preservation of jobs as an advantage within the meaning of Article 101(3) TFEU (para 51)
Metro/Commission	ECJ, 25.10.1977, Case 26/76, ECLI:EU:C:1977:167	The objective of maintaining effective competition can be reconciled with other objectives under Article 101(3) TFEU; no sustainability reference (para 43)
Remia	ECJ, 11.7.1985, Case C-42/84, ECLI:EU:C:1985:327	Safeguarding jobs as a possible efficiency benefit (para 42)
STIM	ECJ, 12.4.2013, Case T-451/08, ECLI:EU:T:2013:178	Cultural diversity as a Union objective must be taken into account in the interpretation of Article 101(3) TFEU (paras 103 et seq.)
Compagnie générale maritime	ECJ, 28.2.2002, Case T-86/95, ECLI:EU:T:2002:50	Efficiencies can also be taken into account if they occur in a market other than the one in which the restriction of competition takes place (para 343)
BBC/Brown Boveri	COM, 11.10.1988, 88/541/ EEC	Promoting technical and economic progress by developing high-performance batteries as an environmentally friendly alternative to the internal combustion engine (para 23)

Name	Reference	Core statement
StichtingBaksteen	COM, 29.4.1994, 94/296/EC	Social conditions and opportunities for continued employment as a means of improving the production of goods and promoting technical and economic progress (paras 27 f.)
EACEM	COM, 16.1.1998, 98/C 12/02	Exempting an agreement by television manufacturers to reduce the standby power consumption of their products to certain limits because the improved energy efficiency also benefits consumers (para 11)
Exxon/Shell	COM, 18.5.1994, 94/322/EC	Consumers increasingly value environmental protection, so that lower consumption of raw materials, energy savings, and waste prevention can be seen as positive aspects of the agreement that benefit consumers (para 71)
KSB/Goulds/Lowara/ITT	COM, 12.12.1990, 91/38/EEC	Improved environmental protection as an argument for a fair share for consumers (para 27)
Assurpol	COM, 14.1.1992, 92/96/EEC	Insurability of environmental damage as a consumer benefit (para 39)
Scottish Nuclear	COM, 30.4.1991, 91/329/EEC	Improving electricity generation and distribution (paras 33 ff.)
Pasteur Mérieux-Merck	COM, 6.10.1994, 94/770/EC	Improving public health through better vaccines as a consumer benefit (paras 89 f.)

practice, efficiency benefits have been defined predominantly in economic terms and set as monetarily quantifiable points. This approach was exemplified clearly by the Dutch competition authority in *Chicken of Tomorrow*. Non-competition sustainability goals can thus only be poorly taken into account. This has also been observed in the literature.[36]

---

[36] Or Brook, 'Priority Setting as A Double-Edged Sword: How Modernization Strengthened the Role of Public Policy' (2020) 16 *Journal of Competition Law & Economics* 435, 486; Assimakis P Komninos, 'Non-competition Concerns – Resolution of Conflicts in the Integrated Article 81 EC' (2005) The University of Oxford Centre for Competition Law and Policy Working Paper (L) 08/05, 10 www.law.ox.ac.uk/sites/default/files/migrated/cclp_l_08-05.pdf accessed 17 August 2023; Gaetano Lapenta and Matteo Giangaspero, 'Greening Antitrust: Lessons from the ACCC's Authorisation of a Recycling Co-Operation Agreement' (2021) 12 JECLAP 758, 763; Giorgio Monti, 'Four Options for a Greener Competition Law' (2020) *Journal of Competition Law & Practice* 2021 124, 125; critically Jaques H J Bourgeois and Jan Bocken, 'Guidelines on the Application of Article 81(3) of the EC Treaty or How to Restrict a Restriction' (2005) 32 *Legal Issues of Economic Integration* 111, 119 ff.

The requirement that there needs to be a fair share for consumers is a key issue for sustainability initiatives with a public benefit: the benefits usually accrue to the general public or other groups (e.g., workers in third countries), but not necessarily to the consumers affected by the restriction of competition.[37] The Commission has allowed such out-of-market efficiencies to suffice in previous decisions, but this is not possible under the 2004 Guidelines.[38]

Current Policy Developments

The debate on exempting sustainability agreements under Article 101(3) TFEU inspired new policy developments on the European level in the form of the Horizontal Guidelines 2023. Two national developments also merit some attention: the Dutch ACM published a far-reaching draft on sustainability and competition, and Austria opted in favour of a statutory exemption.[39]

EU Horizontal Guidelines 2023

In the European Commission's revised Horizontal Guidelines from 2023, the exemption pursuant to Article 101(3) TFEU takes up a great deal of space within the chapter on sustainability agreements.[40] The Commission highlights the special features of such cooperation initiatives compared to other agreements that restrict competition. However, the revision falls short of standards as set in the earlier decisions mentioned above.

In order to determine whether a sustainability initiative is eligible for exemption, it must first be established to what extent the pursuit of sustainability objectives can generate improvements within the meaning of Article 101(3) TFEU. The Commission uses a broad concept but requires objective improvements. The reduction of costs, the increase in product variety, quality improvements, improvements in the production process or innovations are explicitly mentioned. In terms of sustainability initiatives, cleaner production or distribution processes, lower emissions, increased product quality, and greater transparency for consumers are also considered. The guarantee of

---

[37]   Cento Veljanovski, 'Collusion as Environmental Protection – An Economic Assessment' (2020) 18 JCLE 4 f.
[38]   Critically Gaetano Lapenta and Matteo Giangaspero, 'Greening Antitrust: Lessons from the ACCC's Authorisation of a Recycling Co-Operation Agreement' (2021) 12 JECLAP 758, 763.
[39]   Cf Alec J Burnside, Marjolein De Backer and Delphine Strohl, 'Sustainability and Competition Policy' (2023) No 1 Concurrences 10, 11 ff.
[40]   European Commission, 'Guidelines on the applicability of Article 101 of the Treaty on the Functioning of the European Union to Horizontal Co-operation Agreements' [2023] OJ C 259/1, paras 556 ff.

more stable production chains is also mentioned. Nevertheless, the examples in this and other parts of the chapter are strongly geared toward environmental sustainability, i.e., agreements on cooperation for ecological reasons. For the application to other sustainability goals, a transfer is required, which limits the practical usefulness of the new guidelines and means a shortening of the concept of sustainability.

Nevertheless, the concept of efficiency gains in the revised guidelines can be seen as a positive broadening of the practice of the last two decades, which was often based on a narrower understanding.[41] According to this understanding, the necessary efficiency gains were to be sought in qualitative or quantitative improvements of a product or a production process, but not in the promotion of sustainability goals such as increased animal welfare. In this respect, one may cautiously interpret the new wording in the sense that the Commission has at least expanded the concept of efficiencies on a normative basis. However, the still narrow understanding of the criteria 'fair share for consumers' quickly puts a stop to actual broader considerations of sustainability impacts.

This is at the core of the discussion to date: what does it mean that consumers need to receive a fair share of the resulting benefits? The issue is dealt with by the European Commission on several pages in the 2023 Guidelines.[42] In these comments, the Commission stays on familiar paths and thus rejects more far-reaching approaches as proposed by scholars and some national competition authorities.

The fundamental question is whether the criterion of 'fair share' is to be read in such a way that consumers negatively affected by a restriction of competition must be fully compensated for these disadvantages (e.g., by higher prices being offset by higher product quality). The Commission maintains its previous position and stays with this reading of a 'fair share'. For this, it refers to case law of the ECJ.[43] This essentially excludes so-called out-of-market efficiencies from the exemption test. The Commission does mention such advantages under the heading of 'collective benefits' and declares them to be eligible for exemption, provided that the negatively affected consumers

---

[41] Against this broadening cf. Jonas von Kalben, 'Europe's Green Ambition: New Guidelines of the European Commission on the Application of Art. 101 TFEU to Sustainability Agreements – A Critical Account' [2022] Zeitschrift für Wettbewerbsrecht 468, 487.
[42] European Commission, 'Guidelines on the applicability of Article 101 of the Treaty on the Functioning of the European Union to horizontal co-operation agreements' [2023] OJ C 259/1, paras 569 ff.
[43] Case C-382/12 P *Mastercard* ECLI:EU:C:2014:2201 [2014].

are also part of the larger group that benefits.[44] However, even in this case, the Commission emphasises that the 'collective benefits' must be so large, possibly together with other benefits, that the consumers directly affected are compensated for their disadvantages.[45] This severely limits the recognition of out-of-market efficiencies. If the benefits of a restriction of competition accrue to other market participants, the exemption does not apply. This is the essence of the consumer welfare standard.

The Commission essentially stays with the previous practice of assuming a fair share for consumers only with full compensation of the negatively affected consumers in the same market. This could only indeed be a change from the previous practice, if the Commission weighed both sides of this equation in a normative sense, not only by numbers However, there is no indication of this in the revised guidelines.[46] Therefore, the section on 'collective benefits' should probably be understood as a clarification that benefits that accrue to the general public may also constitute consumer benefits, but not if they are out-of-market. This means that reduced externalities are not substantially recognised by the Commission as a justification.[47]

Outside of collective benefits, sustainability initiatives can also produce efficiency benefits for the specific consumers affected. The Commission distinguishes between 'individual use value' and 'individual non-use value' benefits.[48] Individual use value benefits include quantitative and qualitative improvements that directly benefit consumers, e.g., through lower prices or more durable products.[49] Such benefits of sustainability initiatives have so far already been covered by the exemption without any problems.

However, the comments on the so-called non-use value benefits are noteworthy. This covers improvements that do not have any objective benefit for

---

[44]   European Commission, 'Guidelines on the applicability of Article 101 of the Treaty on the Functioning of the European Union to horizontal co-operation agreements' [2023] OJ C 259/1, paras 583 ff.

[45]   European Commission, 'Guidelines on the applicability of Article 101 of the Treaty on the Functioning of the European Union to horizontal co-operation agreements' [2023] OJ C 259/1, paras 584 ff.

[46]   Cf Martijn Snoep, 'What is Fair and Efficient in the Face of Climate Change?' (2023) 11 *Journal of Antitrust Enforcement* 1, 3.

[47]   Cf David Little and others, 'The European Commission's Draft Guidelines on Sustainability Agreements – A Legal Analysis and Practical Implications' (2022) 43 ECLR 403, 410.

[48]   See also Roman Inderst, *Incorporating Sustainability into an Effects-Analysis of Horizontal Agreements* (Publications Office of the European Union 2022) 18.

[49]   European Commission, 'Guidelines on the applicability of Article 101 of the Treaty on the Functioning of the European Union to horizontal co-operation agreements' [2023] OJ C 259/1, para 571.

consumers, but which become a quality feature due to the fact that consumers appreciate them.[50] A good example of this can be an increased animal welfare level: if more species-appropriate conditions do not already lead to qualitatively better animal products, the better conditions can be regarded as an efficiency benefit for consumers, insofar as they value the increased animal welfare.[51] This ultimately integrates the analysis of willingness to pay.

Higher prices due to more sustainable production conditions can therefore be justified if these conditions are worth at least as much to consumers as the product becomes more expensive. This is based on an average consumer in the respective market.[52] How much the more sustainable production is worth to consumers must be investigated empirically, e.g., through surveys.[53] The Commission points to problems with the survey, in particular due to deviations between the stated and actual preferences (so-called attitude-behaviour-gap).[54]

The Commission's comments are similar to the practice of the Dutch competition authority ACM in the *Chicken of Tomorrow* case. The advantage of this method is that it can easily be used for any sustainability target. After all, the starting point and prerequisite is consumers' willingness to pay. It has already been shown that this analysis is methodologically fraught with great difficulties.

Regarding the 'indispensability' criterion, the Commission acknowledges that cooperation between companies may be necessary to achieve sustainability goals.[55] It makes it clear that, in principle, each company should decide independently to what extent it wishes to operate sustainably. As far as consumers value sustainability aspects of their consumer products, it can ultimately be assumed that there is a functioning market mechanism that

---

[50] European Commission, 'Guidelines on the applicability of Article 101 of the Treaty on the Functioning of the European Union to horizontal co-operation agreements' [2023] OJ C 259/1, paras 575 ff.

[51] European Commission, 'Guidelines on the applicability of Article 101 of the Treaty on the Functioning of the European Union to horizontal co-operation agreements' [2023] OJ C 259/1, para 575.

[52] European Commission, 'Guidelines on the applicability of Article 101 of the Treaty on the Functioning of the European Union to horizontal co-operation agreements' [2023] OJ C 259/1, para 578.

[53] European Commission, 'Guidelines on the applicability of Article 101 of the Treaty on the Functioning of the European Union to horizontal co-operation agreements' [2023] OJ C 259/1, para 578.

[54] European Commission, 'Guidelines on the applicability of Article 101 of the Treaty on the Functioning of the European Union to horizontal co-operation agreements' [2023] OJ C 259/1, para 579.

[55] European Commission, 'Guidelines on the applicability of Article 101 of the Treaty on the Functioning of the European Union to horizontal co-operation agreements' [2023] OJ C 259/1, paras 562 ff.

produces sustainable products. Thus, sustainability agreements would not be necessary to achieve sustainability goals per se to the extent that there is a demand for such products.[56] However, they may be necessary to achieve the goals as cost-effectively as possible. In particular, cases should be considered in which there are already regulatory requirements for achieving sustainability goals. Here, the companies should basically achieve the goals independently. Cooperation can be useful however if the objectives can be achieved more efficiently through cooperation.

As a further example of indispensable cooperation, cases are mentioned in which a 'first-mover-disadvantage' applies, i.e., in situations in which a company that is a pioneer in the introduction of a higher level of sustainability is thereby placed at a competitive disadvantage.[57] This includes free rider problems, e.g., when a company incurs large financial expenses to educate consumers about sustainability aspects. When other companies also benefit from this without sharing the costs, there are so-called positive external effects. Cooperation is also said to be useful or even necessary in order to achieve economies of scale, or when consumers make incorrect decisions based on behavioural economics.[58]

However, cooperation can also prevent a higher degree of sustainability and still be considered indispensable. This danger arises when an agreement cooperatively stops individual initiatives that are more ambitious. For example, if a strong food retailer wants to enforce very high animal welfare standards with its suppliers, an industry initiative that agrees only on medium animal welfare standards could put the brakes on that push if the food retailer decides to mitigate its individual risk by cooperating. It is true that the Commission stipulates that a standard setting may only set minimum standards.[59] There are thus no upper limits. However, standard setting can create incentives to set a lower standard than would be possible for individuals. In this case, an agreement may appear 'indispensable' to the outside world and to individual companies, even though it has an ambivalent character: it pulls some along but slows others

---

[56] European Commission, 'Guidelines on the applicability of Article 101 of the Treaty on the Functioning of the European Union to horizontal co-operation agreements' [2023] OJ C 259/1, para 562.

[57] European Commission, 'Guidelines on the applicability of Article 101 of the Treaty on the Functioning of the European Union to horizontal co-operation agreements' [2023] OJ C 259/1, para 566.

[58] European Commission, 'Guidelines on the applicability of Article 101 of the Treaty on the Functioning of the European Union to horizontal co-operation agreements' [2023] OJ C 259/1, paras 567, 563.

[59] European Commission, 'Guidelines on the applicability of Article 101 of the Treaty on the Functioning of the European Union to horizontal co-operation agreements' [2023] OJ C 259/1, para 567.

down. This problem, which is not addressed in the guidelines, would have to be taken into account through a detailed analysis of the sustainability effects.

According to the last condition of Article 101(3) TFEU, an exemption can only be granted if it is ensured that effective residual competition remains in the affected market. In its revised guidelines, the European Commission considers agreements between all companies in a market to be exemptible if they continue to compete for other essential aspects.[60] The Commission considers an agreement on a quality feature to be possible insofar as there continues to be substantial competition on price. In addition, the Commission believes that agreements should be limited in time, after which there is once again unrestricted competition between the companies.

The Commission explicitly does not exclude agreements between all competitors in a market. This is particularly important for sustainability initiatives, as in some cases these can only function or have a large impact if all relevant companies participate. In other cases, the participation of all companies is not necessary, but would have the greatest effect.

Draft Sustainability Guidelines of the Dutch ACM

The Dutch competition authority Autoriteit Consument & Markt (ACM) has made proposals on exempting sustainability agreements in its Draft Sustainability Guidelines.[61] The Draft Guidelines also present a modification of the *Chicken of Tomorrow* approach that had sparked outrage.

It is first clarified that efficiency benefits can be generated by sustainability initiatives, especially if there is a reduction of negative externalities.[62] Such reductions should be quantified using economic methods where possible. If no sufficient data sources are available due to the nature of the efficiency gains, quantification may be left out. Instead, a description that is as specific as possible should be used. The ACM mentions animal welfare aspects in particular.

The guidelines on the 'fair share' requirement are noteworthy. Under certain conditions, the ACM considers a deviation from the principle that consumers must be fully compensated for the disadvantages of the restriction of

---

[60] European Commission, 'Guidelines on the applicability of Article 101 of the Treaty on the Functioning of the European Union to horizontal co-operation agreements' [2023] OJ C 259/1, para 593.

[61] Autoriteit Consument & Markt, 'Second draft version: Guidelines on Sustainability Agreements – Opportunities within competition law' (26 January 2021) www.acm.nl/en/publications/second-draft-version-guidelines-sustainability-agreements-opportunities-within-competition-law accessed 22 June 2023.

[62] Autoriteit Consument & Markt, 'Second draft version: Guidelines on Sustainability Agreements – Opportunities within competition law' (26 January 2021) para 36 www.acm.nl/en/publications/second-draft-version-guidelines-sustainability-agreements-opportunities-within-competition-law accessed 22 June 2023.

competition to be justified. However, only so-called 'environmental-damage agreements' are to be given special treatment: agreements aimed at improving production processes that would otherwise cause damage to people or the environment. In such agreements, a full compensation for affected consumers should not be necessary if 'the agreement helps, in an efficient manner, comply with an international or national standard, or it helps realize a concrete policy goal (to prevent such damage)'.[63]

This condition is reminiscent of the proposal of *Inderst* and *Thomas*, who demanded something similar for a restriction according to *Wouters* (see Chapter 5 above). Under these conditions, full compensation would not be necessary, since the affected consumers caused the societal problem of environmental damage in the first place through their consumption.[64] Thus, the ACM ultimately calls for recognition of benefits to society as a whole (see the policy option EX2 below).

The ACM announced in a 2022 press release that it gave the go-ahead to a cooperation of companies from the energy sector that had agreed on the internalisation of external costs caused by CO_2 emissions.[65] In future, the companies intend to base their purchasing decisions on a price of €100 per metric ton of CO_2. This agreement will make it more attractive to rely on more sustainable energy sources. The ACM applied its draft guidelines and concluded that the expected price increases would be outweighed by the lower environmental impact.

The ACM's draft guidelines also include a new take on any quantification requirement. A time-consuming and expensive quantification of efficiency benefits is dispensable if the following conditions are met:[66]

(a)   the parties have a combined market share not exceeding 30 per cent,

---

[63] Autoriteit Consument & Markt, 'Second draft version: Guidelines on Sustainability Agreements – Opportunities within competition law' (26 January 2021) para 45 www.acm.nl/en/publications/second-draft-version-guidelines-sustainability-agreements-opportunities-within-competition-law accessed 22 June 2023.

[64] Autoriteit Consument & Markt, 'Second draft version: Guidelines on Sustainability Agreements – Opportunities within competition law' (26 January 2021) para 41 www.acm.nl/en/publications/second-draft-version-guidelines-sustainability-agreements-opportunities-within-competition-law accessed 22 June 2023.

[65] Autoriteit Consument & Markt, 'ACM positief over samenwerking bedrijven om duurzaamheid in energiesector te bevorderen' (press release, *ACM*, 28 February 2022) www.acm.nl/nl/publicaties/acm-positief-over-samenwerking-bedrijven-om-duurzaamheid-energiesector-te-bevorderen accessed 28 July 2023.

[66] Autoriteit Consument & Markt, 'Second draft version: Guidelines on Sustainability Agreements – Opportunities within competition law' (26 January 2021) para 54 www.acm.nl/en/publications/second-draft-version-guidelines-sustainability-agreements-opportunities-within-competition-law accessed 22 June 2023.

(b)   the harm to competition is, based on a rough estimate, evidently smaller than the benefits of the agreement.

Simplifying the proof of efficiencies when it is *obvious* that the agreement can ultimately be exempted is welcome. The 30 per cent market share cap will also keep industry-wide agreements that have a significant impact on competition subject to proper scrutiny. Since many sustainability initiatives only work, or at least are particularly effective, when the largest portion of a market is affected, many initiatives will continue to require that scrutiny.

The statutory exemption in Austrian law

The Austrian Cartel Act, which until then provided for an exemption almost identical in wording to Article 101(3) TFEU, was amended in 2021 by adding the following passage in its Section 2(1):[67]

> Consumers shall also be deemed to receive a fair share of the benefits which result from improvements to the production or distribution of goods or the promotion of technical or economic progress if those benefits contribute substantially to an ecologically sustainable or climate-neutral economy.

The explanatory memorandum to the law further explains what is meant by 'ecological sustainability' and climate neutrality.[68] The clarification is limited to environmental sustainability goals and, in particular, does not include social sustainability goals. In addition, the explanatory memorandum makes it clear that it covers only those improvements in sustainability or climate neutrality that are achieved through an innovation. It is therefore not sufficient, for example, to improve the level of environmental protection through territorial agreements or price increases.[69]

Although the amended wording of the law only affects the 'fair share' requirement, it also indirectly affects the concept of efficiency benefits. If a contribution to climate protection may benefit consumers fairly, such a contribution must also be an efficiency benefit in the first place.[70]

---

[67]   Cf Georg Huber, 'Changes to Austrian Competition Legislation' (2022) 43 ECLR N47; Viktoria H S E Robertson, 'Sustainability: A World-First Green Exemption in Austrian Competition Law' (2022) 13 JECLAP 426.

[68]   Austrian Federal Competition Act, as amended effective 10 September 2021, Federal Law Gazette I No 176/2021, 951 of the Supplements XXVII. GP – Government Bill – Explanations www .parlament .gv .at/ PAKT/ VHG/ XXVII/ I/ I _00951/ fname _983231.pdf accessed 18 August 2023.

[69]   Verena Strasser, 'Kartellrecht und Green Deal – der österreichische Weg' (2022) WuW 68, 70.

[70]   Austrian Federal Competition Act, as amended effective 10 September 2021, Federal Law Gazette I No 176/2021, 951 of the Supplements XXVII. GP – Government

The legislative amendment to the Austrian Cartel Act ties in with the dispute over the inclusion of overall societal benefits or out-of-market efficiencies. While under Article 101(3) TFEU it is unclear whether benefits to society as a whole are covered, the Austrian legislator has given its clear acceptance of ecological improvements for the parallel Austrian rule. However, it is not clear from the wording when the contribution is substantial enough. Two approaches are conceivable here: a concrete, economic or quantitative weighing of the disadvantages of the restriction of competition with the ecological benefits, or a more normative, qualitative weighing. The legislative materials, as also depicted in the guidelines of the Austrian Federal Competition Authority on agreements related to sustainability, indicate that the first variant is the basis for the amendment.[71] Sustainability cooperatives can only benefit from the amendment if the disadvantages of restricting competition are outweighed by the ecological advantages of the cooperation.[72] In principle, this must be demonstrated economically, i.e., quantified; this can only be waived if the advantages obviously outweigh the disadvantages.[73]

Summary
The revised guidelines of the European Commission and the Dutch competition authority, as well as the legislative amendment in Austria, impressively illustrate the parallel but nevertheless different legal policy developments on what are essentially the same issues. The Commission remains relatively conservative and, in particular, adheres to the principle that out-of-market efficiencies can only be taken into account to a very limited extent. The Austrian legislator, on the other hand, has taken a completely different decision and clarified that these advantages are covered. In the Netherlands, the Autoriteit Consument & Markt is attempting to bring about a similar result without an amendment to the law.

Bill – Explanations www .parlament .gv .at/ PAKT/ VHG/ XXVII/ I/ I _00951/ fname _983231.pdf accessed 18 August 2023.

[71] Federal Competition Authority, 'Guidelines on the Application of Sec. 2 para 1 Cartel Act to Sustainability Cooperations (Sustainability Guidelines)' [2022], paras 88 ff. Austrian Federal Competition Act, as amended effective 10 September 2021, Federal Law Gazette I No 176/2021, 951 of the Supplements XXVII. GP – Government Bill – Explanations www.parlament.gv.at/PAKT/VHG/XXVII/I/I_00951/fname_983231.pdf accessed 18 August 2023.

[72] Federal Competition Authority, 'Guidelines on the Application of Sec. 2 para 1 Cartel Act to Sustainability Cooperations (Sustainability Guidelines)' [2022], paras 88 ff.

[73] Federal Competition Authority, 'Guidelines on the Application of Sec. 2 para 1 Cartel Act to Sustainability Cooperations (Sustainability Guidelines)' [2022], para 91.

The question of accepting out-of-market-efficiencies is the most prominent issue in applying Article 101(3) TFEU to sustainability agreements. Yet, the three different solutions point to three other defining aspects:

Firstly, the Austrian approach shows that different sustainability goals may be treated differently. The legislator clearly prioritises environmental improvements over other sustainability goals which are not included. This challenges the holistic notion of sustainability.

Secondly, the threshold for benefits may be further defined, e.g. as 'substantial' or 'obvious' with different consequences for their acceptance.

Thirdly, the legal regimes need to clarify how the balancing of negative effects of the restriction and the positive effects of the improvements takes place. A quantitative approach to balancing is seen as the superior solution in all three documents – but it is not necessarily the only one. Qualitative solutions or working with presumptions and other rules on proof may add to the mechanisms employed.

The diversity of approaches in EU, the Netherlands and Austria helps to gain experience, as in a laboratory of legislation, yet there is also a risk of increasing legal fragmentation. If member states of the EU develop divergent legal practices, the actually desired uniform competition law practice is jeopardised. Since, according to Article 3(1) and (2) of Regulation (EC) No 1/2003, national competition law may only deviate from European law to the extent that interstate trade within the meaning of Article 101(1) TFEU is not affected, this adds a further dimension of legal uncertainty for companies, despite all the concessions made by the member states. As soon as a sustainability cooperation in their jurisdiction becomes so significant that it affects trade between member states, their cooperation could suddenly become inadmissible. For this reason, a uniform European solution is ultimately desirable.

OPTIONS

We present six options that have transpired in the past on how to design the exemption under Article 101(3) TFEU.

Option EX 1: (Modified) Willingness to Pay Analysis

One option for better consideration of sustainability aspects in the context of the exemption is the further development of the willingness to pay analysis. The Dutch ACM already tried to combine sustainability aspects with the consumer welfare approach in *Chicken of Tomorrow* using a willingness to pay analysis. This is also an approach taken by the European Commission in the new Horizontal Guidelines. There, the topic is treated as 'individual non-use value benefits'. However, this approach has practical problems and limitations. Difficulties can arise, as the Commission itself indicates, in determining the consumers' benefits. In order to determine the value of a sustainability aspect for consumers, surveys will have to be extensively used. However, the values determined by such surveys will often not reflect the consumers' true willingness to pay.[74]

The advantage of this consumer-driven approach is that it is universally applicable to any sustainability benefit, since anything to which consumers attach value can be seen as an efficiency benefit. However, this reasoning also shows the limitation of this approach. Since sustainability aspects are only recognised to the extent that consumers value them, this approach cannot help to eliminate unsustainable consumer behaviour. The exemption of an agreement under this analysis is not possible if it aims to promote sustainability aspects that are not valued by consumers. Whether such sustainability initiatives are nevertheless desired is another question and might just contradict a consumer welfare approach to which this analysis adheres.

Inderst and *Thomas* propose to retain the willingness to pay approach, but to correct it in detail in order to integrate the specifics of sustainability considerations into the analysis.[75] The starting point of their considerations is that willingness to pay can be determined in different ways, and this can result in different outcomes without any of these outcomes being correct or incorrect.[76] According to *Inderst* and *Thomas*, a so-called reflective willingness to pay analysis could be carried out so as adequately to reflect the importance of sustainability goals.[77] This analysis is not based (only) on actual sales. Instead, it takes into account information deficits and the time taken to make a purchase decision, as well as the context of the decision. Sustainability preferences would therefore be more likely to emerge if consumers were provided with a better factual basis in so-called hypothetical choice experiments and the decision was placed in different contexts.[78] By way of example, consumers

---

[74] See below, Chapter 12, and Roman Inderst, 'Incorporating Sustainability into an Effects-Analysis of Horizontal Agreements' (*SSRN*, 2022) 18 f https://papers.ssrn.com/sol3/papers.cfm?abstract_id=4098476 accessed 28 July 2023.

[75] Roman Inderst and Stefan Thomas, 'Reflective Willingness to Pay: Preferences for Sustainable Consumption in a Consumer Welfare Analysis' (2021) 17 JCLE 848.

[76] Roman Inderst and Stefan Thomas, 'Reflective Willingness to Pay: Preferences for Sustainable Consumption in a Consumer Welfare Analysis' (2021) 17 JCLE 848, 857 f.

[77] Roman Inderst and Stefan Thomas, 'Reflective Willingness to Pay: Preferences for Sustainable Consumption in a Consumer Welfare Analysis' (2021) 17 JCLE 848, 866 ff.

[78] Roman Inderst and Stefan Thomas, 'Reflective Willingness to Pay: Preferences for Sustainable Consumption in a Consumer Welfare Analysis' (2021) 17 JCLE 848, 859 ff.

would be confronted with additional information on the living conditions and slaughter of animals in an animal welfare case.[79]

The advantage of such a modified willingness to pay analysis is that it can be integrated into the existing approach to determine consumer welfare[80] and thus would not require any change in the law or adjustment of the standard.

However, many follow-up questions arise as to how such an analysis would be carried out in practice.[81] It involves an increased effort for competition authorities, private parties, or courts.[82] *Inderst* and *Thomas* themselves are critical of the application of this analysis to externalities (especially non-climate-related externalities).[83] Depending on how this is implemented, taking them into account could lead to measuring the willingness to pay for the behaviour of other consumers. This is the case, for example, if individual consumers attach a value to the fact that other consumers cannot consume meat either.[84] This would lead to distributional problems if the positive effects of a measure were to accrue to these consumers alone. In addition, restricting the freedom of one group of consumers would be justified by the preferences of other consumers.[85]

Consideration of the above findings would have to be reflected in regulatory practice. In fact, it should precisely not be laid down in law, since it is to be expected that methods will change rapidly over time on the basis of the current state of scientific knowledge. Nonetheless, any solution that builds on the willingness to pay analysis must include some explanations on how to make the effort and determine consumer preferences in concrete terms.

---

[79] Cf Roman Inderst and Stefan Thomas, 'Reflective Willingness to Pay: Preferences for Sustainable Consumption in a Consumer Welfare Analysis' (2021) 17 JCLE 848, 861 ff.

[80] Roman Inderst and Stefan Thomas, 'Reflective Willingness to Pay: Preferences for Sustainable Consumption in a Consumer Welfare Analysis' (2021) 17 JCLE 848, 858, 866 ff.

[81] Cf Roman Inderst and Stefan Thomas, 'Measuring Consumer Sustainability Benefits' (*SSRN*, 2021) https://papers.ssrn.com/sol3/papers.cfm?abstract_id=3916070 accessed 28 July 2023

[82] Cf Roman Inderst and Stefan Thomas, 'Reflective Willingness to Pay: Preferences for Sustainable Consumption in a Consumer Welfare Analysis (2021) 17 JCLE 848, 870.

[83] Roman Inderst and Stefan Thomas, 'The Scope and Limitations of Incorporating Externalities in Competition Analysis within a Consumer Welfare Approach' (2022) 45 *World Competition* 351.

[84] Roman Inderst and Stefan Thomas, 'Measuring Consumer Sustainability Benefits' (*SSRN*, 2021) 9 https://ssrn.com/abstract=3916070 accessed 6 July 2023.

[85] Roman Inderst and Stefan Thomas, 'Measuring Consumer Sustainability Benefits' (*SSRN*, 2021) https://ssrn.com/abstract=3916070 accessed 6 July 2023.

Option EX 2: Recognition of Society-wide Benefits

It is conceivable that benefits to society as a whole could be recognised as grounds for exemption under Article 101(3) TFEU.[86] Seen through an economic lens, this could mean an exemption for agreements that lead to price increases, provided that the price increase is lower than the overall saving for society due to lower negative external effects.[87] This could be implemented by changing the practice of the antitrust authorities, ideally the European Commission. New guidance would be needed.

Concept

The recognition of total societal benefits conflicts with the traditional view, which focuses on a consumer welfare standard.[88] The total welfare standard (which is a more encompassing alternative to the consumer welfare standard)

---

[86] Jacques Buhart, 'Think Green Before You Apply: EU Competition Law and Climate-Change Abatement' (2021) 44 *World Competition* 147, 160; Maurits Dolmans, 'Sustainable Competition Policy and the "Polluter Pays" Principle' in Simon Holmes, Dirk Middelschulte and Martijn Snoep (eds), *Competition Law, Climate Change & Environmental Sustainability* (Concurrences 2021) 31; Ella van den Brink and Jordan Ellison, 'Article 101(3) TFEU: The Roadmap for Sustainable Cooperation' in Simon Holmes, Dirk Middelschulte and Martijn Snoep (eds), *Competition Law, Climate Change & Environmental Sustainability* (Concurrences 2021) 47; Lucas Macharis, 'The Exemption of Sustainability Agreements under European Competition Law – Balancing Societal Benefits with Consumer Harm: A New Way Forward' (2022) 43 ECLR 170, 181; see also Martin Gassler, 'Sustainability, the Green Deal and Art 101 TFEU: Where We Are and Where We Could Go' (2021) 12 JECLAP 430, 438; see also Elena Wiese, 'Agenda 2025: Roadmap to Sustainability' (*D'Kart*, 18 May 2022) www.d-kart.de/en/blog/2022/05/18/agenda-2025-roadmap-to-sustainability/ accessed 28 July 2023; Patrick Hauser, 'Agenda 2025: Sustainability Agreement & Private Enforcement' (*D'Kart*, 7 June 2022) www.d-kart.de/en/blog/2022/06/07/agenda-2025-nachhaltigkeitskooperationen-private-enforcement/ accessed 28 July 2023; Richard Whish and David Bailey, 'Horizontal Guidelines on purchasing agreements: Delineation between by object and by effect restrictions' (Publications Office of the EU 2022) paras 2.46 ff.
[87] Maurits Dolmans, 'Sustainable Competition Policy and the "Polluter Pays" Principle' in Simon Holmes, Dirk Middelschulte and Martijn Snoep (eds), *Competition Law, Climate Change & Environmental Sustainability* (Concurrences 2021) 31 f.; Ella van den Brink and Jordan Ellison, 'Article 101(3) TFEU: The Roadmap for Sustainable Cooperation' in Simon Holmes, Dirk Middelschulte and Martijn Snoep (eds), *Competition Law, Climate Change & Environmental Sustainability* (Concurrences 2021) 44.
[88] Cf Roman Inderst and Stefan Thomas, 'The Scope and Limitations of Incorporating Externalities in Competition Analysis within a Consumer Welfare Approach' (2022) 45 *World Competition* 351; Ioannis Lianos, 'Reorienting Competition Law' (2022) 10 *Journal of Antitrust Enforcement* 1, 6.

is conceptually more compatible with the recognition of such benefits, since a total societal increase in welfare is sufficient. The choice between such different paradigms therefore sets the course for the interpretation of the exemption.[89] Here, the conflict between the ban on restrictive business agreements and sustainability goals becomes particularly clear: if only the final prices for consumers are taken into account, negative external effects play no role. They can be completely disregarded in the analysis and an exemption can still be granted if the consumer ultimately pays a lower price or receives a functionally better product. To put it bluntly, it would be in the interest of the end consumer to substitute an environmentally friendly manufacturing process for a cheaper but highly polluting process. This is different if a more normative concept of competition is employed and also the total welfare standard, since negative externalities would also be eligible for consideration. A true consideration of out-of-market efficiencies would be such that externalities would also have to be analysed when considering the fair share for consumers. In such a scenario, a price increase of €3 due to more expensive production processes could be justified by the fact that negative external costs of €30 are avoided due to lower emissions. With a narrow application of a consumer welfare standard, the consumer who has to pay €3 more would benefit only fractionally from the €30 in overall societal benefits, so that the higher prices of €3 would not be compensated in her case.[90] In its 2023 guidelines, the Commission sticks to the consumer welfare standard, although this is in any case not mandatory by law.

Pros and cons
In fact, for economic reasons, there is much to be said in favour of recognising benefits to society as a whole as grounds for exemption. The narrow interpretation of the exemption under Article 101(3) TFEU perpetuates the market failure due to negative externalities.[91] The fact that the Commission is taking this route is surprising in light of the need to internalise external effects through sustainability cooperation, which is also mentioned in the new guidelines.[92] In fact, overall societal benefits are real, measurable consumer

---

[89] For uncertainty about the understanding of Article 101(3) TFEU, see Richard Whish and David Bailey, *Competition Law* (10th edn, Oxford 2021) 165.

[90] Cf Ella van den Brink and Jordan Ellison, 'Article 101(3) TFEU: The Roadmap for Sustainable Cooperation' in Simon Holmes, Dirk Middelschulte and Martijn Snoep (eds), *Competition Law, Climate Change & Environmental Sustainability* (Concurrences 2021).

[91] American Bar Association, *Sustainability and Competition Law – Report of the International Developments and Comments Task Force* (2021) 17.

[92] European Commission, 'Guidelines on the applicability of Article 101 of the Treaty on the Functioning of the European Union to horizontal co-operation agreements' [2023] OJ C 259/1, para 519.

benefits; they are just less immediate.[93] Therefore, it can well be argued that an agreement should be exempted that provides for higher prices but reduces social costs by at least the same amount.[94]

The solution presented here as EX 2, the recognition of such benefits, has the advantage that it is still an economic interpretation of Article 101(3) TFEU, which the Commission has practiced since the turn of the millennium in the context of the exemption. The current approach would not be completely discarded, but it would be developed further. Moreover, this approach leads to case-by-case reviews that are comparatively less open to questions of value.[95] Higher prices on the one hand and lower costs to society as a whole can be calculated with a certain degree of certainty using economic methods. This is the advantage over more normative balancing methods such as those presented here in Option EX 3. This is associated with greater legal certainty for companies.[96]

However, there are also critical voices against the consideration of overall societal benefits. For example, it is argued that the idea of internalising externalities should not be conceptually limited to cases of environmental sustainability, but could ultimately be applied to all aspects of sustainability.[97] This has limits: what is 'priced in' as a negative external effect would then be arbitrary.[98] However, it is well known that it is always difficult to draw boundaries and that counterexamples can always be constructed. Objective,

---

[93]   Maurits Dolmans, 'Sustainable Competition Policy and the "Polluter Pays" Principle' in Simon Holmes, Dirk Middelschulte and Martijn Snoep (eds), *Competition Law, Climate Change & Environmental Sustainability* (Concurrences 2021) 31.

[94]   Maurits Dolmans, 'Sustainable Competition Policy and the "Polluter Pays" Principle' in Simon Holmes, Dirk Middelschulte and Martijn Snoep (eds), *Competition Law, Climate Change & Environmental Sustainability* (Concurrences 2021) 31 f.

[95]   Cf Ella van den Brink and Jordan Ellison, 'Article 101(3) TFEU: The Roadmap for Sustainable Cooperation' in Simon Holmes, Dirk Middelschulte and Martijn Snoep (eds), *Competition Law, Climate Change & Environmental Sustainability* (Concurrences 2021) 47.

[96]   Ella van den Brink and Jordan Ellison, 'Article 101(3) TFEU: The Roadmap for Sustainable Cooperation' in Simon Holmes, Dirk Middelschulte and Martijn Snoep (eds), *Competition Law, Climate Change & Environmental Sustainability* (Concurrences 2021) 47.

[97]   Maarten-Pieter Schinkel and Leonard Treuren, 'Green Antitrust: Friendly Fire in the Fight Against Climate Change' in Simon Holmes, Dirk Middelschulte and Martijn Snoep (eds), *Competition Law, Climate Change & Environmental Sustainability* (Concurrences 2021) 85.

[98]   Maarten-Pieter Schinkel and Leonard Treuren, 'Green Antitrust: Friendly Fire in the Fight Against Climate Change' in Simon Holmes, Dirk Middelschulte and Martijn Snoep (eds), *Competition Law, Climate Change & Environmental Sustainability* (Concurrences 2021) 85.

'technical', quantifiable benefits could in any case be inserted seamlessly into the existing concept. It is true that quantifying benefits is difficult (see Chapter 13).[99] However, this is also the price to be paid for the economic orientation of the exemption provision according to the current reading.

Compatibility with Article 101 TFEU

Option EX 2 can only be implemented if it is compatible with the statutory version of the exemption. According to Article 101(3) TFEU, consumers must have a 'fair share of the resulting benefit'. A distinction must be made here, firstly, between the question of which groups of persons are to be regarded as 'consumers' and, secondly, when these are appropriately involved.

According to recent legal practice, only benefits in the relevant market in each case can be included in the consideration, i.e., only among the consumers concerned in each case.[100] These are regularly the actual end users of the products. The wording in Article 101(3) TFEU is a bit more open, however: 'while allowing consumers a fair share of the resulting benefit'. This can also be understood to mean that the efficiency benefits must accrue to consumers as a social group, with 'consumer' being understood in a broad sense. In 2002, the European Court of Justice stated that 'of course' all positive effects of an agreement had to be taken into account and that there did not have to be any specific relationship to the respective market.[101]

The problem continues with the wording of 'fair share'. According to current legal practice, a fair share requires that the disadvantages suffered by the consumers through the restriction of competition are at least offset by benefits they receive.[102] In other words, consumers need to be fully compensated.

It is easy to understand that consumers receive a fair share if their standing is neutral or even better overall as a result of the agreement. However, the wording is also open enough to assume a 'fair share' even without full compensation of consumers specifically affected by the agreement.[103] The wording

---

[99] Halil Rahman Basaran, 'How Should Article 81 EC Address Agreements that Yield Environmental Benefits?' (2006) 27 ECLR 479, 480.

[100] Case C-382/12 P *Mastercard* ECLI:EU:C:2014:2201 [2014], para 242.

[101] Case T-86/95 *Compagnie générale maritime and Others v Commission* ECLI:EU:T:2002:50 [2002] ECR II-1022, para 343.

[102] Cf Reinhard Ellger, 'Art. 101 Abs. 3 AEUV' in Torsten Körber, Heike Schweitzer and Daniel Zimmer (eds), *Immenga/Mestmäcker, Wettbewerbsrecht*, vol 1 (6th edn, C.H. Beck 2019) paras 235 ff.

[103] Maurits Dolmans, 'Sustainable Competition Policy and the "Polluter Pays" Principle' in Simon Holmes, Dirk Middelschulte and Martijn Snoep (eds), *Competition Law, Climate Change & Environmental Sustainability* (Concurrences 2021) 31; Ella van den Brink and Jordan Ellison, 'Article 101(3) TFEU: The Roadmap for Sustainable Cooperation' in Simon Holmes, Dirk Middelschulte and Martijn Snoep (eds),

only makes it clear that there must be improvements from which consumers benefit. For sustainability initiatives, fair share could be assumed without full compensation. A fair share should not require full compensation of the affected consumers if the market price is otherwise too low due to negative externalities and the specific consumers would benefit from this at the expense of the general public.[104] It would not be in line with economic thinking to allow consumers to free-ride on the external costs at the expense of the general public simply because these types of costs are not priced in.[105] Amending this situation is economically and socially desirable and represents a 'fair' share for consumers.

In this case, a fair share could also be assumed if the consumers affected by the restrictive agreement are also part of the larger group that benefits from the efficiency gains (e.g., lower greenhouse gas emissions). In addition, it must be remembered that 'fair' is a normative legal concept. In any case, it is not mandatory that this is to be understood in the sense of a mathematical offsetting.[106] Full compensation should be required if the efficiency benefits accrue to the undertakings themselves, as this should not be at the expense of consumers. However, if it is a matter of distributing efficiencies between consumers and society, as is the case here, it does not seem appropriate to demand the full

---

Competition Law, Climate Change & Environmental Sustainability (Concurrences 2021) 47; Lucas Macharis, 'The Exemption of Sustainability Agreements under European Competition Law – Balancing Societal Benefits with Consumer Harm: A New Way Forward' [2022] 43 ECLR 170, 178.

[104] Cf Autoriteit Consument & Markt, 'Guidelines on Sustainability Agreements' (2021) para 41; Maurits Dolmans, 'Sustainable Competition Policy and the "Polluter Pays" Principle' in Simon Holmes, Dirk Middelschulte and Martijn Snoep (eds), *Competition Law, Climate Change & Environmental Sustainability* (Concurrences 2021) 35; see also Elena Wiese, 'Agenda 2025: Roadmap to Sustainability' (*D'Kart*, 2022) www .dkart .de/ blog/ 2022/ 06/ 07/ agenda -2025 -nachhalt igkeitskoo perationen -private-enforcement/ accessed 28 July 2023.

[105] Ella van den Brink and Jordan Ellison, 'Article 101(3) TFEU: The Roadmap for Sustainable Cooperation' in Simon Holmes, Dirk Middelschulte and Martijn Snoep (eds), *Competition Law, Climate Change & Environmental Sustainability* (Concurrences 2021) 47.

[106] Maurits Dolmans, 'Sustainable Competition Policy and the "Polluter Pays" Principle' in Simon Holmes, Dirk Middelschulte and Martijn Snoep (eds), *Competition Law, Climate Change & Environmental Sustainability* (Concurrences 2021) 35.

compensation of consumers.[107] 'Consumers, by definition, include us all', as President Kennedy famously said.[108]

The fact that agreements aimed at internalising external effects are supported by European law is shown by the explicit establishment of the so-called *polluter pays principle* in Article 191(2) TFEU.[109] The principle states that the costs of environmental damage must be borne by the polluter. The fact that an agreement which ensures this should constitute a violation of Article 101 TFEU is, at least *prima facie*, a contradiction.[110]

Applicability to different sustainability topics

It should be emphasised that this option is not suitable for all sustainability goals. It is particularly suitable for environmental and climate protection initiatives (e.g., to reduce greenhouse gas emissions), since the problem of negative externalities is regularly particularly serious in these areas but is also already researched in environmental economics. Here, the reduction of these external effects can be particularly effective in generating efficiency benefits for society as a whole.

This is not possible in the same way for other sustainability goals (such as animal welfare or fair wages for farmers), as these are less about externalities, but primarily about ethical or distributional considerations.[111]

Option EX 3: Normative Balancing

In addition to the options presented so far, which all remain within an economic logic, it is also conceivable to opt for a more normative approach to the justification of sustainability agreements.

---

[107] Cf Ella van den Brink and Jordan Ellison, 'Article 101(3) TFEU: The Roadmap for Sustainable Cooperation' in Simon Holmes, Dirk Middelschulte and Martijn Snoep (eds), *Competition Law, Climate Change & Environmental Sustainability* (Concurrences 2021) 46; Martijn Snoep, 'What is Fair and Efficient in the Face of Climate Change?' (2023) 11 *Journal of Antitrust Enforcement* 1, 4.

[108] John F. Kennedy, 'Special Message to Congress on Protecting the Consumer Interest, 15 March 1962 www .jfklibrary .org/ asset -viewer/ archives/ JFKPOF/ 037/ JFKPOF-037-028 accessed 10 August 2023.

[109] Cf. Ioannis Lianos, 'Reorienting Competition Law' (2022) 10 *Journal of Antitrust Enforcement* 1, 8 et seq.

[110] Cf Maurits Dolmans, 'Sustainable Competition Policy and the "Polluter Pays" Principle' in Simon Holmes, Dirk Middelschulte and Martijn Snoep (eds), *Competition Law, Climate Change & Environmental Sustainability* (Concurrences 2021) 26 ff.

[111] Daniel Zimmer and Lara Schäfer, 'Nachhaltigkeitskooperationen in kartellrechtlicher und rechtsökonomischer Betrachtung' (2022) JZ 870, 876.

Legal concept

In the context of the exemption, qualitative improvements (i.e., public welfare considerations) could be weighed up against restrictions of competition. An exemption could then be granted if the restrictive effects on competition are justified on the basis of overriding public interest considerations. This balancing of interests would require a value judgment; it would move away from the stricter approach of calculating numbers currently practiced in the context of Article 101(3) TFEU. At the same time, the public interest would be given priority over competition protection in individual cases.

The European Commission has already attempted to find solutions to conflicting objectives in a similar way in the Guidelines on State Aid for Climate, Environmental Protection and Energy 2022.[112] In principle, subsidies are prohibited under European law for reasons of competition pursuant to Article 107(1) TFEU. However, they can be exempted under Article 107(3) lit. c. The guidelines specify, against the background of the European Green Deal, what applies to subsidies on environmental issues. The guidelines cover numerous categories of aid,[113] such as aid for the reduction of greenhouse gas emissions, for the development of a charging infrastructure for clean vehicles or for the support of the transition to a circular economy. Definitions and justifications for the aid and criteria are provided in each case. The key points are the positive condition that the aid must promote the development of an economic sector and the negative condition that the aid must not entail a change in trading conditions that is contrary to the common interest.

The model of reviewing climate-protective subsidies is mentioned in this context as a model of how competition and sustainability goals are already being balanced at the European level. In this process, the non-competition goals are politically set, defined, and examined. Positive and negative conditions are then defined to ensure a minimum of compatibility with competition. Such a catalogue of safeguarding criteria could also be considered in the context of the exemption under Article 101(3) TFEU.

The normative approach deviates to a certain degree from the efficiency paradigm that is dominant in current competition law theory.[114] Whether this system should be opened up more so that extra-competition issues are taken

---

[112] European Commission, 'Guidelines on State Aid for climate, environmental protection and energy 2022' [2022] OJ C 80/1.

[113] See European Commission, 'Guidelines on State Aid for climate, environmental protection and energy 2022' [2022] OJ C 80/1, para 16.

[114] Cf European Commission, 'Guidelines on the application of Article 81(3) of the Treaty' [2004] OJ C 101/97, para 33; Lars Kjølbye, 'The New Commission Guidelines on the Application of Article 81(3): An Economic Approach to Article 81' (2004) 25 ECLR 566.

into account is, ultimately, a political decision. Institutionally, the argument in favour is that something needs to be done with regard to (at least some) sustainability goals and that it is better to integrate these into a competition-minded approach. Article 101(3) TFEU would provide that framework. Skilled antitrust agencies with a competition and efficiency mindset would remain in the driving seat. If other institutions or laws step in, the fate of competition will probably be worse. Yet, this opens the box: the protection of competition is diluted, and competition agencies are empowered to make decisions that lie outside their actual area of competence. This will, over time, change their expertise and approach. Integrating sustainability concerns in Article 101(3) TFEU to a larger degree is not only a matter of interpreting the term 'improvement', but it is also about the concept of competition. Is competition a purely economic, efficiency-oriented mechanism, or does it have another value in society?

Procedural arrangement

In this approach, particular attention must be paid to the procedural arrangements. In such cases, companies cannot be expected themselves to examine whether their cooperation is exempted. The self-assessment, as is currently provided for under Article 1(2) of Regulation (EC) 1/2003 is not appropriate. Companies are not in a position to assess the public interest benefits of their actions. They cannot be expected to bear the risk that the authorities and courts come to a different conclusion.

For an exemption on normative grounds, a constitutive exemption procedure before a competition authority would therefore be necessary, whereby the competences between the European Commission and the national competition agencies would have to be delimited if necessary. This would ensure the democratic legitimacy of the balancing process on a legal basis. It would also refute arguments that a consideration of non-competition aspects in competition law could lead to legal fragmentation in the Union.[115] A central body and, if necessary, referrals to the ECJ would ensure a uniform application of Article 101(3) TFEU in such cases. The exemption would offer companies legal certainty, which is otherwise criticised as lacking in sustainability initiatives.[116]

---

[115] On this argument, see Halil Rahman Basaran, 'How Should Article 81 EC Address Agreements that Yield Environmental Benefits?' (2006) 27 ECLR 479, 482; Richard Whish and David Bailey, *Competition Law* (10th edn, Oxford 2021) 165.

[116] Christiane Dahlbender, 'Sustaining both the Planet and Competition: A Call for More Guidance' (2021) WuW 392; Ella van den Brink and Jordan Ellison, 'Article 101(3) TFEU: The Roadmap for Sustainable Cooperation' in Simon Holmes, Dirk Middelschulte and Martijn Snoep (eds), *Competition Law, Climate Change & Environmental Sustainability* (Concurrences 2021) 40 f.

For the competition agencies, such an exemption would be uncharted territory, as they would have to assess public benefits, which has not been part of the job description so far. This problem would be solved if further relevant agencies were involved. For example, for environmental initiatives, the Commission's Directorates General for Environmental or Climate Protection could play a role (or respective agencies at the national level). Competitors and relevant associations could also be given participation rights in the procedure. The procedural effort outlined here only in rudimentary form already suggests that this option can only be considered for significant landmark cases. In a certain sense, this would amount to an equivalent of the public interest approval known for merger prohibitions in some countries. However, in the form envisaged here, the procedure would not be transferred to the political sphere but would remain in the area of the competition institutions.

Compatibility with Article 101 TFEU
This option, including a 'normative balancing', raises the question of compatibility with Article 101(3) TFEU. In our view, the current handling of the exemption is not mandated by the text of the law. The prerequisite according to the wording is an improvement in the production or distribution of goods, which could in principle also be assumed without any reference to economic calculations. A production of goods could also be considered 'better' if it is less harmful to the environment, promotes animal welfare or results in fairer wages in developing countries. Insofar as sustainability aspects can be found in European primary law, it does not seem problematic to speak of an 'improvement in the production of goods'.[117] Moreover, the Union institutions are obliged under the horizontal clauses in Articles 7 et seq. TEU to take into account certain public interest objectives when applying European law. This makes it clear that the protection of competition cannot have absolute priority over other Union objectives.

Changes regarding the procedure of exempting certain agreements could be integrated in a reform of Regulation (EC) 1/2003.

Option EX 4: Individual Exemption of Model Cooperation Agreements

Another option under Article 101(3) TFEU would be to open up a notification and exemption system for individual model cooperation agreements.

---

[117] Cf Maurits Dolmans, 'Sustainable Competition Policy and the "Polluter Pays" Principle' in Simon Holmes, Dirk Middelschulte and Martijn Snoep (eds), *Competition Law, Climate Change & Environmental Sustainability* (Concurrences 2021) 31.

In option EX 3 we looked at individual exemptions for agreements that require normative considerations. There is a certain tension, though, since this could in fact be a return to the pre-2004 system of necessary notifications that the European Commission wanted to get rid of for good reason. Returning to a notification system does not seem viable. Yet, a compromise could be to open up this path for certain model agreements with the greatest possible impact. A notification system would of course require strict deadlines.

Eligible initiatives could be such agreements that are transparent and open to all market participants. Solutions of clubs of some companies would not be accepted. For sustainability effects to be achieved there would have to be a material threshold – it would have to be possible to achieve such far-reaching progress through the agreement that a referral to the authorities is justified (and the restriction of competition possibly outweighed). Mere over-fulfilment of legal requirements would not suffice for this purpose; rather, a qualitatively or quantitatively new dimension would have to be reached. What exactly makes a 'quantum leap' of sustainability will depend on a case-by-case assessment, and one could think of a short pre-assessment phase where it is considered whether the agreement can be submitted to the authority. Maybe this could even run with the involvement of other agencies that are better placed to assess the sustainability effects than the competition agency. The idea of this option is to have a formal way to grant legal certainty to such agreements that could propel technology or business models to a new level of heightened sustainability. The model cooperation agreements would need a time limit, monitoring, and evaluation.

We also suggest limiting this approach to initiatives that are intended to pave the way for new binding legal acts. This would be the 'model' character of the agreement: if evaluated positively, i.e. after successful testing, the content of the agreement or further steps would be made mandatory by law as a new legal standard. The model cooperation could therefore serve as a 'laboratory' for huge sustainability gains. Such agreements may be used to initiate a statutory regulation. The right of initiative of the legislature is not affected.

Option EX 5: Statutory Exception

It could also be considered to grant a statutory exception to sustainability agreements or to have some clarifications by statute.

Since it is still disputed whether and to what extent sustainability considerations can have a place within the framework of Article 101(3) TFEU, a legal clarification would be a safe and democratic way out of the problem. A change in the law would remove the existing ambiguities. When agencies simply change their practice, there is still a risk that courts and, in particular, the ECJ would not support the new interpretation of the law.

A statutory exception could take the form of a block exemption regulation (see option EX 6 below) or a change in the wording of Article 101(3) TFEU. Unlikely as a change of Treaty may seem, from an academic perspective it is still important to highlight the different opportunities, not least since our times of crises are times where economic law is substantially challenged.

Possible content
Legislative clarification could be provided in a number of ways. Based on the Austrian solution, a clarification could be made so that benefits to society as a whole can justify an exemption. This would give some types of sustainability activities a comparatively secure standard of review for their cooperation. The substantive advantages and disadvantages of recognising benefits to society as a whole were presented in Option EX 2. Insofar as one is in favour of recognising benefits to society as a whole, it would be desirable to clearly anchor this in the law as well. It should be mentioned here that Option EX 2 would probably work primarily for cases where improvements can be quantified. Sustainability initiatives on animal welfare aspects or fairer wages in the banana sector, for example, would be difficult to take under the umbrella of option EX 2.

A statutory clarification may be more detailed regarding the type of improvements, stating what sustainability goals are recognised, and regarding the level of improvement (e.g. substantial, significant etc.).

It could also be enshrined in law that the weighing process is to be conducted differently, with a normative or political weighing instead of an economic one (cf option EX 3).

An amendment of the law would also need to take a position regarding the question of self-assessment or agency-granted exemption. Without the latter, there would be no official case-by-case assessment. Self-assessment comes with the risk of restraints of competition covered in some greenwashing and little transparency about market activities. A clear-cut statutory exemption would provide more legal certainty.

Feasibility
Such a clarification is possible under national laws of the member states as in Austria, but it would only cover agreements with a purely domestic effect. As stated before, according to Article 3(1) and (2) of Regulation (EC) No 1/2003, European law takes precedence as soon as an infringement is likely to affect trade between member states.

An amendment of Article 101 TFEU would have greater potential but is much more difficult to achieve. As part of European primary law, a change of the European treaties is only possible in accordance with Article 48 TEU, which requires the consent of all member states in accordance with their respective constitutional requirements. A block exemption regulation might be easier to achieve (see below).

When amending the law one challenge lies in properly framing the issue so that the desired agreements are privileged without overshooting the mark and allowing too many restrictions on competition. Admittedly, the legal situation is already so unclear at present that any legislative initiative can contribute at least a little to greater legal certainty. In addition, the amendment of the law can be accompanied by detailed explanations which, together with new official guidelines, will provide sufficient clarity.

SME exemption

Under German national competition law, there is an exemption of certain agreements entered into by small and medium-sized enterprises (SMEs). Section 3 of the German competition act reads:

> Agreements between competing undertakings and decisions by associations of undertakings the subject matter of which is the rationalisation of economic activities through inter-firm cooperation fulfil the conditions of [the national equivalent to Article 101(3) TFEU] if
> (1)   the agreement or the decision does not significantly affect competition on the market, and
> (2)   the agreement or the decision serves to improve the competitiveness of small or medium-sized enterprises.

This allows joint rationalisation to a limited extent in order to give SMEs better competitive opportunities compared with larger competitors. A statutory exemption for sustainability could also tie in with this. The cooperation between would be exempt if they undertake joint efforts to convert their companies to environmental or social sustainability.

This is supported by the fact that the costs of a necessary shift to more sustainability in the company can be a challenge for SMEs in particular. They would gain legal certainty. This also makes sense from a competition point of view if it puts them in a better position to keep up with the big players. However, integrating this exemption on the national level would have limited relevance, again.

Option EX 6: Sustainability Block Exemption Regulation

On the EU level, a well-established instrument for clarifying the requirements of Article 101(3) TFEU are the block exemption regulations (BERs). Currently, there is no such BER specifically for sustainability agreements.

A regulation would give legal certainty to companies and be a much clearer tool than guidelines. Such a BER would have to accomplish the following:

- define the sustainability agreements that fall within the scope;
- grant a general exemption to such agreements;
- establish a market share threshold at which the benefit of the block exemption ceases to apply;
- determine hardcore restrictions and other restrictions that are not permissible even under the BER regime.

Alternatively, sectors could be given individual block exemption regulations exempting specific, typical initiatives. Sector-specific BERs offer models for this.[118] However, such sector-specific BERs are already rather a discontinued model in terms of competition law. It has already been pointed out elsewhere that the sustainability goals require cross-sectoral efforts.

The key issue is the question of market share: sustainability initiatives can have a major impact on the achievement of Sustainable Development Goals precisely when the major market players are involved. Their involvement at the same time poses a greater risk from a competition point of view, which is why the benefit of the block exemption should in principle not accrue to them.[119] This has been the approach in other block exemption regulations.

This dilemma can be resolved in two ways:

First, the market share limits could be maintained analogous to the existing BERs. Then, the advantage of the block exemption would especially benefit companies that do not have high market shares. The sustainability BER would thus provide incentives for small and medium-sized market players to cooperate.

Secondly, in deviation from the current model, companies with larger market shares could also be allowed to participate if the sustainability improvements are so large that the remaining competitive threat is compensated. The extent

---

[118] Regulation (EC) 169/2009 of 26 February 2009 applying rules of competition to transport by rail, road and inland waterway [2009] OJ L 61/1; Regulation (EU) 267/2010 of 24 March 2010 on the application of Article 101(3) of the Treaty on the Functioning of the European Union to certain categories of agreements, decisions and concerted practices in the insurance sector [2010] OJ L 83/1; Regulation (EU) 261/2010 of 25 March 2010 amending Council Regulation (EC) No 297/95 as regards the adjustment of the fees of the European Medicines Agency to the inflation rate [2010] OJ L 80/36.

[119] See Regulation (EU) 2022/720 of 10 May 2022 on the application of Article 101(3) of the Treaty on the Functioning of the European Union to categories of vertical agreements and concerted practices [2022] OJ L 134/4, recitals 6–9.

of the exemption could depend on the market share. In such a model, the prohibited clauses could be different from agreements with less market power.

For the definition of the sustainability targets to be achieved, reference could be made, by way of example, to the Taxonomy that defines this for some environmental sustainability targets.[120] When balancing with the objectives of competition, the State aid guidelines on climate, environmental protection and energy could be an inspiration. The models are similar in that they also use the mechanism of exemptions and non-permissible restrictions. Prioritisation is evident in both models: the Taxonomy and the State aid guidelines select only certain sustainability goals. As much as a comprehensive approach to achieving Sustainable Development Goals is desirable, the broad range of sustainability goals is not suitable for prescribing in a BER.

If the Taxonomy and the State aid guidelines are considered together in light of competition law, this could lead to a sustainability BER that reconciles competition and the common good for some of the sustainability objectives. This would have to be preceded by the insight that these sustainability objectives are indeed partly strengthening competition (namely on the merits), just like the promotion of research and development or the promotion of technology transfer are (each of which is also promoted by its own BER.) BERs are based on the idea that some cooperation fosters competition as is obvious with vertical agreements – they strengthen interbrand competition at the expense of intrabrand competition. For sustainability, a similar pro-competition effect is evident when competition is conceptually defined as sustainable competition. It may be argued that competition with an intergenerational or intragenerational perspective relies on sustainability goals that are taken into account.

If the sustainability objectives are seen as non-competition objectives, the criteria in Article 101(3) TFEU would only be fulfilled if – as already discussed – non-competition objectives are also considered eligible under Article 101(3) TFEU.

A sustainability BER would address the practical problem of companies' self-assessment by providing greater legal certainty. However, a BER would have to position itself on which sustainability goals are a priority, how to deal with companies with market power, to what extent sustainability effects can compensate for competition restrictions, and what the red lines for competition are so that a violation still constitutes a hardcore restriction.

---

[120] For more details see Chapter 10.

7. Abuse of dominance

Abuse of dominance under Article 102 TFEU serves to capture strategies of exclusion and exploitation through unilateral actions by dominant undertakings. When discussing sustainability goals and competition law, abuse of dominance was not in the spotlight.[1] Only a few contributions shed light on this topic.[2] There are no known initiatives by competition authorities, national or European legislators in this area of competition law. Proceedings in which sustainability goals have played a leading role are not known. However, the prohibition of abusive practices provides a strong set of instruments to control the behaviour of companies with a 'special responsibility', which can include sustainability considerations.[3]

---

[1] Simon Holmes, 'How Sustainability Can be Taken into Account in Every Area of Competition Law' in Simon Holmes, Dirk Middelschulte and Martijn Snoep (eds), *Competition Law, Climate Change & Environmental Sustainability* (Concurrences 2021) 8.

[2] Cf Simon Holmes, 'How Sustainability Can be Taken into Account in Every Area of Competition Law' in Simon Holmes, Dirk Middelschulte and Martijn Snoep (eds), *Competition Law, Climate Change & Environmental Sustainability* (Concurrences 2021) 3; Simon Holmes, 'Climate Change, Sustainability, and Competition Law' (2020) 8 *Journal of Antitrust Enforcement* 354; Marios Iacovides and Christos Vrettos, 'Radical for Whom? Unsustainable Business Practices as Abuses of Dominance' in Simon Holmes, Dirk Middelschulte and Martijn Snoep (eds), *Competition Law, Climate Change & Environmental Sustainability* (Concurrences 2021) 91; Marios Iacovides and Christos Vrettos, 'Falling Through the Cracks no More? Article 102 TFEU and Sustainability: The Relation Between Dominance, Environmental Degradation, and Social Injustice' (2021) 10 *Journal of Antitrust Enforcement* 32; Christopher Thomas, 'Exploring the Sustainability of Article 102' in Simon Holmes, Dirk Middelschulte and Martijn Snoep (eds), *Competition Law, Climate Change & Environmental Sustainability* (Concurrences 2021) 105; Julian Nowag, 'Competition Law's Sustainability Gap? Tools for an Examination and a Brief Overview' (2022) 5(1) *Nordic Journal of European Law* 6 https://journals.lub.lu.se/njel/article/view/24504 accessed 18 August 2023; Suzanne Kingston, *Greening EU Competition Law and Policy* (Cambridge University Press 2011) chapter 9.

[3] ECJ in consistent case law, e.g. Case 322/81 *Michelin v Commission* ECLI:EU:C:1983:313 [1983] ECR 3461, para 57; Case C-413/14 P *Intel v Commission* ECLI:EU:C:2017:632 [2017] para 135.

MARKET DOMINANCE

The prerequisite for applying Article 102 TFEU is the dominant position of the undertaking.

Legal Situation

Sustainability considerations are currently not relevant for the assessment of market power. However, they can play an indirect role. This may be the case, for example, if there are barriers to market entry in markets that are directly relevant to individual Sustainable Development Goals, such as the market for waste disposal or for CO_2 certificate trading.

Option AB 1: Changed Preferences and Market Definition

In the context of market definition, sustainability considerations can already play a role if separate product markets are defined for sustainable products and services. This has been discussed by the European Commission, for example, for fair trade coffee compared to conventionally traded coffee.[4] This merely reflects the economic reality. The more strongly sustainability influences the product characteristics or demand relevant for market definition, the more frequently different markets will have to be defined on the basis of such criteria. The European Commission recognises this in the evaluation of the Commission Notice on the definition of relevant market for the purposes of Community competition law.[5]

This is not a legal innovation, but merely a consistent application of previous principles: market definition is about capturing economic reality. This will however only occur if competition authorities, courts and private plaintiffs pay attention to the possible changes in preferences during market definition and specifically identify these preferences.

---

[4] *DEMB/Mondelez/Charger OpCo* (Case M.7292) Commission Decision [2015] C(2015) 3000 final, para 55.

[5] European Commission, 'Commission staff working Document, Evaluation of the Commission Notice on the definition of relevant market for the purposes of Community competition law of 9 December 1997', SWD (2021) 199 final, 8, 31 https://ec.europa .eu/competition-policy/system/files/2021-07/evaluation_market-definition-notice_en .pdf accessed 15 August 2023.

BOX 7.1   SUSTAINABLE BANANAS

The preferences of a large number of consumers may have changed so that bananas from sustainable production (fair wages) are no longer considered interchangeable with bananas from production that does not meet these standards. An increase in the price of 'fair' bananas would not lead these consumers to switch to non-sustainable bananas.

The consequences of such a market definition are that, due to the narrower market, one company will be seen as dominant more quickly.[6] This applies to both the sustainable market and the non-sustainable market that is then to be delineated. This can lead to a stronger protection of competition in both markets, as it is easier to take action against abusive behaviour. This also promotes sustainability. In the sustainable market, the consolidation and expansion of dominant positions can be prevented and thus the functioning of competition can be protected, so that, for example, incentives for innovation are retained to offer even more sustainable products.

Legislative changes are not necessary. However, it can be clarified that it should always be investigated whether preferences for sustainable products or services are already so pronounced that there are separate markets. The procedure for such investigations should be made transparent.

Option AB 2: New Indicators for Dominance

The indicators used to determine market power could be expanded to include aspects that clarify the connection between market power and (lack of) sustainability, e.g. in Article 2(1) Regulation (EC) No 139/2004 (EC Merger Regulation).

Externalisation

The externalisation of costs is a market failure that is particularly relevant for sustainability. Externalisation prevents efficient outcomes from being achieved through market mechanisms. A company that can particularly benefit from externalisation may be able to charge lower costs than a company that foregoes or must forego externalisation. Extensive externalisation (or even the possibility of it) could be considered a relevant indicator for market power. For example, a company would be considered dominant if it could cause emissions without having to take precautions to protect the environment. Such a situation

---

⁶   Critically Michael A Carrier, 'An Antitrust Framework for Climate Change' (2011) 9 *Northwestern Journal of Technology and Intellectual Property* 513, 514.

could arise, for example, if one company (e.g., from another jurisdiction) is subject to less stringent regulations than another. The fact that externalisation may be legal does not change the actual advantages in the market that are at stake. This would provide a starting point – in the sense of a *level playing field* – for the application of competition law to companies from other jurisdictions that are bound by less strict environmental regulations.[7] While these companies would not be bound to comply with the stricter environmental regulations, at least the advantages resulting from the lower level of protection in other jurisdictions would be able to be included in the assessment.

If the externalities are achieved illegally, the effects are stronger and even more relevant for competition, since competitors cannot make use of the externalisation and the illegal externalisation is regarded as particularly undesirable for society. In this respect, it is also irrelevant that the market failure has already been addressed by the legislator, since the specifically competition effects of the infringement must be taken into account here.

It would also be possible to use the internalisation of legal externalities as an indicator that makes it less likely for an undertaking to be considered dominant. It would speak against market dominance if a company did not take advantage of the opportunity to externalise. This would be the case, for example, if a company were to clean the exhaust air, although unfiltered emissions would also be permissible. In this way, the company is taking on more disadvantages in order to protect the general public, although it is not obligated to do so. This can lead to a competitive disadvantage.

Taking (possible) externalisation into account would have positive consequences for sustainability concerns, as an incentive for sustainable behaviour is set. At the same time, non-sustainable companies would be more easily and quickly subject to the control of abusive practices, as their behaviour could be monitored and their market power – and thus the extent of externalisation – could be limited.

Lack of sustainability as an indicator of dominance?

A lack of sustainability could be seen as an indicator for dominance. *Iacovides/ Vrettos* argue that sustainability has increasingly become relevant for competition and therefore companies must strive to produce or offer sustainable products. Companies that nevertheless exhibit non-sustainable behaviour can, they argue, behave independently of the competition parameter of sustainabil-

---

[7]   See Thorsten Käseberg, 'A New EU Level Playing Field Instrument: Potential Goals and Design' (Centre for Economic Policy Research 15 January 2020) https://voxeu.org/article/new-eu-level-playing-field-instrument accessed 22 June 2023.

ity. Their non-sustainable behaviour is therefore an indication of their market dominance.[8]

However, the connection claimed by *Iacovides/Vrettos* has not been proven. In any case, it is not obvious that only companies with market power are currently not violating the Sustainable Development Goals because of the reaction of buyers or competitors. This calls into question the economic justification for the market intervention. As long as this connection cannot be generally assumed or at least proven in individual cases, this criterion thus lacks a connection to competition. The introduction would lead to the application of competition law simply being supplemented by sustainability considerations.

If a corresponding presumption were nevertheless introduced, non-sustainable conduct would then trigger the presumption of market dominance, which would have to be rebutted by the company concerned. To this end, it could be demonstrated that sustainability considerations are not yet a determining competition factor. The presumption would nevertheless create an incentive to make one's own behaviour more sustainable, as otherwise the presumption of market dominance would have to be rebutted independently and the company would expose itself to the risk of falling within the scope of abuse control. This entails increased regulatory costs, as agencies and courts, as well as companies, would need to do more to determine the impact of behaviour on sustainability goals.

JUSTIFICATION

The ECJ allows prima facie justification of abusive conduct where there is an objective need for the conduct,[9] legitimate economic interests,[10] and efficiency gains.[11] The European Commission states in its decisions that justification is possible if the conduct is necessary in order to generate efficiencies that

---

[8]   Marios C Iacovides and Christos Vrettos, 'Falling Through the Cracks no More? Article 102 TFEU and Sustainability: The Relation between Dominance, Environmental Degradation, and Social Injustice' (2021) 10 *Journal of Antitrust Enforcement* 32, 36; see also OECD, 'Techniques and Evidentiary Issues in Proving Dominance/Monopoly Power' DAF/COMP(2006)35 (9 October 2008) 42, 44.

[9]   Case C-418/01 *IMS Health v Commission* ECLI:EU:C:2004:257 [2004] ECR I-5069, para 51.

[10]   Case 27/76 *United Brands v Commission* ECLI:EU:C:1978:22 [1978] ECR 207, paras 189 f.

[11]   Case C-95/04 P *British Airways v Commission* ECLI:EU:C:2007:166 [2007] ECR I-2373, para 69.

outweigh the negative effects of the conduct[12] and do not eliminate effective competition.[13]

European Law

So far, it is not apparent that the courts or antitrust authorities have acknowledged effects on sustainability in the sense of the Sustainable Development Goals when dealing with possible justifications. According to current practice, however, this would be conceivable insofar as sustainability considerations (e.g., lower greenhouse gas emissions) can be regarded as efficiencies or as a legitimate objective.[14] In this respect, reference should be made to the discussion on Article 101(3) TFEU.

Option AB 3: Sustainability as a Factor for Justification

Sustainability concerns could play a greater role as justification in the future. *Holmes* gives the following examples in which he believes sustainability considerations can lead to the justification of abusive behaviour:[15]

- One company charges very high prices by comparison, but this can be explained by the fact that they have internalised the impact on the environment.

---

[12] *Intel* (Case COMP/C-3/37.990) Commission Decision [2009] D(2009) 3726 final, paras 925, 1624; *Telekomunikacja Polska* (Case COMP/39.525) Commission Decision [2011] para 873; *ARA Foreclosure* (Case AT.39759) Commission Decision [2016] para 114.

[13] *Qualcomm (Exclusivity payments)* (Case AT.40220) Commission Decision [2018] C(2018) 240 final, para 387; *Google Android* (Case AT.40099) Commission Decision [2018] C(2018) 4761 final, para 736.

[14] Julian Nowag, 'Competition Law's Sustainability Gap? Tools for an Examination and a Brief Overview' (2022) 5(1) *Nordic Journal of European Law* 6 https://journals .lub .lu .se/ njel/ article/ view/ 24504 accessed 18 August 2023; Christopher Thomas, 'Exploring the Sustainability of Article 102' in Simon Holmes, Dirk Middelschulte and Martijn Snoep (eds), *Competition Law, Climate Change & Environmental Sustainability* (Concurrences 2021) 111.

[15] Simon Holmes, 'Climate Change, Sustainability and Competition Law' (2020) 8 *Journal of Antitrust Enforcement* 354, 388 f, with further examples Marios Iacovides and Valentin Mauboussin, 'Sustainability Considerations in the Application of Article 102 TFEU: State of the Art and Proposals for a More Sustainable Competition Law' in Julian Nowag (ed), *Research Handbook on Competition Law and Sustainability* (2023) 15 ff (forthcoming).

- A company charges higher prices to customers who use the product in environmentally harmful ways.[16]
- A company links the purchase of a product to the purchase of an environmentally friendly product.
- A company refuses to supply goods or provide access to a facility because the buyers want to use them in an environmentally harmful way.

Conversely, it would have to be considered an aggravating factor for the company with market power if it discriminates against precisely those companies that produce in an environmentally friendly manner. If abusive practices are specifically directed against companies that strive for environmental or social sustainability, this would also have to be considered as an aggravating factor.

INFRINGEMENT OF NON-COMPETITION REGULATIONS

Companies that do not comply with the law can gain competitive advantages as a result. This could be seen as a new form of abusive practice.

German Competition Law

In German competition law, there are a few cases in which it is seen as an abuse if an undertaking gains a competitive advantage through the infringement of regulations outside of competition law. The dominant undertaking leaves the 'level playing field'.[17] In the case of dominant undertakings, the infringement of a regulation can be particularly serious due to market power.[18] The most significant recent example is the *Facebook* case (still pending before the courts).[19] This principle could be expanded and applied to regulations promoting and protecting sustainability.

A simple breach of the law by a dominant undertaking cannot automatically constitute an abuse of dominance. Otherwise, competition law would become an enforcement tool for all infringements of the law by dominant companies.

---

[16]   Cf for further details Peter Georg Picht, 'Sell Green Downstream – Sustainable Dual Pricing and Competition Law' (2023) No1 Concurrences 48.
[17]   Maik Wolf and Kathrin Westermann 'GWB § 19' in Franz Jürgen Säcker et al (eds), *Münchener Kommentar zum Wettbewerbsrecht*, vol 2 (4th edn, C.H. Beck 2020) para 35d.
[18]   Maik Wolf and Kathrin Westermann 'GWB § 19' in Franz Jürgen Säcker et al (eds), *Münchener Kommentar zum Wettbewerbsrecht*, vol 2 (4th edn, C.H. Beck 2020) para 35e.
[19]   BGH, KVR 69/19, 23.6.2020, GRUR 2020, 1318 – *Facebook*.

Additional criteria are needed. Under German law, the link to competition is decisive. The question is whether the infringement has particularly serious effects and thus leads to further damage to competition.[20] If the infringement of the law results in a competitive advantage that strengthens the dominant position and thus further harms competition in the affected market, there is a sufficient link to competition. However, the infringement does not have to be the direct result of market power. Due to the broad understanding of causality, the conduct need not have been possible only because the company is dominant. Nevertheless, the key question in such cases remains whether sufficient harm to competition can be proven.

Option AB 4: Infringement of Regulations Protecting Sustainability

With this approach competition law could be used to stop the behaviour of companies that is detrimental to sustainability, when the same behaviour also constitutes an infringement of another regulation.[21] It is essential, however, that a link to competition has to be established.

Example: A dominant undertaking violates environmental regulations and therefore saves production costs. As a result, it can offer products at lower prices and expand its own market share compared to law-abiding competitors.

The advantage of this approach is that sustainability considerations can be taken into account in the context of a competition based review. The decision in the *AstraZeneca* case provides a basis to transfer this concept to European law.[22] In the decision, confirmed by the European courts, the European Commission saw an abuse in the fact that the pharmaceutical company obtained supplementary protection certificates by making unlawful misleading statements to patent offices.

In this way it is possible to address the previously identified market failure of lack of internalisation of cost. It is more difficult to justify preventing any externalisation if it is not prohibited by law. However, if the externalisation takes place through the violation of regulations, this is based on the clear

---

[20] Cf Tobias Lettl, 'Missbräuchliche Ausnutzung einer marktbeherrschenden Stellung nach Art. 102 AEUV, § 19 GWB und Rechtsbruch' (2016) WuW 214, 214 ff; further Jochen Glöckner, 'Wettbewerbsbezogenes Verständnis der Unlauterkeit und Vorsprungserlangung durch Rechtsbruch' (2008) GRUR 960, 965.

[21] Cf Eckart Bueren and Jennifer Crowder, 'Sustainability and Competition Law – Germany' (*SSRN*, 11 November 2022) https://papers.ssrn.com/sol3/papers.cfm ?abstract_id=4365639 accessed 18 August 2023, 12 f.

[22] Case C-457/10 P *AstraZeneca v Commission* ECLI:EU:C:2012:770. Cf Rupprecht Podszun, 'Can Competition Law Repair Patent Law and Administrative Procedures? *AstraZeneca*' (2014) 51 CML Rev 281.

assessment that this externalisation is not protected by law. At the same time, the infringed regulations provide the standard and legal test for sustainability that would otherwise have to be developed by the competition authorities or the courts. For proponents of the approach that competition must be defined as sustainable competition, this category of cases offers an outstanding starting point.

At the same time, challenges remain. The question arises as to whether the competition authorities themselves have the competence to review environmental regulations. In part, this is affirmed and assumed in courts anyway.[23] Nevertheless, it seems advisable to develop a procedure so that the infringement of non-competition regulations can be examined in cooperation with the competent authorities.

This approach will be criticised since the tools of competition law will be used to address non-competition issues.[24] This objection cannot be dismissed entirely. Therefore, the decisive factor remains to establish anti-competition effects in individual cases. The regulation that is being infringed may already have sanctions in place. However, competition law goes beyond this and addresses the particular significance and effects of the infringement on competition. The protection of competition does not take place in a vacuum. To keep non-competition concerns out of competition law does not do justice to other binding goals in European and national law. In addition, there is a danger that, if necessary, new – much stricter – regulation without a focus on competition will be imposed and hinder competition to a higher degree.

EXPLOITATIVE ABUSES

Exploitative abuses (cf Article 102 lit. a) TFEU) cover cases in which the dominant undertaking imposes unreasonably high prices or unreasonably unfavourable contractual terms on customers.

European Law

European competition law subjects market-dominant companies to the control of prices and conditions. Prices and conditions should not deviate from

---

[23] Case C-252/21 *Meta Platforms and Others* ECLI:EU:C:2023:537 [2023], para 178 ff; Maik Wolf and Kathrin Westermann 'GWB § 19' in Franz Jürgen Säcker et al (eds), *Münchener Kommentar zum Wettbewerbsrecht*, vol 2 (4th edn, C.H. Beck 2020) para 35 f.
[24] Cf Eckart Bueren and Jennifer Crowder, 'Sustainability and Competition Law – Germany' (*SSRN*, 11 November 2022) https://papers.ssrn.com/sol3/papers.cfm?abstract_id=4365639 accessed 18 August 2023, 11 ff.

a market where there is effective competition. There are considerable difficulties in determining the 'correct' price or conditions.[25]

Exploitation does not mean the exploitation of natural resources. However, exploitation of customers is not sustainable either; a business relationship based on exploitation is not a fair and stable business relationship, but one that disadvantages one side.

Option AB 5: Unsustainable Behaviour as Exploitation

Holmes suggests that purchase prices that are too low should be considered abusive if they do not include at least the cost of production or allow the seller to make a profit.[26] An example of this might be a company that only buys bananas at such low prices that the producers cannot be paid an adequate wage and thus cannot make a living. The type of exploitative abuse *Holmes* addresses relates primarily to the social and economic dimensions of sustainability. He justifies this with Article 39 TFEU, according to the wording of which the adequate standard of living for persons engaged in agriculture is the objective of European agricultural policy. However, this can also be applied to other sustainability goals. Thus, using similar reasoning, it would be considered abusive if a dominant undertaking only paid its suppliers such low prices that it was not possible for them to internalise their own external effects or avoid them altogether. Here, a parallel could be drawn with abuse through the infringement of non-competition regulations, if a dominant undertaking does not itself commit the breach of law but demands conditions that the market counterparty can only provide in breach of environmental protection regulations.

Exploitative abuse concerns a classic market failure, as it corrects distorted market outcomes due to monopolisation. Despite its anchoring in the wording of Article 102 TFEU and its highlighted importance in the genesis of the norm, it plays a subordinate role in practice. At first glance, it would be unusual to apply its principles to undertakings that pay too low prices. However, this is only an apparent reversal. In the cases described here, the dominant undertaking is the customer, whereas it normally acts as an abusive supplier. Abusive terms may manifest themselves in the form of a price that is too low when the dominant undertaking is the buyer. Nor does previous practice imply any restriction of the application only to suppliers. On the contrary, it should not make any difference in which role the dominant undertaking finds itself. This

---

[25] Cf Richard Wish and David Bailey, *Competition Law* (10th edn, Oxford University Press 2021), 757 ff.
[26] Simon Holmes, 'Climate Change, Sustainability and Competition Law' (2020) 8 *Journal of Antitrust Enforcement* 354, 384 ff.

is also clear from the wording of Article 102 TFEU. There, lit. a) explicitly refers to 'unreasonable purchase or selling prices'. Consequently, a change in the law is not necessary.

This proposal addresses one of the basic concerns of competition law: the concentration of power in markets and its effects. This shows particularly clearly that competition and sustainability can go hand in hand and do not have to be perceived as contradictions. In this respect, the problem of competition law being used to further other goals does not arise. It may be that environmental or occupational health and safety regulations are promoted through competition law. However, it does not matter whether the legislator has already taken measures in this respect. This is because the abusive nature derives from the concentration of power at the dominant company and not from the infringement of other regulations.

At the same time, similar problems arise as in other cases of exploitative abuses. Competition authorities and courts must determine what constitutes a reasonable price. This is fundamentally problematic since the price and the terms and conditions in accordance with the basic economic decisions should actually be left to the market. The appropriate price is therefore the price that would have arisen under normal competitive conditions. However, setting this price presupposes the ability to predict the outcome of competition. A workaround is to compare the price with similar markets where competition exists without the distorting presence of dominant undertaking. *Holmes'* proposal departs from this and sets as a benchmark a price that includes at least the costs of production and allows the seller to earn a profit. This may be easier to determine in individual cases, as no hypothetical market conditions have to be simulated. It remains questionable whether the price determined in this way corresponds to the price under competition. The ECJ has already recognised a similar concept in the *United Brands* decision with the concept of cost-price analysis.[27]

Option AB 6: Exploitation of Public Goods

An entirely new approach is to extend exploitative abuses to the exploitation of public goods.

In other cases, such as under Article 101(3) TFEU, there are discussions about recognising out-of-market efficiencies and therefore extending the scope beyond that of the market. A similar approach could be applied in cases against abusive practices when out of market inefficiencies are recognised. If public

---

[27]   Case 27/76 *United Brands v Commission* ECLI:EU:C:1978:22 [1978] ECR 207, paras 241 ff.

goods, those assigned to the general public, are exploited, this could possibly also constitute a problem under competition law. An example could be the dominant undertaking whose production process is harmful to the environment. The disadvantages do not directly affect the company's customers or business partners. The pollution is at the expense of a public good (environment, air quality) and thus at the expense of the general public.[28]

Recognising an exploitative abuse in this case would be a fundamental extension of the existing understanding. However, it can be justified with an expanded understanding of competition if one wants to recognise such an abuse. The central question is whether not only the market participants should be protected against exploitation, but also the general public. If one takes the economic functions of competition as a basis, competition should lead to an efficient allocation of resources. Those undertakings that can produce in a particularly efficient way should be allowed to use the scarce resources. This principle reaches its limits in the case of public goods. Negative externalities cannot be attributed to the company and therefore there is no incentive to deal with them in a particularly efficient way. It is well recognised that public goods are subject to market failure. The approach presented here could compensate for this deficit, which is exacerbated by competition. The law against abuse of dominance would be the instrument that can at least attribute the negative externalities to dominant undertakings and thus establish competitive conditions for public goods as well. This type of exploitative abuse thus solves classic market failures and addresses sustainability concerns at the same time. The limitation to dominant companies could be justified by their special responsibility for competition and the regularly particularly serious effects. The special responsibility for competition would then include not exploiting public goods to one's own competitive advantage and to the detriment of all other market participants and the general public.

EXCLUSIONARY ABUSE

Exclusionary abuses (cf Article 102 lit. b) and d) TFEU) relate to conduct by dominant undertakings against competitors. In the case of exclusionary conduct, market power is exercised to the detriment of competitors, who as a result fall behind in competition – not because of good performance, but solely because of the market power of the dominant undertaking.[29]

---

[28]   Cf Helen Lindenberg, 'Will Sustainability and Environmental Considerations be the Next Big Hit for Shaping the Application of Article 102 TFEU?' (2022) ZWeR 320, 329 f.

[29]   Case 85/76 *Hoffmann-La Roche v Commission* ECLI:EU:C:1979:36 [1979] ECR 461, para 6.

The *ARA* Case

While no proceedings are apparent in which sustainability considerations
are specifically addressed, the *ARA* decision illustrates how sustainability
is affected by cases against abusive practices. The Commission's decision
deals with a refusal of access to the household waste collection infrastructure
in Austria.[30] The Commission classified ARA's negligent refusal to grant
other companies access to its collection infrastructure as an abusive refusal to
supply. ARA's infrastructure was indispensable for market entry. Duplication
of the infrastructure presented significant legal, practical, and economic
hurdles and was contrary to the public interest.[31] The public interest stemmed
from the fact that duplication would be associated with increased overall costs
and expenses of households.[32]

The procedure allowed competitors to enter the market, which protects
incentives for innovation and efficiencies in this directly sustainability-relevant
market.

Option AB 7: Exclusion and Sustainability

There are established categories and criteria when dealing with exclusionary
abuses that may be open to new interpretations.

Exclusion due to sustainability damage

Iacovides and *Vrettos* propose treating non-sustainable conduct by dominant
undertakings as new categories of abusive conduct. The prerequisite is that
these behaviours have a negative impact on the goals of European competition
law and the prohibition of abusive practices. According to *Iacovides* and
Vrettos, these are not only welfare considerations, but a variety of objectives
inherent to the European Treaties, such as environmental protection, equal
rights, and the protection of employees.[33] This approach can only be convincing if there is a connection between the protection of competition and these
goals. If the tools of competition law are used against conduct that has no connection to competition, this is merely an exploitation of the effective sanctions
without reference to the actual content of the provisions.

---

[30]   *ARA Foreclosure* (Case AT.39759) Commission Decision [2016] para 77 ff.
[31]   *ARA Foreclosure* (Case AT.39759) Commission Decision [2016] paras 78 f.
[32]   *ARA Foreclosure* (Case AT.39759) Commission Decision [2016] paras 86 ff.
[33]   Marios Iacovides and Christos Vrettos, 'Radical For Whom? Unsustainable
Business Practices as Abuses of Dominance' in Simon Holmes, Dirk Middelschulte
and Martijn Snoep (eds), *Competition Law, Climate Change & Environmental
Sustainability* (Concurrences 2021) 98.

There is a high hurdle for establishing new categories of cases under Article 102 TFEU. First, a convincing 'theory of harm' must be formed, which remains within the framework of Article 102 TFEU and clearly focuses on competition.

Sustainability payments in existing case groups

However, the existing categories can be modified to take into account sustainability considerations. This has the advantage that the connection to competition remains, and the law develops gradually without major disruptions. At the same time, these changes also imply that sustainability considerations should be taken more into account in competition law.

The following examples illustrate possible cases where protection of competition and sustainability can converge:

• Abusive refusal to supply: if a refusal to supply affects a sustainable company or prevents sustainable innovation, this may constitute an impediment to competition.

• Abusive impediment of sustainable innovations: this includes circumstances in which the dominant company itself could innovate. If it nevertheless withholds the innovation, this has damaging effects both on innovation, which stagnates as a result, and on sustainability.

• Abusive use of intellectual property rights by dominant undertakings: complex case law exists regarding the abusive use of intellectual property rights.[34] The criteria can be modified by sustainability considerations. In cases of refusal of access, the ECJ has so far required, among other things, the restriction of production, markets or technical development in the face of existing demand.[35] Any increase in sustainability in production could be considered an advantage.

• Abusive discrimination against sustainable companies: if companies are discriminated against because they pursue certain sustainability ideas, no justification could be admissible.

• Abusive denial of access to essential facilities: if a company denies another company access to an essential facility, this is typically only abusive under current law if there are technical, legal or even economic obstacles to the company's own creation of such a facility.[36] Here, it seems reasonable to

---

[34] See only Case C-418/01 *IMS Health v Commission* ECLI:EU:C:2004:257 [2004] ECR I-5069; Case C-170/13 *Huawei* ECLI:EU:C:2015:477 [2015].
[35] Cf Case C-418/01 *IMS Health v Commission* ECLI:EU:C:2004:257 [2004] ECR I-5069, para 52.
[36] Cf Case C-7/97 *Oscar Bronner* ECLI:EU:C:1998:569 [1998] ECR I-7817, para 44.

also recognise ecological obstacles: if it is ecologically unacceptable to build another facility or system, the existing facility would be an essential facility.

The common ground of all these examples is that competitive practices can simultaneously jeopardise the Sustainable Development Goals and thus, in turn, block the path to sustainable competition.

COMMITMENTS

Commitments pursuant to Article 9(1) of Regulation (EC) No 1/2003 are available as an alternative to prohibiting abusive practices. They are characterised by leeway for both the undertakings and for the competition authority.

Commitments can be used to address sustainability considerations. An example of this is provided by the *DE/DK Interconnector* case.[37]

BOX 7.2   SUSTAINABILITY ORIENTED COMMITMENT IN THE *DE/DK INTERCONNECTOR* CASE

The Commission accepted a commitment in the *DE/DK Interconnector* case under which the undertaking, TenneT, agreed to comply with a capacity floor for the interconnector between Germany and Denmark that was higher than the legal requirements.[38]

TenneT operates 40 per cent of the high-voltage grid in Germany and also the interconnector to the grid in Denmark. This 'interconnector' to Denmark is particularly important for international energy trading, as it accounts for 40 per cent of the trade between the Nordic countries and the rest of continental Europe.[39] The Commission accused TenneT of abusing its dominant position by systematically limiting the capacity of the interconnector, thereby partitioning the European energy market.[40] The Commission accepted the commitments offered by TenneT. The commitments were character-

---

[37]   *DE/DK Interconnector* (Case AT.40461) Commission Decision [2018] C(2018) 8132 final.

[38]   *DE/DK Interconnector* (Case AT.40461) Commission Decision [2018] C(2018) 8132 final.

[39]   *DE/DK Interconnector* (Case AT.40461) Commission Decision [2018] C(2018) 8132 final, para 17.

[40]   *DE/DK Interconnector* (Case AT.40461) Commission Decision [2018] C(2018) 8132 final, paras 31 ff, 74.

ised by the fact that they contained a capacity floor, which corresponded to the provisions of the so-called 'Clean Energy Package' and the recast Regulation (EU) 2019/943, which, however, were only available as drafts in the legislative process at the time.[41]

The TenneT Commitment can be seen as an example of over-mandatory efforts by undertakings being made binding in the context of antitrust proceedings that serve non-competition EU objectives (in this case, clean energy supply).

As long as the undertakings submit the proposals for commitments, the competition authority can also accept them, even if they go beyond what is necessary for the protection of competition.[42] However, the extent to which non-competition considerations can be enforced in the context of remedies is disputed.[43]

In the *Greek Lignite* decision[44] the Commission declared commitments binding that contradicted the drafts of the 'Clean Energy Package' and are partly classified as environmentally harmful.[45]

SUMMARY

The prohibition of abuse of market power is initially itself an expression of a sustainable understanding of the economy since exploitation and exclusion

---

[41]   Eleni Diamantopoulou, 'Abuse of Dominant Position and Sustainability – How to Use Article 102 TFEU as a Sword to Promote Sustainability: Lessons Learnt From DE/DK Interconnector' in Simon Holmes, Dirk Middelschulte and Martijn Snoep (eds), *Competition Law, Climate Change & Environmental Sustainability* (Concurrences 2021) 313.

[42]   Cf Richard Wish and David Bailey, *Competition Law* (10th edn, Oxford University Press 2021), 936 ff.

[43]   Cf Rita Leandro Vasconcelos, 'Commitment Decisions: Is the Sky the Limit? – Commentary to Judgment of the General Court (Eighth Chamber) of 15 September 2016, Case T-76/14, Morningstar, Inc. v European Commission' (2017) 1 *Market and Competition Law Review* 195 ff; Dieter Paemen and Victoria S Baltrusch, 'Morningstar v Commission: Raising the Threshold for Challenging Commission Commitments Decisions' (2017) 8 JECLAP 99, 99 f.

[44]   *Greek Lignite* (Case AT.38700) Commission Decision [2018] C(2018) 2104 final.

[45]   Eleni Diamantopoulou, 'Abuse of Dominant Position and Sustainability – How to Use Article 102 TFEU as a Sword to Promote Sustainability: Lessons Learnt From DE/DK Interconnector' in Simon Holmes, Dirk Middelschulte and Martijn Snoep (eds), *Competition Law, Climate Change & Environmental Sustainability* (Concurrences 2021) 313.

strategies do not permit sustainable partnerships. In the context of the sustainability goals, however, the prohibition in Article 102 TFEU has so far been largely ignored. There are, however, some points of contact: the enforcement of Article 102 TFEU could further the Sustainable Development Goals if sustainability considerations were taken into account when deciding on the criteria relevant for Article 102 TFEU (market dominance, abuse, weighing of interests/justification) or on the sanctions (commitments).

This would apply all the more if Article 102 TFEU were also used to enforce non-competition objectives alongside the protection of competition. However, it is also conceivable that abusive practices could be justified with a view to positive effects on sustainability. Within the framework of commitments or remedies, sustainable development can be taken into account within certain limits.

The degree to which sustainability considerations can be taken into account depends on the course set by competition policy as to how extensively competition law is to be opened up: in some cases, the links between competition and sustainability are immediately tangible. In these cases, only clarification may be needed. In other cases, sustainability goals can only be taken into account if competition is defined as sustainable competition.

8. Merger control

With merger control, competition authorities examine the impact of mergers, acquisitions, and the joint ventures on competition.

In the European Union a prominent decision dealing with sustainability in merger control is the acquisition of Monsanto by Bayer.[1] This is Competition Commissioner *Vestager*'s response to the numerous petitioners and NGOs calling for the merger to be prohibited because of negative effects on health, the environment, biodiversity, climate:

> Many of you warn about potential negative effects linked to Monsanto's and Bayer's products, including risks for human health, food safety, consumer protection, the environment and the climate ... While these concerns are of great importance, they do not form a basis for a merger assessment.[2]

In doing so, she clarified that under current law, the Commission solely considers competition effects in its merger review.

PRELIMINARY REMARKS

With Merger control the competition authority examines the change of control of an undertaking. In this respect, two types of effects are conceivable that are related to sustainability: first, mergers in sectors that are relevant for sustainability (e.g., agrochemical, waste management, or energy) change the market structure. This can lead to changes in the structure of the market, most importantly to a higher degree concentration.

On the other hand, a merger can change not only the market but also the parties involved: a merger can speed up market entry that was previously difficult; undertakings can merge their production; corporate cultures change. In both cases, it is conceivable that a change in the control of an undertaking may have repercussions for sustainability. However, these feedback effects are

---

[1] *Bayer/Monsanto* (Case M.8084) Commission Decision 2018/C 459/10 [2018] OJ C 459/10.
[2] Letter from Margrethe Vestager to Petitioners (22 August 2017) http:// ec .europa.eu/competition/mergers/cases/additional_data/m8084_4719_6.pdf accessed 10 August 2023.

largely likely to be indirect. Causal proof of positive or negative sustainability effects is likely to be difficult.

The aim of merger control is to prevent concentration in markets through external growth. This is another way in which competition law has an economically sustainable effect: preventing high concentration in markets is a contribution to sustainable economic development.

Mergers can have three types of impact on sustainability. They can:

- change the structure of markets that have a particularly high relevance for individual sustainability goals;
- lead to efficiencies that have a positive effect on sustainability goals (so-called green deals);
- have a negative effect on sustainability goals (so-called dirty deals).[3]

Sustainability considerations could thus act as a shield against merger control (protection of green deals), or as a sword (protection of sustainability by prohibiting dirty deals). If there is no conflict of objectives between the effects on competition and on the Sustainable Development Goals (green deals without a tendency to restrict competition or dirty deals with a corresponding tendency), no problems arise. However, merger control is neutral with respect to effects on sustainability under the current law, within both the legal requirements and the practice of the European Commission.

MERGER THRESHOLDS

A distinction is made between the thresholds of notification that lead to the application of merger control in the first place, and the substantive criteria for intervention.

EC Merger Regulation

Notification thresholds are defined quantitatively and, in the case of the EC Merger Regulation, relate to turnover in accordance with Article 1(2) and (3) EC Merger Regulation (value of the transaction in some member states). The competition authorities do not have any discretion with regard to the applica-

---

[3]   The terminology 'green deals' and 'dirty deals' follows Nicole Kar, Emma Cochrane and Bella Spring, 'Environmental Sustainability and EU Merger Control: EU Competition Policy's Dark Horse to Support Green Investment' in Simon Holmes, Dirk Middelschulte and Martijn Snoep (eds), *Competition Law, Climate Change & Environmental Sustainability* (Concurrences 2021) 126 ff; cf Emanuela Lecchi, 'Sustainability and EU Merger Control (2023) 44 ECLR 70.

tion of these thresholds – in contrast to the application of Articles 101 and 102 TFEU and corresponding national provisions. In the case of these quantitative thresholds, there is no scope in current law for considerations of sustainability.

In 2021, the European Commission opened up the criteria for referral by changing the interpretation of Article 22 of the EC Meger Regulation.[4] Mergers that do not have to be notified in the member states can now also be referred to the European Commission, where they would not have to be notified either. This referral leads to the application of European merger control. In addition to criteria relating to competition, the Commission cites 'other criteria' that could lead to such a referral. Accordingly, cases should be referred to the Commission in which the undertakings involved carry out important research or have access to important raw materials. Primarily, cases from the digital economy and the pharmaceutical industry are being considered. Cases that are classified as particularly important with a view to the Sustainable Development Goals could also come within the scope of merger control via this new practice.

Option MC 1: Sustainability-relevant Mergers

Consideration should be given to amending the thresholds so that mergers are subject to notification that have not been subject to notification so far but are particularly relevant to sustainability. Separate criteria could be developed for mergers in sectors relevant to sustainability.

This could be achieved in a number of ways:

- a list of undertakings that are particularly relevant for sustainability or a notification obligation for all mergers analogous to Article 14 Digital Markets Act; special consideration of such companies in referrals pursuant to Article 22 EC Merger Regulation;
- the introduction of a supplementary quantitative threshold based on CO_2 emissions; if these thresholds are exceeded, lowered turnover thresholds could apply, so that companies with particularly high emissions would be subject to especially strict criteria;
- the possibility for the competition authority to take up non-notifiable mergers if requested by certain actors (e.g., specifically designated NGOs or a large number of petitioners).

---

[4] European Commission, 'Guidance on the application of the referral mechanism set out in Article 22 of the EC Merger Regulation to certain categories of cases' [2021] OJ C 113/1.

The first two paths mentioned are designed to ensure a high degree of legal certainty, so that companies know ex ante which merger projects must be notified. The instrument of a notification by other parties deviates significantly from this and would represent a considerable innovation. However, in other jurisdictions and due to the new interpretation of Article 22 of the EC Merger Regulation, taking up non-notified cases is not entirely uncommon.

In the literature, as far as can be seen, notification thresholds have not yet been identified as relevant for sustainability. It is also not apparent at present that there are mergers relevant for sustainability which did not have to be notified. In this respect there seems to be no need for a change in the notification criteria. However, transparency for sustainability-relevant cases would possibly be increased.

CRITERIA FOR INTERVENTION

According to Article 2(2) of the EC Merger Regulation a merger can be prohibited if it would significantly impede effective competition ('significant impediment of effective competition' = SIEC test). If a merger increases an undertaking's ability to exert pressure on suppliers and exploit them, this is an impediment to competition, which at the same time poses a threat to economic and social sustainability goals. Beyond that, however, the consideration of sustainability goals in merger control has hardly been developed.

No Consideration of Non-competition Interests

Currently only the competition effects of the merger can be taken into account.[5] Non-competition effects, e.g., environmental protection or job security, are not taken into account. This follows the wording of the provision, which focus on the impediment of competition, the recitals, and the legislative history of the EC Merger Regulation.[6] There is also a broad international consensus for the

---

[5]   Cf Richard Wish and David Bailey, *Competition Law* (10th edn, Oxford University Press 2021), 913.
[6]   See Council Regulation (EC) 139/2004 on the control of concentrations between undertakings (EC Merger Regulation) [2004] OJ L 24/1, recitals 2–7.

strict focus on competition effects.[7] However there are suggestions that consideration be given to including various other interests in the SIEC test.[8]

No Balancing with Other Objectives

In practice, objectives of other provisions are not taken into account. There is often no conflict between the application of merger control and the objectives of the European Union and the fundamental rights and freedoms. Something else could apply to the horizontal clauses, for example, on environmental protection (Article 11 TFEU). However, the horizontal clauses only define policy objectives and principles in general terms; unlike Articles 101 and 102 TFEU and the EC Merger Regulation derived from these, they are not designed as rules that are to be applied to individual cases.[9] So far, there are no standards for the application of these objectives in individual cases within merger control in case law and literature. For example, the concept of striking a careful balance is suitable for conflicting fundamental rights of individuals, but not for the integration of general policy objectives into a case-by-case analysis under competition law. Operationalisation in the context of merger control is therefore out of the question.[10] Finally, Article 21 of the EC Merger Regulation and Article 2(1) of the EC Merger Regulation also prevent this. According to these provisions, other legitimate interests are not to be taken into account within European merger control.

---

[7]   See International Competition Network, 'ICN Recommended Practices for Merger Analysis' (2008), I.A.Comment 1 www .ftc .gov/ system/ files/ attachments/ merger -workshop -competition -authorities -caribbean/ rec -practices -merger -analysis .pdf accessed 15 August 2023.

[8]   See Ioannis Lianos, 'Merger Activity in the Factors of Production Segments of the Food Value Chain: A Critical Assessment of the Bayer/Monsanto merger' (2017) UCL Centre for Law, Economics and Society, Policy Paper Series 2017/1 www .Lianos_cles-policy-paper-1-2017.pdf accessed 10 July 2023.

[9]   Bernhard W Wegener in Bernhard W Wegener (ed), *Europäische Querschnittspolitiken* (Nomos 2014) § 1 para 7.

[10]   Cf Heike Schweitzer, 'Die Bedeutung nicht-wettbewerblicher Aspekte für die Auslegung von Art. 101 AEUV im Lichte der Querschnittsklauseln' in Monopolies Commission (ed), *Politischer Einfluss auf Wettbewerbsentscheidungen* (Nomos 2015) 26 f.; Wolfgang Kirchhoff, 'Außerwettbewerbliche Aspekte bei Entscheidungen nach Art. 101 AEUV, insbesondere im Licht der Querschnittsklauseln des AEUV' in Monopolies Commission (ed), *Politischer Einfluss auf Wettbewerbsentscheidungen* (Nomos 2015) 12, who rejects further considerations – e.g., with a view to restricting the very facts of Article 101(1) TFEU (13).

Decisions

Sustainability considerations were discussed in particular with regard to the *Bayer/Monsanto* merger. This merger is in line with the other agrochemical mergers *Dow/Dupont* and *ChemChina/Syngenta*.[11]

In Bayer/Monsanto, the Commission took an in-depth look at what non-competition concerns could be considered. It was called upon to address environmental concerns, food safety, sustainable development, public health, and agricultural sector objectives.[12] In particular, the loss of biodiversity in seeds as a damage to the environment should be included in the competition assessment. In the assessment of dynamic efficiencies, the focus should be on high-quality innovations, with quality measured by the contribution to food safety and public health.[13]

The theory of harm in the agrochemical cases is much more focused on safeguarding innovations in the future and therefore dynamic competition than was previously the case. The approach represents a departure from the focus on static efficiencies (increasing output, lowering price).[14] *Various* paths to innovations that undertakings can take are protected.[15] This may be seen as significant also for the path to more sustainable technology.

On the other hand, the Commission stated that, although it had to take into account the horizontal clauses and policy goals of the European Union, it could only act within the scope of its specific powers according to Article 5(1), (2) TEU.[16]

---

[11] *Bayer/Monsanto* (Case M.8084) Commission Decision C(2018) [2018] OJ C 459/10; *ChemChina/Syngenta* (Case M.7962) Commission Decision [2017] C(2017) 2167 final; *Dow/DuPont* (Case M.7932) Commission Decision [2017] C(2017) 1946 final, cf Emanuela Lecchi, 'Sustainability and EU Merger Control' (2023) 44 ECLR 70.

[12] *Bayer/Monsanto* (Case M.8084) Commission Decision C(2018) [2018] 1709 final, para 3006.

[13] *Bayer/Monsanto* (Case M.8084) Commission Decision C(2018) [2018] 1709 final, para 3007.

[14] *Dow/DuPont* (Case M.7932) Commission Decision C(2017) [2017] 1946 final, paras 1990 ff; Nicolas Petit, 'Significant Impediment to Industry Innovation: A Novel Theory of Harm in EU Merger Control?' (2017) International Center for Law & Economics, Antitrust & Consumer Protection Research Program White Paper https://orbi.uliege.be/bitstream/2268/207345/1/SSRN-id2911597.pdf accessed 10 July 2023.

[15] Cf Wolfgang Kerber, 'Competition, Innovation and Maintaining Diversity through Competition Law' in Josef Drexl, Wolfgang Kerber and Rupprecht Podszun, *Competition Policy and the Economic Approach – Foundations and Limitations* (Edward Elgar 2011) 173 ff.

[16] *Bayer/Monsanto* (Case M.8084) Commission Decision C(2018) [2018] 1709 final, para 3015.

The Commission was also unable to identify a conflict with the provisions on agriculture in Articles 39, 42 TFEU. These are indeed provisions that can claim priority over competition law. It is not clear, asserts the Commission, which of the many objectives in Article 39 TFEU could lead to the merger between Bayer and Monsanto being prohibited.[17]

Option MC 2: Sustainability and the SIEC Test

Sustainability considerations could be given greater weight in the SIEC test. This can be done within the framework of a narrow price-oriented interpretation or through a stronger integration of other objectives.

Consumer welfare

Consumer welfare is often seen as central to the SIEC test. Therefore it is based on an analysis of whether the merger will lead to higher prices or lower quality/innovation. *Dolmans* writes:

> This consumer welfare analysis should include whether the concentration can be expected to raise or lower the environmental price that consumers pay, which is not reflected in the market price in monetary terms or in quality.[18]

This should include externalities that are not reflected in the price.

A more far-reaching approach would be to include in the analysis whether the merger creates market power for a less sustainable player that cannot be controlled by sustainably operating competitors.[19] It could be taken into account that a competitor has just invested in environmentally friendly technologies and thus falls behind.[20]

With a similar argument a merger could be cleared if, for example, environmental costs are reduced, such as if a competitor is acquired that uses a more

---

[17]   *Bayer/Monsanto* (Case M.8084) Commission Decision C(2018) [2018] 1709 final, para 3023.

[18]   Maurits Dolmans, 'Sustainable Competition Policy' (*SSRN*, 2020) 12 https://papers.ssrn.com/sol3/papers.cfm?abstract_id=3608023 accessed 10 July 2023. See also Stefan Thomas, 'Normative Goals in Merger Control' (*SSRN*, 2021) https://papers.ssrn.com/sol3/papers.cfm?abstract_id=3513098 accessed 15 August 2023.

[19]   Maurits Dolmans, 'Sustainable Competition Policy' (*SSRN*, 2020) 12 https://papers.ssrn.com/sol3/papers.cfm?abstract_id=3608023 accessed 10 July 2023.

[20]   Maurits Dolmans, 'Sustainable Competition Policy' (*SSRN*, 2020) 12 https://papers.ssrn.com/sol3/papers.cfm?abstract_id=3608023 accessed 10 July 2023.

environmentally friendly technology that will be utilised post-merger by the whole undertaking.[21]

Also consistent with the consumer welfare approach would be models that identify consumers' hypothetical willingness to pay and incorporate that into the analysis.[22]

With the help of this approach, the shortcomings of the current practice can be addressed without breaking the system. External effects are a market failure and are not taken into account so far. Integration into the merger control assessment would reflect the actual effects of the merger. This applies both to external effects with a market connection and to external effects outside the market. However, the question again arises of whether effects outside a market should still be covered by competition law.[23]

New interpretation of the SIEC test
It would also be conceivable to reinterpret the SIEC test. There is no reason to reduce the SIEC test to an economic analysis of consumer welfare. An expanded interpretation of the SIEC test could include, for example, the following:

- considering long-term consumer preferences rather than focusing on short-term monetary effects; such long-term customer interests could include, for example, respect for planetary boundaries;
- definition of competition protected under the SIEC test as 'sustainable competition';
- analysis of sustainable innovation, e.g., if environmentally friendly tech-nologies or research into sustainable solutions are to be phased out after an acquisition;'[24]

---

[21]   Maurits Dolmans, 'Sustainable Competition Policy' (*SSRN*, 2020) 12 https://papers.ssrn.com/sol3/papers.cfm?abstract_id=3608023 accessed 10 July 2023.
[22]   Roman Inderst and Stefan Thomas, 'Reflective Willingness to Pay: Preferences for Sustainable Consumption in a Consumer Welfare Analysis' (2021) 17 JCLE 848.
[23]   Cf the problem of out-of-market efficiencies when looking at an exemption, Chapter 6.
[24]   See Elias Deutscher and Stavros Makris, 'Sustainability Concerns in EU Merger Control: From Output-Maximising to Polycentric Innovation Competition' (2022) *Journal of Antitrust Enforcement* 1, 13 ff, 33 ff; Maurits Dolmans, 'Sustainable Competition Policy' (*SSRN*, 2020) 12 https://papers.ssrn.com/sol3/papers.cfm?abstract _id=3608023 accessed 10 July 2023; Francisco Costa-Cabral, 'Reply to European Commission Call on "Competition Policy Supporting the European Green Deal"' (*SSRN*, 2021) 2, 8 https:// papers .ssrn .com/ sol3/ papers .cfm ?abstract_id = 3778154 accessed 10 July 2023. Critically Stefan Thomas, 'Normative Goals in Merger Control' (*SSRN*, 2021) https://papers.ssrn.com/sol3/papers.cfm?abstract_id=3513098 accessed 15 August 2023.

- greater consideration of structural effects, such as reducing the number of potentially innovative firms and potential competition on innovation.[25]

Neither of the models mentioned under this option MC 2 requires any legislative changes. However, they would need to be implemented in practice. This would require guidelines from the authorities specifying such approaches, giving further examples and developing further criteria. However, this would not guarantee that such a development would be supported by the courts. Whether there is a need for such new interpretations of the SIEC test is unclear. In any case, they are accompanied by increased regulatory costs, which would at least have to be outweighed by the positive sustainability effects.

Legislative action

If it is to be ensured that a new interpretation of the SIEC test is supported by the courts, a change in the law is required. New criteria would have to refer to the sustainability effects that result from the merger. Thus, a rule would be conceivable according to which a significant impediment to effective competition also exists if ecologically and socially sustainable competition is impaired by the merger.

Alternatively or as a supplement, references to sustainable development could be included in the list in Article 2(1)(b) EC Merger Regulation.

So far, ecologically and socially sustainable competition has not been explicitly protected by competition law. However, the frequent reference to 'competition on the merits' is already open to such an interpretation. However, it would have to be defined in more detail (possibly in guidelines or by the legislators) what 'environmentally and socially sustainable competition' is and in which scenarios there are merger-related restrictions. The specifications of the Sustainable Development Goals could be used for this purpose. The characteristic of this option is that the focus on competition is retained, but an expansion of the guiding principles is undertaken.

Option MC 3: Non-competition Goals

Even further, non-competition goals could be included in merger control.[26] For example, it could be required that a merger should not impede the achievement of the UN Sustainable Development Goals, that biodiversity must be

---

[25] Elias Deutscher and Stavros Makris, 'Sustainability Concerns in EU Merger Control: From Output-Maximising to Polycentric Innovation Competition' (2022) *Journal of Antitrust Enforcement* 1, 35 ff, 41 ff.

[26] In contrast, especially Stefan Thomas, 'Normative Goals in Merger Control: Why Merger Control Should Not Attempt to Achieve "Better" Outcomes than Competition'

safeguarded,[27] or that no harmful climate impacts should be associated with a merger. Conversely, such mergers that have a positive impact on the achievement of Sustainable Development Goals could be privileged.

Such an approach is set out in the Commission's 2022 Guidelines on State Aid for climate, environmental protection and energy.[28] This is also conceivable for merger control that pursues corresponding objectives. For example, mergers that are intended to make a significant contribution to climate protection (e.g., by adopting and rolling out a climate-friendly technology or by concentrating on the charging station infrastructure) could be privileged, provided that certain minimum competition related requirements are met.

The requirements for positive effects on sustainability would have to be specified. The guidelines on state aid could serve as a model. However, it is questionable to what extent the Directorate General for Competition can be legitimised to analyse sustainability concerns in merger cases.[29]

In particular, it is also questionable to what extent there are cases in which it is precisely the merger that is required in order to achieve the corresponding objectives. In cases of doubt, contractual cooperation should suffice. However, something else may apply if a company is endangered without a takeover.[30] It would be questionable whether there is then an SIEC at all and whether the existing instruments do not allow for exceptions.[31]

EFFICIENCY DEFENCE

European law (cf recital 29 of the EC Merger Regulation) recognises that mergers can also bring about an improvement in competition and generate efficiencies. What has been established with regard to Article 101(3) TFEU applies also to merger control: the concept of efficiencies is to be understood in economic terms; here, there can be a synchronisation of economic and sustainability goals.

(*SSRN*, 2021) https://papers.ssrn.com/sol3/papers.cfm?abstract_id=3513098 accessed 3 August 2023.

[27] On this example, affirmatively Tommaso Valletti and Hans Zenger, 'Should Profit Margins Play a More Decisive Role in Merger Control? – A Rejoinder to Jorge Padilla' (2018) 9 JECLAP 336, 336 ff.

[28] European Commission, 'Guidelines on State Aid for climate, environmental protection and energy 2022' [2022] OJ C 80/1.

[29] For the legitimacy issue, see Chapter 13.

[30] Cf Emanuela Lecchi, 'Sustainability and EU Merger Control' (2023) 44 ECLR 70.

[31] Cf European Commission, 'Guidelines on the assessment of horizontal mergers under the Council Regulation on the control of concentrations between undertakings' [2004] OJ C 31/5, paras 89 ff.

European Law

Companies are free to present efficiencies brought about by mergers that outweigh the negative effects. Positive effects on sustainability could be recognised to a greater extent than before. Currently the 'efficiency defence' faces a high standard of proof. In particular, long-term positive effects for sustainability that are not reflected in short-term price reductions for consumers are rarely recognised.[32]

Option MC 4: Sustainability and Efficiencies

If positive effects for sustainability are to be recognised to a greater extent in order to clear mergers that would otherwise be prohibited, this should be clarified in the law.

To this end, it would be conceivable, on the one hand, to amend the wording of the efficiency defence in the statutory provisions. Recital 29 of the EC Merger Regulation would have to be amended in a way that efficiencies also include improvements to sustainability. This could be narrowed down further and specified in guidelines. The discussion corresponds in part to that on Article 101(3) TFEU. On the other hand, it could also suffice if guidelines on the interpretation of the efficiency defence were adapted to include effects on sustainability. For this purpose, the sustainability effects would have to be incorporated into the economic test. However, the efficiencies must always be specific to a merger.[33]

REMEDIES

In practice, the vast majority of all notified mergers are cleared. In cases where competition concerns are identified, commitments can avert a prohibition.

Basics

Typical commitments are the divestiture of business units or granting competitors access to intellectual property or technologies. The commitments must address the competition concerns and be proportionate.[34] The competition

---

[32]   Tilman Kuhn and Cristina Caroppo, 'Sustainability in merger control – time to broaden the discussion' (2020) 41 ECLR 596, 599.

[33]   Cf Simon Holmes, 'Climate change, sustainability, and competition law' (2020) 8 *Journal of Antitrust Enforcement* 354, 392.

[34]   Cf European Commission, 'Commission notice on remedies acceptable under Council Regulation (EC) No 139/2004 and under Commission Regulation (EC) No 802/2004' [2008] OJ C 267/1.

authority cannot impose obligations on companies that do not directly serve to eliminate restrictions on competition.[35] However, remedies are negotiated, especially in early stages of the merger.[36] By negotiating, companies and authorities have some leeway. It is questionable whether sustainability aspects can be taken into account when examining the commitments offered by companies willing to merge, or whether commitments that would address the competition concerns can be rejected on the basis of sustainability concerns.

Decisions

In all three major agrochemical merger cases, the European Commission granted clearance only under far-reaching conditions. In the *Bayer/Monsanto* case, among other things, all overlaps in seeds and pesticides were eliminated by divesting Bayer's portfolio; Bayer had to divest its global research and development unit for seeds and traits, as well as research activities competing with Monsanto's glyphosate.[37] In addition, access to Bayer's digital agronomy activities had to be granted. The review was limited purely to competition concerns. In any case, the decision does not indicate whether the environmental impact also played a role.

In the *Veolia/Suez* case, the Commission examined a merger in the water treatment and waste management sectors and cleared it under structural conditions.[38] Vice President *Vestager* stated in the press release:

> By this decision, the Commission ensures that this transaction will not adversely affect competition in the water and waste markets, two sectors that are key to the European Green Deal and the circular economy.[39]

This statement makes it clear that the competition assessment is crucial, but effects of mergers and remedies for achieving sustainability goals should not be underestimated.

---

[35] See European Commission, 'Commission notice on remedies acceptable under Council Regulation (EC) No 139/2004 and under Commission Regulation (EC) No 802/2004' [2008] OJ C 267/1, para 9.
[36] Cf Simon Holmes, 'Climate Change, Sustainability, and Competition Law' (2020) 8 *Journal of Antitrust Enforcement* 354, 394 f.
[37] *Bayer/Monsanto* (Case M.8084) Commission Decision C(2018) [2018] 1709 final, Annex 3.
[38] *Veolia/Suez* (Case M.9969) Commission Decision C(2021) [2021] 9666 final (unpublished).
[39] European Commission, 'Mergers: Commission approves the acquisition of Suez by Veolia, subject to conditions' (press release 14 December 2021) https://ec.europa.eu/commission/presscorner/detail/en/IP_21_6885 accessed 30 June 2023.

Option MC 5: Strengthening Sustainable Remedies

In the future, remedies with effects on sustainability could be taken into account to a greater extent. This is possible, as the commitments are offered by the undertakings and to that extent are voluntary. Additionally, the commitments will not always be able to only address the competition concern and will have effects on other goals anyways. There could be positive effects on sustainability and competition at the same time, for example, if a company is obliged to grant a license to competitors for the use of an environmentally friendly technology.[40] There is no conflict here.

A broader example that would involve the extension of the previous concept would be the following: it is often the case that certain parts of a company have to be divested. This requirement is mostly directed against the purchaser.[41] Up to now, the sustainability of the acquirer has not played any role. For example, it is not yet required that the purchaser produces with a climate-neutral technology. Including this as a criterion would be extensive. However, such a requirement could possibly already be read into the existing requirements. The Commission requires in its guidelines:

> ... the purchaser must possess the financial resources, proven relevant expertise and have the incentive and ability to maintain and develop the divested business as a viable and active competitive force in competition with the parties and other competitors ...[42]

It could be argued that a viable, active competitor in competition only emerges if it is sustainable and does not rely on expiring technologies or is exposed to high risks due to significant compliance concerns in the supply chain.

MINISTERIAL AUTHORISATION

Under German law, a merger prohibited by the Federal Cartel Office can be permitted by the Federal Minister of Economics with a ministerial authorisation (Section 42 GWB) due to macroeconomic advantages or an overarching interest of the general public. This has no equivalent at the European level.

---

[40] Cf Tilman Kuhn and Cristina Caroppo, 'Sustainability in merger control – time to broaden the discussion' (2020) 41 ECLR 596, 599.

[41] European Commission, 'Commission notice on remedies acceptable under Council Regulation (EC) No 139/2004 and under Commission Regulation (EC) No 802/2004' [2008] OJ C 267/1, para 48.

[42] European Commission, 'Commission notice on remedies acceptable under Council Regulation (EC) No 139/2004 and under Commission Regulation (EC) No 802/2004' [2008] OJ C 267/1, para 48.

The wording in German law is broad enough to include sustainability concerns. Environmental protection concerns can be a public interest within the meaning of Section 42 GWB. The positive effects of the merger must be permanent and attributable to the merger.[43] How the public interest is to be examined, quantified if necessary, and weighed against the restriction of competition is a serious problem.[44]

Decision

Environmental aspects were decisive in the *Miba/Zollern* ministerial authorisation. The Federal Minister of Economics granted the authorisation on the basis of the public interest 'know-how and innovation potential for energy transition and sustainability'.[45] The authorisation was linked to the condition that investments amounting to €50 million be made in Germany to realise this public interest. The bearings produced by the merging parties are used in wind turbines, among other things. Environmental policy objectives were expressly recognised as a paramount public interest, in particular also with reference to the sustainability strategy of the German government as well as the international climate commitments of the German government, UN Sustainable Development Goal 7 and Article 20a of the German constitution (Grundgesetz).[46]

In this case the minister made a qualitative, not a quantitative, assessment of the effects on sustainability. It was accepted that the benefits to the public good are more likely to be achieved in the medium to long term.[47] Nevertheless, these benefits were found to outweigh the competition concerns of the Federal Cartel Office. The decision was met with criticism.[48] However, it is not disputed that sustainability can constitute a public interest that can be taken into account in the context of ministerial authorisation.

---

[43]   Gunnar Kallfaß, '§ 42 GWB' in Hermann-Josef Bunte (ed), *Kartellrecht*, vol 1 (14. Auflage Hermann Luchterhand Verlag 2021) para 5.

[44]   See Maximilian Konrad, *Das Gemeinwohl, die öffentliche Meinung und die fusionsrechtliche Ministererlaubnis* (Duncker & Humboldt 2019).

[45]   German Federal Ministry for Economic Affairs and Energy (BMWi), 19 August 2019, IB2-20302/14-02, para 167.

[46]   German Federal Ministry for Economic Affairs and Energy (BMWi), 19 August 2019, IB2-20302/14-02, paras 172 ff., 251.

[47]   German Federal Ministry for Economic Affairs and Energy (BMWi), 19 August 2019, IB2-20302/14-02, para 258.

[48]   Maximilian Konrad, 'Die Ministererlaubnis Miba/Zollern und die Reform der Ministererlaubnis mit der 10. GWB-Novelle' WuW 2020 244; see also Oliver Budzinski and Annika Stöhr, 'Ministererlaubnis für Kartellfälle: Kooperation im Sinne des Gemeinwohls?' (2020) ZWeR 437.

The European Debate

Opening European merger control to non-competition aspects is not only relevant for sustainability. A variety of non-competition interests could be taken into account. In recent years, with a view to the prohibition of the *Siemens/ Alstom* merger, there have been prominent calls to open up European merger control to such considerations (creating European champions).[49] This has been met with unanimous criticism in academia.[50]

Option MC 6: Overriding Political Decision on Merger Cases

If merger control essentially remains a competition-oriented tool, the question arises of whether, outside of merger control, public interest considerations can be used to intervene and correct the outcome of the competition analysis. This can happen in two ways:

- An instrument such as the German ministerial authorisation (Section 42 GWB) clears mergers that were prohibited on competition grounds.
- Conversely, a political veto could also be imposed on such mergers, which, although unobjectionable from a competition point of view, should be prohibited for reasons of public welfare.

The ministerial authorisation has been strongly criticised.[51] However, proponents emphasise that it makes sense to have an outlet for non-competition considerations that cannot be dealt with under merger control.[52] The German model has the advantage of creating transparency, so that a clear distinction can be made between competition and public interest considerations.

---

[49] See German Federal Ministry for Economic Affairs and Energy (BMWi) and MINEFI – French Ministry of Economy and Finance (Ministère de l'Économie et des Finances) (2019), A Franco-German Manifesto for a European industrial Policy Fit For the 21st Century, 19 February 2019.

[50] Massimo Motta et al, 'More, Not Less, Competition is needed in Europe' (*D'Kart*, 15 February 2019) www.d-kart.de/en/blog/2019/02/15/europa-braucht-mehr -nicht-weniger-wettbewerb/ accessed 10 August 2023.

[51] Cf Rupprecht Podszun, 'Ministererlaubnis – Einbruch der Politik ins Recht der Wirtschaft' (2016) NJW 617; Maximilian Konrad, *Das Gemeinwohl, die öffentliche Meinung und die fusionsrechtliche Ministererlaubnis* (Duncker & Humboldt 2019).

[52] Florian Bien, 'Die Berücksichtigung nichtwettbewerblicher Aspekte in der Fusionskontrolle – Gibt es Alternativen zur Ministererlaubnis?' (2016) NZKart 445, 446 with further examples of similar regulations from abroad.

Sustainability can be taken into account within this framework – as seen with *Miba/Zollern*.[53]

In the context of European merger control, political considerations can be decisive in the Commission. However, this is hardly transparent. So far, there does not seem to be any real need for an overriding political decision because of public interest at the European level. Given the even more divergent notions of what constitutes the public interest in the European Union than at the national level, political interference in merger control appears even more problematic than it already is at the national level.

There also seem to be hardly any reason for the prohibition of a cleared merger for sustainability reasons. The sustainability concerns have to be linked specifically to the merger. Apart from the fact that such a prohibition also raises many legal problems (e.g., with regard to compatibility with Article 21 of the EC Merger Regulation, the fundamental freedoms and world trade law), hardly any cases seem conceivable in which significant sustainability problems arise precisely as a result of a merger, which are not in some way also competition concerns and can therefore be the subject of merger control. If companies operate non-sustainable business models, this can possibly be prohibited politically. However, it is then not an issue of merger control.

SUMMARY

The initial finding from *Bayer/Monsanto* that the powerful instrument of merger control has nothing to do with sustainability is not correct: there are already options for taking sustainability issues into account in merger control. The connection between market power and sustainability can be analysed or competition could be understood as sustainable competition. In the context of the efficiency defence and remedies, a broader recognition of sustainability is conceivable. However, a stronger consideration of non-competition goals jeopardises the focus on competition concerns. This can only be done – if at all – within extremely narrow limits. Where a connection between market power and negative effects on sustainability can be demonstrated, it makes particular sense to combat both at the same time. Where there is no such connection, merger control is the wrong tool to deal with the problems.

---

[53] Cf also Matthias Karl and Philipp Pichler, 'Ministererlaubnis – Ein Baustein ökologischer Wettbewerbspolitik?' in Sozietät Gleiss Lutz (eds), *Festgabe für Rainer Bechtold zum 80. Geburtstag* (Nomos 2021) 123, 137 with reference to Article 20a GG and the investment requirement in the *Miba v Zollern* case.

9.   Procedure and sanctions

Sustainability could also play a role in more procedural aspects of competition law or in the sanctioning of violations. This is what we explore in this chapter.

PRIORITY SETTING

The European Commission and national competition agencies have a wide margin of discretion whether to open proceedings for violation of competition law.[1] This means that the agencies can pick their cases. In this very important, first procedural step, the consideration of sustainability objectives is not excluded from the outset.[2]

Basics

The competition authorities must decide how to use their limited resources in the prosecution of violations of the prohibition of restrictive business agreements and abuses. Therefore, they can refrain from prosecuting violations or pursue certain violations with vigour. Legal standards for this are virtually non-existent. For the European Commission, a review of the scope for action is only possible by means of the complaints procedure under Chapter IV of Regulation (EC) No 773/04.

The way in which the discretion to select cases is exercised is of enormous importance in practice: if the authority decides to pursue a case, this can have hefty consequences under competition law, ranging from remedies to fines. If the authority refrains from doing so, the leeway for the companies concerned is much greater. Then essentially 'only' private enforcement is a potential threat.

In its 'Strategic Plan 2020–2024', the Directorate General for Competition announced that it will exercise its antitrust enforcement powers on a case-by-case

---

[1]   Or Brook and Kati Cseres, 'Priority Setting in EU and National Competition Law Enforcement' (*SSRN*, 2021) 12 ff https://papers.ssrn.com/sol3/papers.cfm?abstract_id=3930189 accessed 3 August 2023.
[2]   Richard Whish and David Bailey, *Competition Law* (10th edn, Oxford 2021) 166.

basis in a way that supports the European New Green Deal.[3] It is difficult to understand to what extent this announcement actually influences the decisions to take cases. Nor can any conclusions be drawn from the rejection decisions in this respect for a special consideration of sustainability objectives.[4]

The discretion can be exercised in different directions:

- The antitrust agencies can decide not to prosecute agreements or potential abuses if they relate to sustainability initiatives. This means that the agencies can give companies greater leeway when it comes to the design of sustainable economic activities.
- Agencies can also actively support sustainability initiatives by advising formally or informally how the most legally secure arrangement possible could be designed. This would not only save the initiative from public enforcement, but also provide help in private enforcement, at least morally.
- Competition agencies may also prioritise the prosecution of agreements or abuses that are potentially harmful to sustainability. In this third dimension, competition law is used as a sword to fight for more sustainability by sanctioning anti-competition practices that also harm sustainability.

Non-opening of Proceedings as a Strategic Step

In Germany, the Bundeskartellamt used its discretion as a strategic tool to look into cases and then to declare explicitly not to take them up. In this way, it refrained from initiating proceedings in three exemplary, high-profile cases of sustainability-oriented cooperations.

- In its 2017/2018 activity report, the Bundeskartellamt stated that it had not initiated proceedings against the Fairtrade system and that it had exercised its discretionary power in this respect. The Fairtrade system concerns trade in agricultural products from third countries, in particular those of the Global South. It defines standards on the basis of which the Fairtrade label is awarded. Parts of the standards are organisational and product-related criteria. In addition, there are price elements that prescribe a minimum price for certain product groups and the payment of a Fairtrade premium. Despite these pricing elements – which are problematic from a competition

---

[3]   DG Competition, Strategic Plan 2020–2024, Ref. Ares (2020)5180558 – 02/10/2020, 13 https://commission.europa.eu/system/files/2020-10/comp_sp_2020 _2024_en.pdf accessed 15 August 2023.
[4]   Or Brook and Kati Cseres, 'Priority Setting in EU and National Competition Law Enforcement' (*SSRN*, 2021) 43 ff https://papers.ssrn.com/sol3/papers.cfm?abstract_id= 3930189 accessed 3 August 2023.

point of view – the Bundeskartellamt refrained from intervening.[5] It stated that it is a voluntary, non-exclusive system with a small market share and high transparency.

- The Initiative Tierwohl (Animal Welfare Initiative) is an industry alliance of agriculture, the meat industry, and food retailers that has repeatedly been dealt with by the Bundeskartellamt since 2015.[6] The Initiative organises a sustainability agreement that is essentially financed by the four major retailers in Germany. To this end, a few cents have been paid to the initiative for every kilogram of pork and poultry meat sold since 2015.[7] This money is used to reward livestock farmers for implementing animal welfare measures, such as more space in barns in particular. Producers can join the initiative and use its label, which classifies each animal's living conditions into levels 1–4.[8] In 2022, the Bundeskartellamt took sustainability concerns into account when exercising its discretion by not initiating proceedings for the time being in spite of antitrust concerns.[9] The express aim was to use the Initiative to develop a compliant design 'in a transitional phase', e.g., before extending it to cattle fattening.[10] A uniform surcharge is no longer to be tolerated in the future; instead, more competitive elements are to be used.[11] Common labels for animal welfare criteria and the payment of a small sum as compensation for better farming conditions are seen as compatible with the prohibition of restrictive business agreements,

---

[5] Bundeskartellamt, 'Activity Report 2017/2018' (2019) 52.

[6] Bundeskartellamt, 'Activity Report 2017/2018' (2019) 52; Bundeskartellamt, 'Activity Report 2015/16 and Annual Report 2016 of the Bundeskartellamt' (Press release 28 September 2017) www.bundeskartellamt.de/ SharedDocs/ Publikation/ EN/ Pressemitteilungen/28_06_2017_TB_und_JB.pdf accessed 15 August 2023.

[7] Bundeskartellamt, 'Activity Report 2015/16 and Annual Report 2016 of the Bundeskartellamt' (Press release 28 September 2017) www .bundeskartellamt .de/ SharedDocs/ Publikation/ EN/ Pressemitteilungen/ 28 _06 _2017 _TB _und _JB .pdf accessed 15 August 2023.

[8] For details, see https://initiative-tierwohl.de accessed 10 August 2023.

[9] Bundeskartellamt, 'Achieving sustainability in a competitive environment – Bundeskartellamt concludes examination of industry initiatives' (Press release 18 January 2022) www .bundeskartellamt .de/ SharedDocs/ Publikation/ EN/ Pressemitteilungen/2022/18_01_2022_Nachhaltigkeit.pdf accessed 15 August 2023.

[10] Bundeskartellamt, 'Achieving sustainability in a competitive environment – Bundeskartellamt concludes examination of industry initiatives' (Press release 18 January 2022) www .bundeskartellamt .de/ SharedDocs/ Publikation/ EN/ Pressemitteilungen/2022/18_01_2022_Nachhaltigkeit.pdf accessed 15 August 2023.

[11] Bundeskartellamt, 'Achieving sustainability in a competitive environment – Bundeskartellamt concludes examination of industry initiatives' (Press release 18 January 2022) www .bundeskartellamt .de/ SharedDocs/ Publikation/ EN/ Pressemitteilungen/2022/18_01_2022_Nachhaltigkeit.pdf accessed 15 August 2023.

as they increase transparency for consumers when choosing meat according to animal welfare criteria. The non-opening of formal proceedings was combined in this case with a pledge to continuously monitor the sustainability initiative.

- In 2022, the Bundeskartellamt dealt with the Living Wages Initiative of food retailers.[12] They agreed on joint standards along the supply chain for private label bananas. The goal was to monitor wages and increase the sustainability of sourcing practices. In addition, the sales volume of bananas meeting these standards is to be gradually increased. The Bundeskartellamt saw no reason to open proceedings, as there was no exchange on prices or costs and no binding minimum prices or price premiums as part of the initiative.

Option PR 1: Sustainability-oriented Priority Setting

Exercising priorities with reference to sustainability is already possible now and without changing the legal situation. Priorities in selecting cases can be set politically; they are usually not subject to judicial scrutiny. Priorities could be set according to the value of economic activity for (certain) sustainability goals. Where the agency has the impression that an initiative should be tested and explored, it can refrain from enforcement action. Where it is convinced that the activity is helpful and should be strengthened, it can use its advisory potential to make the initiative waterproof. Where behaviour is detrimental to sustainability goals, it can decide in favour of vigorous enforcement. These three ways and thresholds could be further defined, yet do not need a clear-cut mandate from a legal perspective. The importance of the Sustainable Development Goals, in the international discourse and in policy documents on the European and national level, speaks in favour of greater consideration of such concerns. If more cases are looked into (and potentially closed again or not even formally opened), this would shed more light on the connection between competition and sustainability – a welcome by-product.

If more certainty is to be provided, the agencies could commit more strongly to certain priorities or the use of discretion in a certain way. However, this would necessitate the formulation of clear criteria. Moreover, it is precisely the flexibility and the element of surprise that make the intervention of the competition agencies effective. It is also conceivable that at other times there

---

[12] Bundeskartellamt, 'Achieving sustainability in a competitive environment – Bundeskartellamt concludes examination of industry initiatives' (Press release 18 January 2022) www .bundeskartellamt .de/ SharedDocs/ Publikation/ EN/ Pressemitteilungen/2022/18_01_2022_Nachhaltigkeit.pdf accessed 15 August 2023.

may be other issues or cases that appear particularly urgent. Therefore, a more explicit intervention, be it by the agency itself or the lawmakers, in the field of priority-setting, may be problematic. The fact, however, that exercising this discretion of selecting a case for investigation or not has an enormous influence, not least on sustainability goals, must be very clear to the officials. Here is the room for 'Sustainability Awareness': it depends on this first decisive step whether competition and sustainability becomes a topic or not.

ANTITRUST MONITORING OF SUSTAINABILITY INITIATIVES

In the practice of the antitrust agencies, there are further ways to clarify the admissibility of certain practices.[13]

Legal Situation

The spectrum ranges from informal discussions without any binding effect to statements and decisions pursuant to Article 10 of Regulation (EC) 1/2003 (or respective national rules). 'Comfort Letters', signalling a non-opposition to the parties of an agreement, are no longer in use on the European level (as they were under Article 2 of the old Regulation 17/62), but were re-introduced by Article 210a (6) CMO for restrictive agreements on agricultural issues (see above, Chapter 4). In Germany, letters by the chairperson of the responsible decision division in the Bundeskartellamt, detailing the approach of the division in a certain matter, have become a commonly used instrument to provide some guidance to specific sectors. Section 32c (4) of the German competition act empowers companies to ask for such a letter under certain circumstances, very comparable to Article 210a (6) CMO. Courts are not bound in any way, but such letters nevertheless have a certain persuasive effect, also for private enforcement. Pursuant to Article 10 of Regulation (EC) No 1/2003, the European Commission has the power to make a binding finding that conduct does not infringe Articles 101(1) and 102 TFEU or is exempt pursuant to Article 101(3) TFEU because of Community public interest. As far as can be seen, the Commission has not yet taken a decision pursuant to Article 10 of Regulation (EC) No 1/2003.

---

[13] Cf also Elise Provost, 'Sustainability and competition policy' (2023) No 1 Concurrences 31, 34 f.

Option PR 2: Entitlement to Comfort Letters

An extension and, above all, an expanded application of these possibilities for the agencies would partially overcome the difficulties of self-assessment and provide greater clarity for competition law as a whole.[14] The agencies could practice this without further legal changes, but there could also be an entitlement to ask for comfort letters when an economic activity aims at strengthening sustainability. The hurdles of Article 10 of Regulation (EC) 1/2003 are too high at present. A revised version of Regulation 1/2003 could provide for the possibility of a consultation with the Commission for sustainability initiatives below the threshold of a decision according to Article 10. This may include a written opinion that would not have a binding effect.[15]

Two further aspects are important for the guidance this provides: first, it must be clarified to what extent the authority should involve third parties in the procedure. There is no legal obligation to do so. However, in view of the sometimes considerable effects, those who are affected should be consulted. In sustainability cases, those who represent sustainability interests (e.g., NGOs or environmental protection agencies) could also have the right to be heard.

In order to achieve the necessary effect in markets, all decisions and informal statements of the agencies should be published on a mandatory basis. Without publication of informal guidance it is difficult to understand the reasoning of the agencies or the developing line of cases in the field. Sustainability initiatives can encourage imitation. This alone speaks in favour of publication. In addition, smaller market participants in particular are otherwise most likely to be cut off from important information.

Option PR 3: Sustainability Sandbox

Another model could be the introduction of a Sustainability & Competition Sandbox along the lines of the model proposed by the Hellenic Competition

---

[14]   Also in favour is the American Bar Association, 'Sustainability and Competition Law' (2021) Report of the International Developments and Comments Task Force 20.

[15]   Competition Law Forum, 'Reform of Regulation 1/2003: Correcting the Current Lack of Effective Communication' (British Institute of International and Comparative Law 2008) 3 ff www .academia .edu/ 1943367/ Reform _of _Regulation _1 _2003 _Correcting _the _Current _Lack _of _Effective _Communication _The _Competition _Law _Forums _Submission _to _the _European _Commission _in _relation _to _its _Consultation_on_Regulation_1_2003 accessed 15 August 2023.

Authority.[16] This would imply closer monitoring of sustainability initiatives by the antitrust agencies.

Sandboxes are regulatory 'safe spaces' in which innovative activities and business models are implemented under supervision and evaluation.[17] Companies can try out cooperative ventures for a limited period of time without fear of regulatory intervention. If the evaluation is positive, the approach can be permanently established in the market. In this respect, the Hellenic Competition Authority speaks of a 'supervised space for experimentation ... for the promotion of innovative business initiatives in favour of sustainable development'.[18] After a proposal has been submitted, the competition authority is supposed to give the green light by means of a 'no-enforcement action letter'. On this basis, the concrete project is to be implemented, but it is subject to monitoring by the competition authority. The analysis includes not only the competition impact, but also the achievement of key performance indicators (KPIs) for sustainability. The Greek competition authority intends to define these KPIs in a technical report.

The model of the Sustainability Sandbox follows other regulatory sandboxes, which aim to open up scope for companies and encourage them to test innovative solutions. The difference to the practice of informal consultancy for example, with 'comfort letters', is the structured procedure. Companies can – at least for reasons of self-commitment on the part of the authority – make a claim for treatment in the sandbox procedure. Sandbox models become even more attractive when accompanied by a dispensation from regulatory restrictions. For example, if a conduct were exempted from competition law for five years (including a corresponding effect also in private enforcement), this would increase the incentive for companies to try. At the same time, a high degree of transparency would be provided.

Nevertheless, the question remains as to what will happen after the end of the test phase. With a time frame of approximately five years, larger investments may not be made unless there is legal certainty that the investment can be operated for a longer period of time.

A genuine exemption from the prohibition of restrictive agreements would have to be in line with higher ranking EU law. National solutions, like the

---

[16] See Hellenic Competition Commission, 'Sustainability Sandbox' (July 2021) www.epant.gr/en/enimerosi/sandbox.html accessed 22 June 2023; OECD, 'Note by Greece, Environmental Considerations in Competition Enforcement' DAF/COMP/WD(2021)482021 (15 November 2021).

[17] OECD, 'Note by Greece, Environmental Considerations in Competition Enforcement' DAF/COMP/WD(2021)482021 (15 November 2021) para 20.

[18] OECD, 'Note by Greece, Environmental Considerations in Competition Enforcement' DAF/COMP/WD(2021)482021 (15 November 2021) para 30.

Greek one, have only limited effect here. In this respect, a European initiative for a sandbox would be welcome.

SECTOR INQUIRY

With the instrument of the sector inquiry pursuant to Article 17 of Regulation (EC) No 1/2003 and respective national powers, the competition agencies have an important investigation option for systematically screening markets.

Legal Situation

The requirements for initiating a sector inquiry are not high. Nevertheless, they are focused on price developments and competition issues. Previous sector inquiries have on several occasions been devoted to topics with a high relevance for sustainability. For instance, the European Commission investigated the energy sector.[19] The German Bundeskartellamt undertook inquiries in the energy industry, on charging infrastructure or waste management.[20] The agencies could deliberately select topics that enable them to shed more light on the relationship of competition and sustainability.

Option PR 4: Sector Inquiries on Sustainability and Competition

The competition agencies can start sector inquiries even now if they find some indications of 'restricted or distorted' competition. This is the wording employed in Article 17 of Regulation (EC) No 1/2003. In a reform, this wording may be reworded in a broader way so as to encompass the possibility to conduct a sector inquiry to examine the sustainability effects in a sector or market. The knowledge gathered on this basis would be helpful for the future design of the relationship. However, this would also impose a burden on companies, which would be obliged to provide information. Possibly, the powers during a sector inquiry (including searches) could be scaled down in these cases.

---

[19]   See European Commission, 'Sector inquiries' https:// competition -policy .ec .europa.eu/antitrust/sector-inquiries_en accessed 10 August 2023.
[20]   See Bundeskartellamt, 'Sector inquiries' www .bundeskartellamt .de/ EN/ AboutUs/ Publications/ Sectorinquiries/ sectorinquiries_node .html accessed 10 August 2023.

THIRD-PARTY PARTICIPATION AND COOPERATION WITH AUTHORITIES

Competition agencies, courts and directly affected companies are not the only players in competition law proceedings. Third parties may also be involved, for instance other undertakings or non-governmental organisations, be it environmental activists or small enterprises.

Legal Situation

Pursuant to Article 27(3) Regulation (EC) No 1/2003, third parties may be involved 'where they show a sufficient interest'. Pursuant to Article 18(4) EC Merger Regulation, third parties may be heard in merger control proceedings. Third parties can also be involved at an early stage of the proceedings.

In the *Bayer/Monsanto* proceedings, the Commission gave several non-governmental organisations from the agricultural and environmental sectors the status of interested parties in Phase II.[21] Interests of a non-competition nature sufficed as a sufficient interest. The views of these NGOs are reflected and acknowledged in the decision.[22] They have thus been given the opportunity to officially influence the Commission in its view. The submission was addressed, and even though non-competition aspects were not taken into account for the decision, there was heightened transparency and political discussion of the merger case.

In addition, the competition agencies have opportunities and obligations to cooperate with other institutions: the EU's Directorate General for Competition coordinates with the Legal Service within the Commission, for example. In a 2023 decision on the interplay of privacy and competition, the ECJ asked the competition agency to liaise with the data protection bodies.[23]

Option PR 5: Strengthening Third-party Rights

The role of stakeholders who bring sustainability-related aspects into procedures could be strengthened. For example, NGOs that advocate for the achievement of Sustainable Development Goals could be considered as potential third parties. The preconditions for participation already exist at present,

---

[21] *Bayer/Monsanto* (Case M.8084) Commission Decision C(2018) [2018] 1709 final, para 27.
[22] *Bayer/Monsanto* (Case M.8084) Commission Decision C(2018) [2018] 1709 final, e.g., paras 3005 ff.
[23] Case C-252/21 *Meta Platforms* ECLI:EU:C:2023:537 [2023] para 57.

but could be safeguarded (e.g., by a legal clarification that any interest in the case is sufficient and that it does not have to be a dedicated antitrust interest). Participation would have to ensure that the parties have extended access to information and must be heard in the proceedings. In the *Bayer/Monsanto* case, NGOs have made significant contributions that have broadened the view of the issues.

The law of procedural participation is currently only regulated in rudimentary fashion, so that special regulations for sustainability NGOs would be a systematic innovation. Against this background, attention should be paid to the consideration of the role of NGOs, especially in the case of a comprehensive amendment of the law of procedural participation, for example, in the course of the reform of Regulation (EC) No 1/2003.

Option PR 6: Cooperation with Other Authorities

The institutional and legal limitations of antitrust authorities (on this, see Chapter 13 below) can be mitigated by greater cooperation with other relevant authorities. There is some potential here. The Directorate General for Competition already has a close cooperation with the Directorate General CONNECT in the digital sector. This could become a blueprint for similar cooperation, e.g., with the Directorate General for Climate Protection or the Directorate General for the Environment. Such cooperations could contribute the necessary expertise, for example, for the evaluation of sustainability initiatives, and mitigate the legitimacy problem. However, cooperations are always associated with efficiency losses and increased regulatory costs.

TRANSPARENCY AS A SECONDARY PURPOSE

Antitrust and merger control proceedings are intended to protect competition. In addition, the aim is to create transparency regarding the development of companies and markets. This secondary purpose of competition law, which is hardly associated with any burdens for companies, opens up the possibility of strengthening transparency also with a view to sustainability impacts.

Legal Situation

The public investigation of competition violations and the advertising of mergers open up a view of what is happening in the economy. So far, however, neither in the process nor ex post are correlations with sustainability goals systematically examined.

Option PR 7: Sustainability Assessment, Climate Check and Ex-post Evaluation

The antitrust proceedings could be used as a reference point to increase transparency for sustainability issues.

It is conceivable that a sustainability assessment will be published with a merger control decision or in other competition law cases. The US Federal Communications Commission (FCC) carries out a 'public interest, convenience and necessity' test for mergers in the telecommunications sector.[24] This results in a comprehensive assessment based on non-competition standards. As little as this model seems suitable for legal enforcement, it is conceivable that – without legal effect – a sustainability report could be attached to decisions. In this way, it could be shown to what extent the companies involved in the process are hindering or promoting the development of sustainability in certain areas and to what extent this is changed by the merger. It remains to be decided whether the companies may also conduct their own investigations for this assessment, whether they can comment and who would be responsible for such a report (the companies themselves, the competition agency, other sovereign bodies, associations commissioned by the state).

Such an assessment could be limited to climate protection (as possibly the most pressing current issue). Every action of the antitrust agency could be checked for its climate impact (climate check for authorities). In the same way, corporate activities could be analysed accordingly (climate check for companies). The climate check would have to result in a kind of 'footprint' for the respective action – be it an official decision or a corporate guarantee.

Such reporting would also be a benchmark for subsequent ex-post evaluations of decisions. How have emissions developed five years after the merger/ following the approval of the agreement, and to what extent is the development due to the antitrust decision? By way of example, this would be a question that could be examined. Ex-post evaluation should be strengthened regardless, to allow for learning effects.[25] This seems particularly important for novel issues such as the integration of sustainability into the audit grid.

---

[24] See the accounts in Rachel E. Barkow and Peter W. Huber, 'A Tale of Two Agencies: A Comparative Analysis of FCC and DOJ Review of Telecommunications Mergers' (2000) 1 University of Chicago Legal Forum 29; James R. Weiss and Martin L. Stern, 'Serving Two Masters: The Dual Jurisdiction of the FCC and the Justice Department Over Telecommunication Transactions' (1998) 6 CommLawConspectus 195.

[25] See, e.g., for the energy sector, Tomaso Duso, Jo Seldeslachts and Florian Szucs, 'The Impact of Competition Policy Enforcement on the Functioning of EU Energy Markets' (2019) 40 *The Energy Journal* 97.

The antitrust proceedings would merely be an occasion to create greater transparency. The aim would be to shed light on the connection between competition and sustainability. Such measures would be considered primarily as a duty in individual sectors or as an option in outstanding cases. Regulatory costs would thus increase.

SANCTIONS LAW

Violations of competition law usually lead to cease and desist orders, but they may also be subject to fines and claims for damages. The fines, which can be substantial, and the claims for damages (including the associated proceedings), which can be high in some cases, could have a considerable deterrent effect in areas where 'trying out' innovative solutions would be helpful. The incentive for companies to develop sustainability activities in legal grey areas is thus reduced – especially if there is no legally secure exception for the activity. Sanctions could be adjusted accordingly.

Option PR 8: Sustainability Effects in the Assessment of Fines

The assessment of fines is based on the 'gravity … of the infringement' (Article 23(3) of Regulation (EC) 1/2003). This gravity is determined 'taking into account all the relevant circumstances of the case'.[26] In appropriate cases, the extent to which sustainable development has been harmed could be taken into account as an aggravating factor.[27] Equally, it would be conceivable to see a mitigating factor in the fact that the companies are pursuing sustainability goals with an agreement that was held to be anti-competitive.[28]

In the draft guidelines of the Dutch ACM, the antitrust authority provides for cartel violations having privileges through sustainability initiatives.[29] If companies have tried in good faith to comply with the guidelines or have even received positive feedback from the ACM, no fine is to be imposed in the event

---

[26]   European Commission, 'Guidelines on the method of setting fines imposed pursuant to Article 23(2)(a) of Regulation No 1/2003' [2006] OJ C 210/2, para 20.

[27]   In the case of car emissions, the Commission did not address the aspect of environmental damage when assessing the fine, cf *Car Emissions* (Case AT.40178) Commission Decision C(2021) [2021] 4955 final, para 233.

[28]   Maurits Dolmans, 'Sustainability agreements and antitrust – three criteria to distinguish beneficial cooperation from greenwashing' (*SSRN*, 2021) https://papers.ssrn.com/sol3/papers.cfm?abstract_id=3920369 accessed 3 August 2023.

[29]   Autoriteit Consument & Markt, 'Guidelines on Sustainability Agreements', 2nd draft version (2021) para 72 www.acm.nl/sites/default/files/documents/second-draft-version-guidelines-on-sustainability-agreements-oppurtunities-within-competition-law.pdf accessed 15 August 2023.

of the discovery of an infringement. As in the Dutch model, the consequences of an act (and, if applicable, efforts to limit negative consequences) can be taken into account.

However, the fine must correspond with the legal fault. Effects that have nothing to do with competition can therefore not be taken into account, as they are not covered by the protective purpose of the rule (under current law). (This could change if a Sustainable Competition was the new standard of competition law.) Such consequences, which are, however, closely related to market events, could be taken into account as one factor. However, this would have to be clarified in the fining guidelines issued by the competition authorities.

Option PR 9: Increasing or Limiting the Risk of Damages

Consideration could also be given to adjusting the risk of private damages claims. In cases where special damage to sustainability goals has occurred as a result of anti-competitive behaviour, the antitrust infringement could also be the starting point for claims for damages that have occurred outside the context of competition. This would, of course, link two extremely difficult aspects of private damages – liability for damages under competition law and liability for further-reaching consequences for public goods.

Conversely, one may consider protecting companies from claims for damages if they have pursued sustainability goals in good faith but this has resulted in a restriction of competition that harmed others. However, such a limit of private claims by third parties would probably only be justified in extremely few cases. In addition, it is doubtful whether a corresponding regulation would be doctrinally tenable and compatible with European law.

In sum, we think that considering sustainability goals at the level of damages remains a distant prospect.

PART III

Overarching issues

10. Definition of sustainability goals

Charlotte Kreuter-Kirchhof and Rüdiger Hahn

BASIC UNDERSTANDING

What does 'sustainability' mean? The concept of sustainable development has its historical roots in the eighteenth century in the idea of a permanent preservation of natural goods for economic purposes. According to *von Carlowitz*, wood is to be cultivated in such a way that 'there is a *sustainable* steady and lasting use' (emphasis added).[1] Accordingly, sustainability serves economic, *intergenerational* use. In the principle of sustainability, ecological and economic concerns complement each other. Sustainability is oriented toward the long term and permanence.

The WCED Definition

This ties in with the modern understanding of the term. Sustainable development is development that seeks to meet the needs of people living today and, at the same time, the concerns of future generations. According to this, sustainable development is an anthropocentric concept that combines ecological, economic and social goals. Thus, as early as 1972, the 'Stockholm Declaration' of the United Nations called for the environment to be protected 'for present and future generations'.[2] The World Commission on Environment and Development (WCED; the so-called Brundtland Commission) defined the term sustainability for the first time in 1987. Sustainable, it said, is develop-

---

[1] Hans Carl von Carlowitz, *Sylvicultura oeconomica oder Haußwirthliche Nachricht und Naturmäßige Anweisung zur Wilden Baum-Zucht* (Verlag Kessel 1713) 105 f.

[2] United Nations, *Report of the United Nations Conference on the Human Environment* (1972) 4, Principles 1, 2.

ment 'that meets the needs of the present without compromising the ability of future generations to meet their own needs'.[3]

This broad characterisation covers the two main pillars on which the modern understanding of sustainable development rests: intra- and intergenerational justice.

Intragenerational justice aims to meet current needs (i.e., within the current generation) globally. This idea, especially with a view to countries of the Global South, is often less present in many discussions of sustainable development, although it is a central concept in the WCED report. According to this, sustainable development is not possible without meeting the needs of poorer population groups, for example, in the form of sufficient food, clean drinking water, sanitary facilities or a minimum level of social security and health care.

Through the idea of *intergenerational* justice, the needs of future generations gain weight at the same time: social and ecological systems are to be maintained in a way that does not hinder future generations in their development.

Weak, Strong and Critical Understanding

While the WCED definition is widely used and accepted, its generality leaves much room for interpretation as to how sustainability can be achieved.[4] The main objective of a 'weak' understanding of sustainability is to keep at least the total sum of anthropogenic (i.e., man-made) capital and natural capital constant. Accordingly, natural capital can in principle be replaced by anthropogenic capital. Natural resources can be used indefinitely if the use value of the goods and services produced compensates for the loss of natural capital. The drawback of this concept of sustainability is that a complete substitutability of natural capital by man-made capital is probably impossible due to technical limitations and natural laws. When all of the Earth's non-renewable resources, biodiversity, and biocapacity are depleted, it is unlikely that humanity will survive at the same level of prosperity as before.

The counterpart is a 'strong' understanding of sustainability. The basic idea is to live only from the 'interest' of natural capital, i.e., to use only those natural goods and services that are continuously being added without diminishing the natural capital stock. Accordingly, non-renewable resources may not be used (because they do not renew themselves in time periods relevant to humanity and therefore do not generate 'interest'), while renewable resources may only

---

[3]   World Commission on Environment and Development, *Report: Our Common Future* (1987) 42.

[4]   Robert Ayres, 'On the Practical Limits to Substitution' (2007) 61 *Ecological Economics* 115; Eric Neumayer, *Weak Versus Strong Sustainability: Exploring the Limits of Two Opposing Paradigms* (4th edn Edward Elgar Publishing 2013).

be used within their regenerative capacity. The disadvantage of this concept of sustainability is that it has a rather metaphorical character. A complete renunciation of any use of non-renewable resources does not seem feasible and would also mean that intragenerational justice would only be possible through a very drastic (and thus probably unrealistic) redistribution of global wealth.

A middle ground is taken with an understanding of 'quasi', 'critical' or 'environmental' sustainability. It is based on the principle of prudence and not exceeding critical limits.[5] An example of such a critical limit is the goal of limiting global warming to 1.5°/2°C relative to pre-industrial times, if possible. One rationale for this limit is that an increase in the Earth's temperature beyond 1.5°/2°C will lead to various so-called 'tipping points' that could irreversibly change the Earth's climate.[6]

Other Approaches

There are other attempts to concretise sustainable development. One widely used approach to reduce complexity and illustrate different options for improving intergenerational justice is the so-called 'IPAT formula'.[7] The equation illustrates the impact of human activity on ecological systems through the equation: impact = population x affluence x technology. Human 'impact' refers to the ecological footprint. 'Population' includes the number of people leaving an ecological footprint. 'Affluence' is determined by the level of individual consumption, i.e., the impacts associated with our lifestyle and the associated material and energy consumption and emissions. The 'technology' factor describes the impact per unit of consumption. It refers to the damage caused by technologies chosen to support our level of affluence. This consequently relates to the energy required to produce and deliver material multiplied by the environmental impact per unit of energy.

Another approach to making sustainable development more tangible, which is frequently pursued in the context of economics, is the so-called triple bottom line (or three pillars) approach.[8] The economic pillar is usually understood as the responsibility of a company to generate profits to be able to operate sus-

---

[5] Will Steffen et al, 'Planetary Boundaries: Guiding Human Development on a Changing Planet' (2015) 347 *Science* 736.

[6] Timothy Lenton et al, 'Climate Tipping Points – Too Risky to Bet Against' (2019) 575 *Nature* 592.

[7] Donella Meadows, Jorgen Randers and Dennis Meadows, *Limits to Growth: The 30-year Update* (Earthscan 2014) 124 ff. The abbreviation IPAT stands for Impact = Population x Affluence x Technology.

[8] John Elkington, *Cannibals with Forks: The Triple Bottom Line of 21st Century Business* (Capstone 1999).

tainably in the long term. In addition, aspects such as economic prosperity and development are mentioned here. Regarding the ecological pillar, topics such as environmental protection, conservation of resources, and corporate measures to achieve these goals are discussed. The social dimension includes topics such as social justice and equal opportunities and often refers to employees and supplier companies and their fair remuneration, diversity, working conditions and work-life balance.

THE CONCEPT OF SUSTAINABLE DEVELOPMENT IN LAW

Regardless of the specific interpretation, the idea of sustainability has long been entrenched in law.

International Law

International law refers to the principle of sustainability in a large number of treaties. For example, the Framework Convention on Climate Change, the Paris Agreement on Climate Change and the Convention on Biological Diversity are all based on the principle of sustainable development. This guiding principle already formed the basis of the Rio Declaration of the United Nations in 1992. According to this, environment and development are inseparably linked.[9]

In 2015, the international community concretised the principle of sustainable development in 17 Sustainable Development Goals (SDGs) in the United Nation's 2030 Agenda. These global development goals are divided into 169 sub-targets which are to be achieved by the year 2030. The Sustainable Development Goals are based on a comprehensive understanding of sustainable development, which is addressed to all states in the world, to the private sector, civil society and other actors. The goals pursue social, ecological, and economic concerns in an integrated manner. The concept of sustainability is not a justiciable legal concept, but a guiding principle of international environmental and development law.

The colourful illustration of the 17 Sustainable Development Goals by the United Nations became iconographic. The 17 goals are, very briefly, defined with the following slogans – please be aware that the goals are defined in more detail, and as we said, are specified with concrete targets and indicators. The list, nonetheless, provides a first idea of these goals:

   '1 – No Poverty

---

[9]   United Nations Conference on Environment and Development, *Rio Declaration on Environment and Development, Agenda 21* (1992).

2 – Zero Hunger
3 – Good Health and Well-being
4 – Quality Education
5 – Gender Equality
6 – Clean Water and Sanitation
7 – Affordable and Clean Energy
8 – Decent Work and Economic Growth
9 – Industry, Innovation and Infrastructure
10 – Reduced Inequalities
11 – Sustainable Cities and Communities
12 – Responsible Consumption and Protection
13 – Climate Action
14 – Life below Water
15 – Life on Land
16 – Peace, Justice and Strong Institutions
17 – Partnerships for the Goals.'[10]

Whether the 17 goals are being achieved is monitored based on 231 indicators.[11] The Secretary-General of the United Nations submits an annual report on the implementation of the Sustainable Development Goals.[12] The Sustainable Development Goal Report 2021 shows that the COVID-19 pandemic has made it much more difficult to achieve the Sustainable Development Goals. This is exemplified by the following developments:[13]

• For the first time in 20 years, the number of people living in extreme poverty increased. As a result, an additional 119 to 124 million people were pushed into extreme poverty in 2020. This reverses the progress made since 2016 in the fight against extreme poverty.[14]
• The pandemic also likely contributed to an additional 70 million to 161 million people going hungry worldwide in 2020.[15] Around 2.37 billion

---

[10]   For further information see United Nations, 'Sustainable Development Goals' www.un.org/sustainabledevelopment/ accessed 15 August 2023.

[11]   The United Nations defines 247 indicators, see UNGA Res 71/313 (10 July 2017) UN Doc A/Res/71/313. However, some indicators are duplicated in this list. See https://unstats.un.org/sdgs/indicators/indicators-list/ accessed 10 August 2023.

[12]   These reports can be found at United Nations Statistic Division 'Reports' https://unstats.un.org/sdgs/ accessed 10 August 2023.

[13]   United Nations, *The Sustainable Development Goals Report 2021* (United Nations 2021) https://unstats.un.org/sdgs/report/2021/The-Sustainable-Development -Goals-Report-2021.pdf accessed 15 August 2023.

[14]   United Nations, *The Sustainable Development Goals Report 2021* (United Nations 2021) 26 f https:// unstats .un .org/ sdgs/ report/ 2021/ The -Sustainable -Development -Goals-Report-2021.pdf accessed 15 August 2023.

[15]   United Nations, *The Sustainable Development Goals Report 2021* (United Nations 2021) 28 https://unstats.un.org/sdgs/report/2021/The-Sustainable-Development-Goals -Report-2021.pdf accessed 15 August 2023.

people have nothing to eat or are unable to eat a healthy, balanced diet on a regular basis.
• COVID-19 also reversed 20 years of progress in education: An additional 101 million children (i.e., 9 per cent) have not achieved minimum reading proficiency.[16]

In September 2019, at their summit in New York, heads of state and government noted that the Sustainable Development Goals will not be achieved by 2030 if current trends continue. They therefore proclaimed the current decade as a Decade of Action for the implementation of the 2030 Agenda.[17]

The Sustainable Development Goal Report 2022 does not draw a more optimistic picture. According to this report, the interlinked crises of today including the COVID-19 pandemic, the war in the Ukraine as well as climate change put the achievement of the Sustainable Development Goals in grave danger.[18]

European Law

The European Union and its member states are also committed to the Sustainable Development Goals and the guiding principle of sustainable development. This is required by European primary law: the European Union shall work for the sustainable development of Europe (Article 3(3) sentence 2 TEU) and contribute to global sustainable development (Article 3(5) sentence 2 TEU). According to Article 11 TFEU, environmental protection requirements must be integrated into the definition and implementation of the Union policies and activities, particularly with a view to promoting sustainable development. According to the principle of sustainable development, a high level of environmental protection and the improvement of the quality of the environment shall be ensured (Article 37 Charter of Fundamental Rights).

To implement the 2030 Agenda, the European Commission presented the European Green Deal in December 2019.[19] Through this strategy, Europe is to become 'a fair and prosperous society, with a modern, resource-efficient and

---

[16]   United Nations, *The Sustainable Development Goals Report 2021* (United Nations 2021) 34 f https:// unstats .un .org/ sdgs/ report/ 2021/ The -Sustainable -Development -Goals-Report-2021.pdf accessed 15 August 2023.

[17]   UNGA Res 74/4 (21 October 2019) UN Doc A/Res/74/4.

[18]   United Nations, *The Sustainable Development Goals Report 2021* (United Nations 2021) 2 https://unstats.un.org/sdgs/report/2021/The-Sustainable-Development -Goals-Report-2021.pdf accessed 15 August 2023.

[19]   European Commission, 'The European Green Deal' (Communication) COM(2019) 640 final; see already European Commission, 'Next steps for a sustainable European future – European action for sustainability' (Communication) COM(2016) 739 final.

competitive economy'. By 2050 Europe shall become the first carbon-neutral subcontinent, with net zero greenhouse gas emissions.[20] The Green Deal was followed in November 2020 by the Commission's comprehensive approach to implementing the Sustainable Development Goals. This comprises six core areas, of which the Green Deal is one.[21] The concept of sustainability is defined in more detail, among others, in Regulation (EU) 2020/852 (Taxonomy Regulation).[22] It establishes criteria for classifying the extent to which an investment can initially be regarded as environmentally sustainable (especially in relation to climate change). The regulation thus contributes to operationalising the concept of sustainability, particularly for the financial sector. The aim is to determine the degree of environmental sustainability of an investment to promote private sustainable investment.[23]

BOX 10.1 MECHANISM OF THE TAXONOMY REGULATION

Article 3 of the Taxonomy Regulation specifies four criteria for investments into economic activities that are seen as environmentally sustainable:

First, economic activity must make a substantial contribution to achieving an environmental goal as set out in Article 9 of the Regulation.

The environmental objectives are defined in Article 9 as follows:

(a) climate change mitigation;
(b) climate change adaptation;
(c) the sustainable use and protection of water and marine resources;
(d) the transition to a circular economy;
(e) pollution prevention and control;
(f) the protection and restoration of biodiversity and ecosystems.

What constitutes a substantial contribution is defined in Articles 10–16 based on more specific requirements for each of the stated environmental

---

[20] European Commission, 'The European Green Deal' (Communication) COM(2019) 640 final.

[21] European Commission, 'Delivering on the UN's Sustainable Development Goals: A comprehensive approach' (Commission Staff Working Document) SWD(2020) 400 final.

[22] Regulation (EU) 2020/852 of the European Parliament and of the Council of 18 June 2020 on the establishment of a framework to facilitate sustainable investment, and amending Regulation (EU) 2019/2088 [2019] OJ L 198/13.

[23] Regulation (EU) 2020/852 of the European Parliament and of the Council of 18 June 2020 on the establishment of a framework to facilitate sustainable investment, and amending Regulation (EU) 2019/2088 [2019] OJ L 198/13, Article 1.

objectives.

Secondly, there must be no significant harm to the environmental objectives. What is considered significant harm is defined in Article 17.

Thirdly, Article 18 defines minimum safeguards that may not be undermined.

Fourthly, the technical screening criteria of the Commission must be complied with to make the concretisation of contributions and harm as comprehensible as possible.

Thus, balancing economic activities with sustainability goals works in the Taxonomy Regulation by managing investments and keeping in mind specifically selected environmental goals, setting prohibitions, defining a minimum standard, and technical specifications.

National Law

Apart from international and European law, there are national rules on sustainable development. For example, the German government and courts have defined the principle of sustainable development in more detail. One outstanding contribution is the decision on climate protection, handed down by Germany's Federal Constitutional Court in 2021. According to this ruling, there are intertemporal guarantees of freedom enshrined in fundamental rights.[24] This effect (partly based on Article 20a of the German constitution, the Grundgesetz) obliges the legislature to safeguard fundamental freedoms over time and to spread the opportunities associated with freedom proportionately across generations.[25] Measures that the legislature takes or refrains from taking today to protect the Earth's climate system have an effect for future generations that may have similar effects as an intervention today.[26] Article 20a of the constitution requires that the burden of mitigating greenhouse gases not be offloaded unilaterally onto the future.[27] The legislature must initiate the transition to climate neutrality in good time. This decision of the Federal Constitutional Court concretises the principle of sustainability in its intergenerational dimension for climate protection in a cross-generational protection

---

24   BVerfG, 1 BvR 2656/18 et al, 24.3.2021, BVerfGE 157, 30, paras 1–270.
25   BVerfG, 1 BvR 2656/18 et al, 24.3.2021, BVerfGE 157, 30, para 183. See also
Principle 4 and paras 116 ff.
26   BVerfG, 1 BvR 2656/18 et al, 24.3.2021, BVerfGE 157, 30, para 184.
27   BVerfG, 1 BvR 2656/18 et al, 24.3.2021, BVerfGE 157, 30, para 183. See also
Principle 4 and paras 116 ff.

mandate. The ruling is but one example for the strong role that sustainability nowadays plays in various fields of law and policy.

MULTI-STAKEHOLDER APPROACH TO THE SUSTAINABLE DEVELOPMENT GOALS

The 17 Sustainable Development Goals, their 169 sub-targets and 231 indicators form the globally recognised benchmark of sustainable development. The core elements of sustainability are intergenerational and intragenerational justice: sustainable development meets the needs of present and future generations alike and enables them to live in full dignity. The goal is an economically efficient, socially balanced and ecologically compatible development. In this context, planetary boundaries, together with a life of dignity for all, provide the outer constraint. Thus, the Sustainable Development Goals follow a comprehensive approach to sustainability. Unlike the eight Millennium Development Goals (MDGs), which were adopted in 2000 and should have been achieved by 2015,[28] they are addressed to all states worldwide. However, this comprehensive concept of sustainable development is directed not only at states, but also at the private sector, civil society, and other actors.[29] Companies are becoming key players in sustainable development.[30] They are to take responsibility for implementing the 2030 Agenda. States 'call upon all businesses to apply their creativity and innovation to solving sustainable development challenges'.[31] This 'multi-stakeholder approach' expands the circle of addressees of the Sustainable Development Goals. Just as the principle of sustainable development combines economic, ecological, and social concerns, companies are asked to integrate the goals of sustainable development into their business activities and contribute to the achievement of the Sustainable Development Goals through their economic activities. They are not only addressees of government regulation on sustainability but are themselves actors in global sustainability.

The Sustainable Development Goals thus tie in with global initiatives that require companies to exercise due diligence and act responsibly. These include the United Nations Guiding Principles on Business and Human Rights and the United Nations Global Compact. Further initiatives at different levels try to bring companies to commit to sustainable development. Moreover, many companies today refer individually to the Sustainable Development Goals to

---

[28]   UNGA Res 55/2 (18 September 2000) UN Doc A/Res/55/2.
[29]   UNGA Res 70/1 (21 October 2015) UN Doc A/Res/70/1 paras 39, 41, 43, 52, 60, 62, 70, 76, 79, 84. See also target 17.17.
[30]   UNGA Res 70/1 (21 October 2015) UN Doc A/Res/70/1 para 41.
[31]   UNGA Res 70/1 (21 October 2015) UN Doc A/Res/70/1 para 67.

express their commitment to sustainability and illustrate their own progress and actions. In doing so, many companies initially refer to the goals that best fit their business model and activities.

EXEMPLARY TOPICS

Both the definition of sustainability and the possible market interventions and legitimation patterns for it are broad. To make the subject matter of this report more tangible, three exemplary topics are presented to demonstrate sustainability issues, problems, tools for resolution, potential consequences, and wider implications. These three cases are discussed in more detail below. They do not cover the full range but allow for a more in-depth illustration of the mechanics of sustainability and competition protection.

Topic 1: CO_2 Reduction

BOX 10.2 THE CO_2 PROBLEM

CO_2 is a chemical compound of carbon and hydrogen that contributes significantly to the anthropogenic greenhouse effect. CO_2 emissions come from a number of sources, including the combustion of fossil fuels for power generation and in industry, heat generation, mobility, and the LULUCF[32] sector.

The increase of CO_2 in the atmosphere leads to an increase in the average earth temperature. This man-made greenhouse gas effect is already measurable today and is a major factor in man-made climate change.[33]

Climate protection plays a central role in the context of sustainability. One of the greatest challenges in climate protection is the reduction and avoidance of CO_2 emissions. To effectively protect the earth's atmosphere, economy and society must be greenhouse gas neutral by 2050 at the latest.[34] Protecting the climate system is a task for states as well as companies and civil society. This applies irrespective of stage or industry, as corporate activities currently regularly cause CO_2 emissions. Aspects of climate protection or climate resil-

---

[32]   LULUCF stands for land use, land use change and forestry.
[33]   See IPCC, *Climate Change 2021, The Physical Science Basis* (Cambridge University Press 2021); IPCC, *Climate Change 2022: Impacts, Adaptation and Vulnerability* (Cambridge University Press 2022).
[34]   See IPCC, *Six Assessment Report – Synthesis Report* (IPCC 2023).

ience are accordingly mentioned very comprehensively in various Sustainable Development Goals and the respective indicators,[35] either as a goal in its own right (Goal 13: Climate action) or as a means of achieving other goals (Goals 1.5, 2.4, 11.b, 12.a). Goal 7, a clean and affordable energy supply for all people worldwide, is particularly relevant. An indicator directly relevant in the corporate context is, for example, '13.2.2 Total greenhouse gas emissions per year'.

Topic 2: Fair Pay in Banana Production

BOX 10.3 LIVING WAGES

The sustainability initiative of the Deutsche Gesellschaft für Internationale Zusammenarbeit (GIZ) GmbH and the working group of the German retail sector to promote living wages and incomes in the banana sector has already been the subject of an investigation by the German competition agency.[36] The aim of the cooperation is to achieve living wages and incomes in the banana sector along the supply chain. The starting point for the initiative is Ecuador, where there is a statutory minimum price per banana crate and a minimum wage, but these are mostly not respected in practice. With a view to the new obligations to monitor the supply chain coming into force at the time of writing, four objectives in particular are being pursued: responsible procurement practices by retailers, active worker representation in the producer country, development of processes for monitoring transparent wages and working conditions as well as complaints bodies, and cooperation between stakeholders in the banana sector and food retail for a joint agenda for living wages.[37]

A second sustainability issue is the remuneration of workers in the banana-growing regions. This is about fair working conditions. Regarding the Sustainable Development Goals, direct references can be found in SDG 1 (No poverty), SDG 2 (No hunger), SDG 3 (Health and well-being), SDG 8 (Decent work and economic growth) and SDG 10 (Reduce inequalities). The

---

[35]   UNGA Res 71/313 (10 July 2017) UN Doc A/Res/71/313.
[36]   Bundeskartellamt, B2-90/21, 25.11.2021, for case summary see www .bundeskartellamt.de/SharedDocs/Entscheidung/EN/Fallberichte/Kartellverbot/2022/ B2-90-21.pdf accessed 15 August 2023.
[37]   Bundeskartellamt, B2-90/21, 25.11.2021, case summary 1 www.bundeskartellamt .de/ SharedDocs/ Entscheidung/ EN/ Fallberichte/ Kartellverbot/ 2022/ B2 -90 -21 .pdf accessed 15 August 2023.

indicators directly relevant in the business context are accordingly diverse, e.g., '2.3.2 Average income of small-scale food producers, by gender and indigenous group membership', '8.5.1 Average hourly earnings of employees, by gender, age, occupation, and persons with disabilities', or '8.8.2 Level of national compliance with labour rights (freedom of association and collective bargaining) based on International Labor Organisation (ILO) text sources and national legal frameworks, by gender and migration status'.

Topic 3: Animal Welfare

BOX 10.4   ANIMAL WELFARE INITIATIVE

In German competition law, Initiative Tierwohl (German for Animal Welfare Initiative) gained prominence. Representatives from the agricultural and meat industries joined forces with food retailers with the aim of improving animal welfare in livestock farming by, among other things, paying a so-called 'animal welfare surcharge' per kilogram of pork or poultry meat sold. This surcharge is a financial subsidy for participating livestock farmers who implement certain criteria from a predefined catalogue.[38] These include, for example, requirements for drinking water, barn climate, feeding, and the obligation to provide ongoing training for livestock farmers.[39]

In Germany, animal welfare is more frequently the subject of discussions on competition policy. Animal welfare can be linked to the climate protection goal, for example, when greenhouse gas emissions are reduced. On the other hand, it is about issues of animal welfare as part of the fauna to be protected, sustainable agriculture, and biodiversity. However, animal welfare as such is not a direct objective of the Sustainable Development Goals, even though it is regularly discussed in the antitrust debate on sustainability and is also subsumed under the topic of sustainability in the revised guidelines on horizontal block exemptions.[40] Indirectly, individual references may be found in

---

[38]   Bundeskartellamt, B2-72/14, 08.03.2022, for case report see www .bundeskartellamt.de/SharedDocs/Entscheidung/EN/Fallberichte/Kartellverbot/2022/ B2-72-14.pdf accessed 15 August 2023.

[39]   Additional criteria are available at Initiative Tierwohl, 'Criteria' https://initiative -tierwohl.de/tierhalter/kriterien/ accessed 10 August 2023.

[40]   European Commission, 'Guidelines on the applicability of Article 101 of the Treaty on the Functioning of the European Union to horizontal co-operation agreements' (Communication) [2011] OJ C 11/1, para 517.

SDG 12 (Sustainable consumption/production) as well as SDG 15 (Life on land) and in indicators related to biodiversity, but usually with a focus on nation-state targets that cannot be directly applied in the business context (e.g., 15.9.1.a. Number of states that have included national targets in line with or similar to the Aichi Biodiversity Target 2 of the Strategic Plan for Biodiversity 2011–2020 in their national biodiversity strategies and action plans). Despite this actual lack of direct references to animal welfare in the Sustainable Development Goals, the topic can nevertheless serve as an example due to its prominence in the antitrust debate – not least to illustrate the conceptual ambiguities around sustainability.

11. Government intervention in markets

Competition law serves as a tool for sovereign intervention in markets and the regulation of entrepreneurial behaviour. Within commercial law, the presence or potential of market failures justifies governmental intervention in the realm of entrepreneurial autonomy.

MARKET FAILURE AS A REASON FOR INTERVENTION

The concept of market failure, though not novel, is long established in the theory of general economic policy.[1]

Definition of Market Failure

From an economic perspective, market failures, alongside distributional policy objectives, constitute a primary rationale for government intervention in markets. In economic theory, the term 'market failure' encompasses any deviation from efficient market outcomes that arises independently from governmental market intervention. In practical terms, perfect market efficiency often remains elusive, rendering market failure a nearly ubiquitous phenomenon. Thus, market failure only becomes an issue for economic policy when the failure reaches a certain level or dimension. According to the theory of market failure, government market interventions become viable precisely when (1) without market interventions there is a threat of (not insignificant) market failure *and*, at the same time, (2) market interventions result in superior outcomes with reasonable certainty compared to the status quo.[2]

Traditional instances of market failures include significant competition issues (in extreme cases, a natural monopoly), negative or positive externalities (with public goods serving as a specific case), and information asymmetries. In addition, insights from behavioural economics may also justify regulatory

---

[1]   Cf Francis M Bator, 'The Anatomy of Market Failure' (1958) 72 *Quarterly Journal of Economics* 351.

[2]   Cf Ronald Coase, 'The Problem of Social Cost' (1960) 3 *Journal of Law and Economics* 1; Harold Demsetz, 'Information and Efficiency: Another Viewpoint' (1969) 12 *Journal of Law and Economics* 1.

intervention, particularly where a significant number of consumers (or suppliers, where relevant) suffer from distorted perceptions or systematically commit decision errors ('biases') that are difficult to correct ex post.

The Various Market Failures

The paradigmatic example of a systematic competition problem are so-called 'natural monopolies'. This phenomenon arises organically when monopolies are manifested due to subadditive cost functions – often associated with increasing returns to scale and typically with decreasing average costs. In other words, in the case of a natural monopoly production and distribution costs are lowest when there is only one single supplier in the market – the natural monopoly. This is particularly evident in network-dependent utilities such as water, electricity, or district heating. The operation of a second network would typically be inefficient in these industries. Optimal market functioning therefore requires a single supplier to meet market demand. Given the lack of contestability and the enduring monopolistic landscape that characterise these markets, they are invariably subject to state regulation.

> ## BOX 11.1 NATURAL MONOPOLY IN NETWORK INFRASTRUCTURE
>
> In Germany, electricity and gas networks, the railroad infrastructure (which includes the railway tracks, the stations, and the rail-specific electricity network), and parts of the telecommunications network and the postal service are subject to public regulation. The specific regulatory measures are largely – although not always exclusively – implemented and monitored by the Federal Network Agency, and the framework is designed to achieve two interrelated objectives. Firstly, it aims at protecting competitors of (often vertically integrated) infrastructure providers from being hindered or even excluded from competition in upstream or downstream markets through unfair foreclosure practices. Second, the framework seeks to protect consumers from excessive pricing and other forms of exploitative practices. Through such regulation, a societal equilibrium is established, which serves as a potential channel for promoting a sustainable economic landscape.

Second, market failures may occur in the case of public goods. In economic theory, public goods are those for which (a) the use by an additional user does not cause additional costs so that, in particular, the utility of the good for existing users is not affected by the presence of new users (commonly known as non-rivalry in consumption), and (b) the exclusion of users who refrain from paying for the use is not possible by reasonable means (known as non-excludability). These conditions give rise to the so-called free-rider problem: if non-paying users (the free-riders) cannot be excluded from using the public good, the market provision of public goods is often inefficiently low. In economic terms, not all publicly provided goods are public goods, however. In other words, not all services that are commissioned or produced by the state – for example, by public enterprises – are also public goods. Nevertheless, there is typically a need for government interventions in the case of true public goods, due to their inadequate provision by the market.

BOX 11.2   CONSERVATION OF NATURE AS A PUBLIC GOOD

The protection of nature can be interpreted as a public good, since no one can be excluded from the benefits of an intact environment and nature through established means. At the same time, the costs associated with nature conservation remain unchanged, even when others share the benefits from an intact nature. In the absence of government mandates for nature conservation, companies and consumers alike tend to show insufficient regard for the environment and nature.

Closely related to the public goods dilemma is the notion of externalities, where significant positive or negative consequences of an action spill over to unrelated third parties without these effects on third parties being sufficiently taken into account by the acting parties. Externalities are thus presented as a third potential market failure. Pollution and noise are the classic examples of negative externalities, while vaccinations are the archetypal example of positive externalities, typically protecting not only the vaccinated person but also third parties from infection. Market failure in such scenarios arises from the fact that individuals do not take into account the consequences, whether negative or positive, for third parties when making individual decisions.

BOX 11.3   EXTERNALITIES OF CLIMATE CHANGE

A prominent example of negative externalities is the emission of greenhouse gases. In the absence of regulatory measures such as carbon pricing, individual companies would not take sufficient account of the wider societal costs associated with greenhouse gas emissions in their production decisions. Similarly, many consumers would fail to internalise these costs in their purchasing decisions. Consequently, in the absence of corrective market interventions, greenhouse gas emissions would be excessive.

The fourth type of market failure relates to information asymmetry. If one side of the market lacks sufficient information about the quality of a service or other transaction attributes relevant to the other side, mutually beneficial transactions may be discouraged due to a lack of trust.

BOX 11.4 FAIR REMUNERATION AND INFORMATION ASYMMETRIES

Many consumers are concerned about the fair remuneration of producers of agricultural products such as milk, meat, or bananas. However, buyers often lack information about the remuneration received by these producers from their direct buyers and are, therefore, unable to express their preferences through their purchasing decisions. The introduction of seals and labels can mitigate potential market failures. Similarly, mandatory labelling of product ingredients can serve similar functions. In the absence of such mandatory labelling, consumers may find it very costly (e.g., due to search and information costs) to determine the content of products.

The fifth factor that can induce market failures is limited rationality among market participants. Behavioural biases can lead some market participants consistently to make wrong decisions that are not in their own best interests. This can happen when individuals do not fully understand the context in which they are making a decision, or when they are overwhelmed by the complexity of the decision.

BOX 11.5 BEHAVIOURAL FAILURE AND HEALTHY EATING

A common behavioural bias is consistently to prioritise the short-term benefits of an action over its long-term costs. A classic example is the tendency to consume insufficient amounts of healthy foods and excessive amounts of stimulants in the short term, and to regret it later. By taxing (and thus increasing the price of) the corresponding goods (such as tobacco, alcohol, sugar, fatty foods), advertising bans and other measures, sovereigns try to intervene in a corrective manner and reduce consumption. Similar strategies are applied to electricity, water, and transport such as air travel. Despite knowledge and learning, consistent changes in behaviour do not always occur.

In practice, it is possible to encounter a combination of market failures. As early as 1969, Nobel laureate *James Buchanan* pointed out that imperfect competition leads to fewer negative externalities than perfect competition.[3] Information asymmetries, on the other hand, may be more pronounced in the absence of competition than in the presence of competition – due to a lack of comparative opportunities. In cases where several market failures coexist, multiple policy instruments are usually required to address them effectively. Competition law mainly addresses the market failure of imperfect competition, while consumer protection law has, by and large, mainly addressed information asymmetries and behavioural biases of consumers. Various negative externalities are addressed by specific environmental, nature conservation and climate-protection regulations, which do not per se target competition deficits. Information asymmetries are also often addressed in special legislation, e.g., for financial markets, insurances, or food products.

Market Failures and Sustainability Goals

Several sustainability goals are closely linked to externalities and the concept of public goods. In particular, climate protection and a clean environment can be regarded as public goods because individual or even national contributions cannot be excluded, especially in global climate policy. For example, if global warming is limited to 1.5°C, the benefits accrue to all, regardless of individual contributions. Environmental, nature and climate protection are areas where the primary economic concern is the effective internalisation of external effects, including intergenerational considerations.

The regulation of natural monopolies and the reduction, of competition deficits can also be interpreted as supporting a sustainable economy by promoting social equilibrium as a facet of sustainable development.[4] In addition, regulated network industries such as railways and energy have inherent natural monopolies with significant potential to contribute to sustainability. In the (sector-specific) regulation of these networks, therefore, climate and environmental objectives in particular play a not inconsiderable role.

---

[3]   James Buchanan, 'External Diseconomies, Corrective Taxes, and Market Structure' (1969) 59 *American Economic Review* 147.

[4]   United Nations, *The Sustainable Development Goals Report 2021* (United Nations 2021) https://unstats.un.org/sdgs/report/2021/The-Sustainable-Development -Goals-Report-2021.pdf accessed 15 August 2023.

Information asymmetries are also relevant to achieving sustainability goals. Consumers often lack the means to easily identify or verify the conditions under which products are produced, including compliance with environmental standards, labour practices or producer compensation – elements that are important to consumers. Seals or mandatory labelling requirements can help reduce such information asymmetries and facilitate the transition to a sustainable economy.

SOCIAL OBJECTIVES AS A REASON FOR MARKET INTERVENTION

State interventions in markets are not always linked to classical market failures. From a political point of view, market interventions can also be justified in a democracy if the majority of a population wants such a measure, for instance, in order to achieve distribution policy goals. In this case, there is a tension between the preferences of the majority and potential restrictions on the freedom of minorities. Market interventions then aim at distributional goals or at implementing ideals of fairness and justice. For example, the goal of paying higher prices to producers in economically less developed countries should not be understood as a correction of classic market failures. In any case, it is not easy to subsume this issue under one of the five market failures. It is neither about competition deficits/natural monopolies nor about (measurable) externalities and public goods nor about information deficits and consumer misbehaviour. Rather, it is about correcting market outcomes that are perceived as unfair, i.e., from an economic point of view, a distribution of exchange rents that does not correspond to certain notions of justice.

Put simply, the problem in these cases is not that markets and competition do not produce *efficient* outcomes, i.e., that there is market failure in the economic sense, but that markets and competition do not produce outcomes that are *perceived* as *equitable*. These two problems – lack of efficiency and lack of equity – may coincide, but they may also occur separately. An inefficient market outcome may correspond to different perceptions of fairness.

The recognition that efficient market outcomes may not always be consistent with perceptions of fairness is not new. Thus, to the extent that a distribution of resources perceived as fair is part of a definition of the common good, market outcomes regularly deviate from outcomes that are perceived as fair. In a social market economy – and even in other market-based systems – various redistributive mechanisms are, therefore, employed, mainly through tax and transfer systems at local, national and, in some cases, international levels. These redistributive mechanisms are ultimately based on a wide variety of taxes and transfers, ranging from income taxes and corporate taxes to various consumption taxes (such as tobacco taxes, energy taxes, etc.), the revenues of which flow into public budgets. However, as we will discuss in the following section, taxes and transfers are not in principle incompatible with competition in markets.

From an economic perspective, another difference is that inefficiencies resulting from market failures are relatively easy to measure and quantify to a certain degree, whereas deviations from fairness ideals are much more difficult if not impossible to quantify.

Consequently, the reason for intervening in the market is relevant for the choice of the most appropriate instrument. It is important to categorise the problem to be addressed as either a market failure or a societal objective. However, the broad concept of sustainability as it is used as the basis for this report cannot be placed into a single category. Some sustainability objectives can be linked to market failures, including to a limited extent, the market failure of imperfect competition. Many sustainability concerns can be attributed to negative externalities. However, some of these are primarily fairness equity concerns that require government intervention.

GOVERNMENT INTERVENTION

Governmental interventions in markets address market failures or uphold societal goals through diverse means, including regulations (such as bans or the specification of production or product standards), subsidies or taxes on consumption or production, the definition and limitation of (tradable) pollution rights such as emission certificates, information obligations, and the granting of legal claims, e.g., arising from product liability. More recently, it has also become common practice to require internal company compliance, which includes documentation and monitoring obligations. One possibility for Government intervention is competition law, which was described in more detail above.

However, the presence of market failure does not imply that the market and competition do not themselves develop solutions to overcome market failure. Especially in the case of information asymmetries, the market can overcome market failure independently by establishing brands with recognition value, quality labels and seals of approval.

BOX 11.6 OVERCOMING INFORMATION ASYMMETRIES WITH A 'SEAL OF APPROVAL'

Quality seals or quality labels are symbols attached to products indicating a recognised product standard or regulation and that the manufacturer of the product has verified compliance with these standards or regulations. These symbols convey not only specific product attributes like quality, but also compliance with safety and environmental criteria. Typically, these labels are visually represented as seals or written descriptions. A quality seal can provide consumers with information about the product's features, but also about the manufacturer's trustworthiness. However, the proliferation of numerous seals in certain sectors can lead to confusion, as consumers may struggle to assess the relevance and legitimacy of these labels independently.

However, in the case of public goods and externalities that affect many people, such as global warming induced by greenhouse gases, market-immanent solutions without sovereign intervention are unrealistic. Measures like the introduction of CO_2 pricing, whether through emissions trading schemes such as the European Union Emissions Trading System (EU ETS) or through CO_2 taxes, are required from an economic perspective to foster efficient market outcomes.

BOX 11.7 EU EMISSIONS TRADING SCHEME

Introduced in 2005, the European Union Emissions Trading System (EU ETS) serves as a cornerstone of the EU's climate change mitigation efforts. It stands as a pivotal instrument for the cost-effective reduction of greenhouse gas emissions within the EU, functioning under the so-called 'cap and trade' principle. This mechanism involves an upper limit ('cap') on the total allowable greenhouse gases emitted across all participating parties. Within this cap, emission allowances can be bought and traded ('trade'). The artificial cap on allowances guarantees their value. In addition, the total quantity of certificates is reduced over time so that certain goals, such as climate neutrality, can be achieved.

In general, two primary forms of market intervention can be distinguished: regulatory and pricing instruments. These will first be outlined in a general context before delving into their application for the pursuit of sustainability objectives.

Regulatory Market Intervention

'Regulatory' market interventions encompass a spectrum of measure, ranging from product regulation to outright prohibitions on certain products and/or

Table 11.1   Regulatory instruments

Regulatory instrument	Examples
Quota regulations	Statutory biofuel quota, statutory recycling quota for packaging
Prohibition on products	Ban of traditional light bulbs, ban of products containing CFCs
Ban on production technologies	Legal phase-out of nuclear power, lignite, and hard coal-fired power generation, ban of cars with combustion engines
Specification of minimum standards for production	Specifications for livestock farming, minimum standard for the assessment of the recyclability of packaging subject to system participation
Advertising bans and regulations	Regulation of tobacco advertising, alcohol advertising
Market access restrictions	Environmental assessment for construction projects, approval procedures for power plants
Documentation requirements	Risk assessment and documentation in the supply chain due diligence act
Labelling obligations	Energy consumption labelling, food labelling (contents)
Public labelling standards	Nutri-Score, EU Organic Logo

production technologies and rules for corporate governance, e.g., regarding production methods, distribution, or market behaviour. Closely related to this are legal mandates for liability, for instance, in cases of consumer harm. The scope of such interventions is vast and multifaceted across industries, with diverse regulations addressing products and production practices. Table 11.1 provides – without any claim to completeness – an overview of common market interventions that are not based on price and are here referred to collectively as 'regulatory' measures.

There are numerous detailed sector-specific regulations for all areas of the economy. For instance, within the food industry, the Act on Strengthening Organisations and Supply Chains in the Agricultural Sector, influenced by the UTP Directive, anchors a ban on various trade practices in the food chain that the legislator considers unfair. In the financial domain, the EU has introduced a taxonomy to appraise the environmental (especially climate-related) sustainability of investments.[5] The range of options for market regulation, encom-

---

[5]   For more details see Chapter 10.

passing varying degrees of stringency and flexibility, is almost unmanageable[6] and is used differently by the legislature from sector to sector.

Whether the legislative intent behind these actions is to cure market failures in all cases in the economic sense will not be discussed in depth here. Of importance is the recognition that the legislature employs an array of diverse regulatory interventions to counter perceived market deficiencies that would arise in the markets without the corresponding interventions.

The above-mentioned sovereign interventions possess the potential to restrict competition to varying extents. For example, actions such as establishing barriers to market entry or enforcing product bans are more likely to impose stricter constraints on competition compared to labelling obligations. Generally, regulatory provisions inherently restrict competition in at least one competition parameter, otherwise their enactment would be redundant.

However, in the case of market failures, the (legislative) restriction of unregulated competition can indeed yield efficiency and serve the common good, particularly when these measures overcome or at least alleviate market failures. Given that one of the objectives of competition is also to facilitate efficient market outcomes, there does not need to be an inherent conflict between competition and regulatory measures from an economic perspective. In other words, unregulated or unrestricted competition would lead to inefficiencies in the presence of market failures, making the legislative restriction of competition desirable.

In this respect, regulatory requirements determine the framework conditions within which competition between companies takes place; it is not a necessary outcome that such interventions will introduce of competition. This presupposes that the measures affect all market participants equally and under the same conditions.

Pricing Instruments

In addition to regulatory provisions, market interventions that address relative prices, encompassing taxes, subsidies, and other price-mechanism adjustments, predominantly serve the purpose of rectifying instances of market failure.

In principle, price-related instruments can be designed to maintain a neutral impact on competition among companies. Particularly, in the context of carbon levies – whether in the form of a tax or as part of a CO_2 price derived from an emissions trading system – concerns related to any distortion of competition

---

[6]   Other possibilities for regulation include regulating locations (e.g., arcades, supermarkets), restrictions on certain consumers (such as age restrictions on alcohol, tobacco, or gambling), or regulating opening hours, to name but a few.

are typically minimal from an economic perspective, provided no individual company receives preferential treatment. In this scenario, CO_2-intensive production methods may experience a competitive setback compared to environmental-friendly alternatives, resulting in a disadvantage. However, if CO_2 prices reflect the external costs of CO_2 emissions, this competitive disadvantage is socially desirable and promotes efficiency.

Depending on their design, taxes and levies can have a distorting effect on competition in a market if certain companies are selectively treated differently from their competitors in terms of taxation. Additionally, these interventions can also affect competition dynamics between different markets. Regarding the implications of price-oriented market interventions for competition, it is observed that the degree of competition distortion intensifies as the substitution relationship between the affected products and services becomes closer. When the substitution relationships are sufficiently close, competition law may consider these products to be part of the same market. Conversely, if products are only in a weak substitution relationship the distortions of competition are likely to be minimal, signifying that these products do not compete within the same relevant market. However, when consumers are more willing to substitute, competition distortions in favour of the lower-taxed option become more pronounced.

Cooperation initiatives between companies may become necessary in scenarios such as deposit and return systems. When such systems are mandated by laws, as for example, in Germany under the Packaging Ordinance or the Closed Substance Cycle and Waste Management Act (KrW-/AbfG), the German Federal Cartel Office (Bundeskartellamt) has approved such cooperation in the past. As indicated by the Bundeskartellamt itself, several take-back systems for packaging have been established due to legislative actions, resulting in the creation of new market relations or markets through these take-back systems. When the establishment of such systems requires essential cooperation among competitors, the Federal Cartel Office (Bundeskartellamt) has imposed measures to ensure that this cooperation is confined to what is necessary. Moreover, the Federal Cartel Office (Bundeskartellamt) has aimed to structure the emerging market relationships as competitively as possible.[7]

This illustrates the tension between sovereign measures and competition and the remaining scope of intervention of antitrust regulations.

---

[7]   Bundeskartellamt, *Offene Märkte und nachhaltiges Wirtschaften – Gemeinwohlziele als Herausforderung für die Kartellrechtspraxis* (2020) 15.

Table 11.2   Types of market intervention

Type of market intervention	Examples
Excise taxes	Tobacco tax, alcohol tax, energy tax
Minimum prices with purchase guarantees	Guaranteed feed-in tariffs for renewable energies
Obligations to acquire licences or rights for consideration	Emissions trading systems
Direct subsidies (various forms: fixed contribution, premium, credit subsidies ...)	Purchase premiums for electric cars, subsidies for energy efficiency measures
Indirect subsidies	Tax benefits for electric cars as company cars
Deposit and return obligations	Can deposit, bottle deposit

Market Intervention in Sustainability Goals

In principle, there is no inherent conflict between competition and sustainability objectives. When addressing market failure or pursuing societal goals, the legislature possesses a variety of tools that can be employed without necessarily causing distortions of competition while still maintaining effective competition in markets.

The above-mentioned instruments can equally be found in the context of sustainability. Regulatory requirements concerning production methods and permissible products are established, for instance, by the Eco-Design Directive (2009/125/EC), by the so-called ban on traditional light bulbs, by restrictions on the so-called fleet consumption of passenger cars,[8] by the mandatory decommissioning of coal-fired power plants in Germany, and many other legal provisions.

Subsidies, such as those directed towards renewable energy generation or the purchase of electric cars, constitute a prevalent tool within sustainability policies. Similarly, taxes on items such as mineral oil or particularly unhealthy foods, high in sugar, fat, and/or salt content, are employed to further sustainability goals. These taxes are found in various countries, including the United Kingdom, Norway, and France. The European Emission Trading System (EU ETS), designed to regulate CO_2 emissions, also functions as a price mechanism. Other measures include mandatory recycling quotas, can deposits and information requirements – such as disclosure on animal husbandry conditions

---

[8]   Regulation (EU) 2019/631 setting CO_2 emission performance standards for new passenger cars and for new light commercial vehicles, and repealing Regulations (EC) No 443/2009 and (EU) No 510/2011 [2019] OJ L 111/13 stipulates that carbon dioxide emissions from new cars are to be reduced by 15 per cent by 2025 and by 37.5 per cent by 2030 compared with 2021. This means that so-called fleet emissions in 2030 may only be 59.4g CO_2/km.

or energy consumption classifications for products. The range of sovereign market interventions intended to correct market failures is diverse, especially in the area of sustainability.

Tensions with competition law

The above-mentioned measures are prone to potential conflicts with competition law when subsidies are granted, triggering the intervention by European State aid control. However, State aid law can consider sustainability objectives within the scope of broadly defined exemption provisions in Article 107(3) TFEU. Notably, the recently reformed Climate, Environmental and Energy Aid Guidelines (KUEBLL) provide a framework that makes subsidisation possible to achieve environmental goals.[9] Through this approach, the EU Commission aims to strike a balance between competition concerns induced by subsidies and the desired sustainability effects. Similar subsidy guidelines are in place for measures targeting other public interest goals.

Competition law in the narrower sense – encompassing the prohibition of cartels, abuse control and merger control – remains unaffected by these requirements. No exemptions from competition law are necessary for the concerned producers to comply with these regulations. Competition law upholds competition within the framework of existing legislation, ensuring that mandatory adherence has a competition-neutral impact on companies.

The compatibility of legislative measures with overriding European competition law must be assessed under State aid law, as well as under Article 106 TFEU and Articles 101, 102 TFEU in conjunction with the principle of 'effet utile'."

Tinbergen rule

From an economic-theoretical perspective, it is generally preferable to use a separate instrument for each independent economic policy objective (so-called *Tinbergen rule*).[10] Combining two objectives under a single instrument typically results in an uneven achievement of both objectives, with one often being compromised. When two economic policy instruments are utilised for a single objective, the risk of (costly) redundancies and inefficiencies arises. While individual economic policy instruments may have weaknesses, employing multiple instruments in a complementary manner to attain one goal is not uncommon. However, pursuing multiple objectives with a solitary

---

[9]   European Commission, 'Guidelines on State Aid for climate, environmental protection and energy 2022' [2022] OJ C 80/1.
[10]   See Jan Tinbergen, *On the Theory of Economic Policy* (North-Holland Publishing Company 1952).

instrument is more problematic, since in this case incomplete achievement of objectives is basically unavoidable and executive institutions are granted discretionary leeway that can easily lead to arbitrary decisions. In this respect, many economists advocate the adoption of independent instruments to pursue sustainability goals.[11]

Nevertheless, there are also economists and legal scholars who consider the so-called 'multiple goals' approach to be less problematic. *Inderst/ Thomas*, for instance, are notably more optimistic that – especially in the area of sustainability – transparent metrics can be found for specific case groups, which, for example, within the framework of a methodologically expanded consumer welfare approach, allow a sufficiently robust 'accounting' within the framework of efficiency considerations.[12] However, this requires complex evaluation of the value a sustainability measure holds for consumers and potentially other individuals who may not directly consume the relevant good. *Inderst/Thomas* assume that this assessment can indeed be undertaken, even acknowledging the inherent methodological challenges involved.[13]

Regulatory failure

Government interventions are not universally efficient, nor are they necessarily the optimal solution for correcting market failures or achieving societal goals. Instead, the potential for regulatory failure must always be weighed against any market failure. Regulatory failures can arise for a variety of reasons, including information asymmetries and knowledge gaps, the influence of lobby groups, bureaucratic tendencies to entrenchment or limited rational behaviour in political decision-making processes.[14] A challenge particularly relevant for the pursuit of sustainability goals is the short-term perspective of political

---

[11] Cf Robert Solow, 'The Economics of Resources or the Resources of Economics' (1974) 64 *American Economic Review* 1; more recently Maarten Pieter Schinkel and Yossi Spiegel, 'Can Collusion Promote Sustainable Consumption and Production?' (2017) 53 *International Journal of Industrial Organization* 371.

[12] Roman Inderst and Stefan Thomas, 'Integrating Benefits from Sustainability into the Competitive Assessment – How Can We Measure Them?' (2021) 12 JECAP 705, 709; Roman Inderst and Stefan Thomas, 'The Scope and Limitations of Incorporating Externalities in Competition Analysis within a Consumer Welfare Approach' (2022) 45 *World Competition* 351.

[13] For a critical survey of methods for identifying unknown value estimates, see Lucy Kanya et al, 'The Criterion Validity of Willingness to Pay Methods: A Systematic Review and Meta-analysis of the Evidence' (2019) 232 *Social Science & Medicine* 238, for an example.

[14] Cf Richard Whish and David J Bailey, *Horizontal Guidelines on purchasing agreements: Delineation between by object and by effect restrictions* (Publications Office of the European Union 2022) para 2.25.

decision-makers. According to political economy theory, politicians tend to prioritise the period up to the next election and often neglect the period(s) after that, thereby overlooking longer-term considerations.[15] As a result, measures that incur costs in the short term (e.g., through necessary investments) but generate benefits only in the long term are then neglected.

The influence of existing lobby groups can contribute to maintaining the status quo for an extended period.[16] This problem is likely to be particularly relevant to measures where today's voters or existing companies bear the costs, while future generations will benefit. This dynamic holds even if the adverse effects disproportionately impact their own voters less or affect people in other regions, such as the global South.

The decision of the German Federal Constitutional Court on the Climate Protection Act of 24 March 2021, may not represent robust evidence for the proposed hypothesis, but it is nevertheless consistent with the theory. The court urges the legislature to uphold civil liberties over time, stressing that fundamental rights, coupled with Article 20a of the Basic Law for the Federal Republic of Germany, oblige the legislature to distribute opportunities for freedom in a future-oriented and proportionate manner.[17] The measures that regulators take or fail to take today to protect the Earth's climate system have an antecedent effect similar to that of an intervention. Greenhouse gases emitted today will no longer be available in the 'budget' tomorrow. The intertemporal safeguarding of freedom of fundamental rights dictates that the burden of mitigating greenhouse gases should not be shifted unilaterally into the future. This climate-protection obligation aims to prevent 'regulatory failure' and mandates that the legislature act responsibly to safeguard the Earth's climate system. Similar concerns arise in other policy domains, like pension policy, where experts frequently critique the shift of burdens onto

---

[15]   Cf Kenneth Rogoff, 'Equilibrium Political Budget Cycles' (1990) 80 *The American Economic Review* 21; Iconio Garrì, 'Political Short-termism: A Possible Explanation' (2010) 145 *Public Choice* 197; Torsten Persson and Guido Tabellini, *Political Economics: Explaining Economics Policy* (The MIT Press 2000).

[16]   Cf Raquel Fernandez and Dani Rodrik, 'Resistance to Reform: Status Quo Bias in the Presence of Individual-Specific Uncertainty' (1991) 81 *The American Economic Review* 1146; Gene M Grossman and Elhanan Helpman, *Special Interest Politics* (The MIT Press 2001); R Emre Aytimur, 'Importance of status quo when lobbying a coalition government' (2014) 15 *Economics of Governance* 203; Frédéric Varone, Karin Ingold and Charlotte Jourdain, 'Defending the Status Quo across Venues and Coalitions: Evidence from California Interest Groups' (2017) 37 *Journal of Public Policy* 1; Linda Flöthe, 'Representation Through Information? When and Why Interest Groups Inform Policymakers about Public Preferences' (2020) 27 *Journal of European Public Policy* 528.

[17]   BVerfG, 1 BvR 2656/18 et al, 24.3.2021, BVerfGE 157,30.

future generations. Overall, this incentive-based explanation sheds light on why sovereign interventions may not be comprehensive enough in the short term when pursuing sustainability goals.

12. Economic assessment and quantification

How can common good and sustainability concerns be economically evaluated and quantified?[1] What forms of quantitative assessment are available not only to account for the benefits to society today, but also the benefits to future generations?

Many of the methods and analytical techniques discussed below relate to environmental aspects of sustainability. However, the concepts and tools presented are also applicable, at least in part, to other aspects of sustainability. The aim is to provide an overview of possible measurement tools and to critically assess their advantages and disadvantages with a view to comparing the potential competition effects of certain competitive behaviours with the possible societal benefits of greater sustainability.

Competition law can take sustainability concerns into account in various contexts, such as the assessment of mergers and acquisitions, abuse of a dominant position (Article 102 TFEU), or anti-competitive agreements between competitors (Article 101 TFEU).

In particular, agreements between competitors have played a prominent role in the discussion so far. An agreement can take various forms, such as a consensus between companies agreeing to phase out the production and sale of a less sustainable product variant. On the one hand, such an agreement can serve the public good by phasing out the production and sale of a less sustainable product, thereby avoiding environmental costs. On the other hand, it reduces consumer choice and may lead to higher prices. Other agreements may involve a more efficient allocation of scarce resources.

There are several methods that can be used to assess environmental costs and benefits, depending on the situation. Some of these methods are based on approaches already known from environmental economics. One such method is the so-called welfare analysis. This involves weighing the social benefits of a measure against possible restrictions on competition, regardless of the

---

[1]   See also Theon van Dijk, 'A New Approach to Assess Certain Sustainability Agreements under Competition Law' in Simon Holmes, Dirk Middelschulte and Martijn Snoep (eds), *Competition Law, Climate Change & Environmental Sustainability* (Concurrences 2021) 61 ff.

type of restriction. A fundamental assumption (and at the same time possible limitation) of welfare analysis is that individual preferences can be aggregated to social welfare.

The concept of Total Economic Value (TEV) is used to assess environmental costs and benefits. It attempts to capture the total welfare gains that can be attributable, for example, to improvements in environmental quality or other environmental factors that contribute to human well-being. The TEV is based on the analysis of use values and non-use values. In this context, use value refers to the actual, potential, or planned use of the good in question by the consumer himself or others. Non-use value, on the other hand, is the value attributed to the good even if it is not used by the consumer itself. In other words, non-use value is the willingness to pay to maintain a good even if there is no actual, potential, or planned use. In the climate context, for example, this valuation may be based on an ethical or religious desire to protect nature 'for its own sake' or to preserve it for posterity. Non-use values include existence values, bequest values, and altruistic values.[2]

METHODS OF EVALUATION USING CASE-SPECIFIC DATA

For most environmental goods and services, TEV is measured using a variety of valuation techniques. These can be based on either 'revealed' or 'stated' preferences. Both approaches have different advantages and disadvantages, which will be discussed later.

Revealed Preferences: Methods Based on Market Decisions

Revealed preferences methods are based on the analysis of observed market data. For example, a product may be offered in two different versions, one more and one less environmentally friendly. Based on real purchase data, the customers' preferences for the attribute (in this case environmental friendliness) of the product can then be recorded.

The choice of this method has major disadvantages. Firstly, many sustainability analyses refer to products that have not yet been produced, for example, in the case of an agreement between companies aimed at a new product variant with a higher environmental standard. In such cases, consumers cannot make a real decision, so there is no real purchase data and, thus, no revealed prefer-

---

[2]   David W Pearce and R Kerry Turner, *Economics of Natural Resources and the Environment* (Johns Hopkins University Press 1990).

ences. This also makes analysing potential mergers and their impact on consumer behaviour difficult to assess directly, especially ex ante to the merger.

Another disadvantage occurs when the environmental good in question is not directly traded. The use of real purchase data may then be ruled out for the analysis. However, the use of an environmental good usually leaves a behavioural trace in the markets for non-environmental goods. Accordingly, it may be possible to use the revealed preferences method to estimate utility values even when the good in question is not itself traded.

Despite these problems, there are significant advantages to using methods based on revealed preferences. For example, by observing consumers' actual behaviour, the 'intention-behaviour-gap'[3] can be avoided. This gap can arise in surveys when consumers exhibit positive attitudes toward sustainability but fail to translate them into action, purchasing fewer sustainable products than they profess to. For the measurability of real demand, approaches that measure revealed preferences prove superior to those based on expressed preferences. However, relying solely on actual demand might exhibit shortsightedness in evaluating sustainability aspects. For instance, if consumers perceive their actions as inconsequential in the overall context, actual purchasing behaviour might not align with their preferences. For example, considering the scenario where consumers opt for air travel as a mode of transportation; this choice does not necessarily imply an indifference to the environment or a lack of preference for eco-friendly transportation. Yet, their behaviour may appear insignificant when viewed in the broader context of all air travel or in comparison to individuals who frequently fly.

Another problem associated with methods measuring explicit preferences are information asymmetries. If consumers do indeed favour products with elevated environmental standards but are unaware or do not comprehend that a specific item aligns with this criterion, their actual purchasing behaviour will not reflect these preferences. For example, these may be products that protect particularly endangered species or products cultivated through sustainable shifting farming practices. Despite biodiversity decline being a pressing concern, many consumers remain oblivious to this issue. Products boasting biodiversity preservation or ecosystem protection might not experience heightened demand – particularly if their prices exceed those of conventional alternatives due to these attributes.

---

[3]   Pat Auger and Timothy M Devinney, 'Do What Consumers Say Matter? The Misalignment of Preferences with Unconstrained Ethical Intentions' (2007) 76 *Journal of Business Ethics* 361; Hyun Jung Park and Li Min Lin, 'Exploring Attitude-behaviour Gap in Sustainable Consumption: Comparison of Recycled and Upcycled Fashion Products' (2020) 117 *Journal of Business Research* 623.

Accordingly, careful selection and application of preference measurement approaches is crucial when assessing specific issues, in order to reduce the likelihood of misinterpretation of results. The following sections address the practical challenges of implementing preference measurement approaches. First, the focus shifts to methods rooted in actual market choices – the realm of revealed preferences. Subsequent discussions examine survey-based tools, including their advantages and disadvantages.

Travel Cost Method (TCM)

The Travel Cost Method (TCM)[4] has been developed to assess the value of non-market goods, particularly when these goods have no quantifiable price, such as a nature park in a recreational setting – a non-market environmental good. While the park itself lacks a monetary value, the cost of travel to and from the park, as well as on-site lodging, incurs expenses for users. TCM acknowledges the diverse factors that contribute to the creation of a good, factors that might not be inherently captured by its price. Nonetheless, the value of the good can be deduced from these elements. Fundamentally, TCM operates under the assumption of weak complementarity between the good and its consumption output. This means that the marginal utility of the public good (here, natural park) is zero when consumption expenditure is zero (i.e., when people stop taking trips to natural areas). That is, if trips to natural areas become so expensive that no one goes there anymore, the marginal social cost of a decline in the quality of the natural area is also zero. This bears significant implications.

Notably, TCM exclusively assesses use values, excluding non-use values associated with the mere existence of the natural area.

Hedonic Price Method (HPM)

The Hedonic Price Method (HPM)[5] estimates the value of a non-market good by observing the behaviour in the market for a related good. Thus, a market good is leveraged as a reference point, and it is within this market that the

---

4   Harold Hotelling, 'Letter of June 18, 1947', in Land and Recreating Planning Division National Park Service (ed), *The Economics of Public Recreation: An Economic Study of the Monetary Evaluation of Recreation in the National Parks* (United States. National Park Service 1949); Robert C Lucas, 'Clawson and Knetsch, Economics of Outdoor Recreation' (1969) 8 *Natural Resources Journal* 738; Nancy E Bockstael and Kenneth E McConnell, *Environmental and Resource Valuation with Revealed Preferences* (Springer 2007); George R Parsons, 'The Travel Cost Model' in: Patricia A Champ, Kevin J Boyle and Thomas C Brown, *A Primer on Nonmarket Valuation* (Springer 2017).

5   Sherwin Rosen, 'Hedonic Prices and Implicit Markets: Product Differentiation in Pure Competition' (1974) 82 *Journal of Political Economy* 34.

non-market good is indirectly traded. The underlying principle rests on the notion that the price of numerous market goods is a function of the bundling of their attributes. For example, the attractiveness of a location may be reflected as a function of its attributes. Similarly, a car's price encompasses its attributes, encompassing aspects like engine performance, fuel efficiency, safety, reliability, and other considerations. Employing statistical methodologies, HPM disentangles the implicit price of any characteristic linked to non-market goods, such as local air quality. This method allows for the quantification of the value attributed to particular non-market features, offering insight into how these features influence market behaviour and pricing dynamics.

Nevertheless, the implementation of HPM in practical settings can give rise to various challenges stemming from its statistical procedures. These challenges encompass issues like omitted variable bias, multicollinearity, selection of a suitable functional form, market segmentation, and spatial correlation, among others. Precise parameter selection becomes paramount in order to paint an accurate and dependable representation when employing this method.

Avoidance behaviour, defensive expenditures and medical costs

The valuation based on various costs, such as avoidance costs, defensive expenditures, or medical costs, finds application in scenarios where protection against an increase in non-market damage (e.g., environmental damage) can be achieved by purchasing a market good.[6] In this context, the price of the market good to be purchased is considered a substitute or replacement for the non-market damage.

Avoidance or averting behaviour operates on the premise that individuals can shield themselves from non-market detriment by opting for costly avoidance measures, which may involve purchasing market goods or utilising other non-market commodities. These avoidance actions entail expenses that would not be incurred if, for instance, the risk of environmental health hazards was absent. As an example, the purchase of bottled water or water filters is contingent upon the presence of drinking water contamination risk.[7]

Defensive expenditures denote financial outlays whose value signifies the implicit price of the non-market good or damage under consideration. Consider the instance of noise pollution along a road, which can be deemed

---

[6]   Guy Garrod and Kenneth G Willis, 'Economic Valuation of the Environment' (2002) 21 *Environmental and Resource Economics* 101; Mark Dickie, 'Defensive Behavior and Damage Cost Methods' in Patricia A Champ, Kevin J Boyle and Thomas C Brown, *A Primer on Nonmarket Valuation* (Kluwer Academic Publishers 2017) 293.

[7]   Glenn C Blomquist, 'Self-Protection and Averting Behaviour, Values of Statistical Lives, and Benefit Cost Analysis of Environmental Policy' (2004) 2 *Review of Economics of the Household* 89.

as detrimental. Households residing in apartments or houses along that road might invest in double-glazed windows to mitigate exposure to traffic noise. The double-glazing serves as the market good that acts as a surrogate for the non-market good, namely, freedom from noise pollution.

Comparable to defensive costs, costs of illness also pertain to financial expenses. However, they focus on expenditure relating to medical services and products necessitated by morbidity and other health repercussions. The health impacts of air pollution, for instance, can be evaluated in terms of funds allocated to medication for managing health-related symptoms. Yet, a challenge emerges from the fact that changes in this type of spending are often not directly observable.

Dose-response method

The cost of illness described above can be ascertained by estimating the production loss attributed to the illness. The approach for determining this production loss employs the observed or estimated market price as the valuation metric. For instance, this could involve utilising the farm price for evaluating variations in farm yields or the wage rate for assessing changes in labour supply. Accurate data pertaining to the relationship between damages, like air pollution levels, and health impact is required for these calculations. This relationship is also referred to as the dose-response or exposure-response relationship.

Nonetheless, translating a physical impact often necessitates comprehensive insights into the potential ecological consequences of the estimated physical responses. This requirement is particularly relevant for commodities such as agricultural products, where the translation can be relatively straightforward due to the direct economic impact of yield changes. In contrast, other situations, such as health impacts, may involve a less evident and very complex translation process.

Expressed Preferences: Methods Based on Hypothetical Choices

Methods aimed to determine stated preferences rely on hypothetical decisions, typically collected through surveys or experiments. These gauge people's intended, rather than actual, conduct in artificially constructed or hypothetical markets. The effectiveness of these preference assessment methods hinges on the availability of valid and reliable data. A key concern in analysis is whether the hypothetical nature of the market introduces bias, potentially mirroring the intention-behaviour gap previously discussed. This bias could prevent meaningful interventions.

However, the hypothetical nature of these methods is not necessarily only a drawback. Constructed markets can be harnessed to examine agreements among competitors to introduce more sustainable products. Here, consumers are presented with a hypothetical choice involving a new product variant adhering to higher environmental standards, yet not currently available in the market. This feasibility is contingent upon the hypothetical nature of the methods, which contrasts with the use of expressed preferences. Even if a product variant boasting higher environmental standards were already present in the market, relying solely on revealed preferences from existing purchases might yield an incomplete depiction. Various factors, including limited product availability or information asymmetries regarding specific attributes, could contribute to this shortfall. Moreover, the widespread adoption of the more environmentally friendly alternative among consumers may influence their willingness to pay, offering a novel reference point for their own assessment.

The following sections delve into the methodologies employed to determine and evaluate stated preferences.

Contingent valuation (CV) method

The predominant technique for ascertaining expressed preferences is contingent valuation (CV).[8] This method is applicable across the spectrum of non-market goods and can encompass the entire array of benefits associated with a non-market good or service, including those unlinked to present or future use (i.e., non-use value). In this context, all parameters related to the good itself can be defined: the design of the market structure, the characteristics of the good and its various facets, the institutional framework for its provision, and the financing mechanism. Through random sampling, individuals are subsequently selected and directly asked about their Willingness to Pay (WTP). This metric measures what individuals are willing to pay for a hypothetical improvement in environmental quality and, conversely, what they are willing to give up in order to forego such an improvement.

The generation of data for this type of evaluation is done by means of a questionnaire. This contains the description of the good and all other relevant general conditions. In addition to the actual survey about the willingness to pay, information about the socio-economic and demographic characteristics of the respondents are gathered. These are mainly used to control for various characteristics when analysing the data. To ask the actual core question about willingness to pay, there are various question types that may be more appropriate depending on the situation. These include open-ended questions, restricted

---

    [8]   Siegfried von Ciriacy-Wantrup, 'Capital Returns from Soil-Conservation Practices' (1947) 29 *Journal of Farm Economics* 1181; Robert K Davis, 'Recreation Planning as an Economic Problem' (1963) 3 *Natural Resources Journal* 239.

dichotomous choices, double-bind dichotomous choices, and others. The selection of an appropriate response mode is pivotal, mitigating issues in analysis such as hypothetical market bias (e.g., overestimating individual's WTP).

When analysing the data, econometric techniques are applied to the survey outcomes to capture the mean or median WTP and its key determinants. This can be done when WTP is directly collected by estimating a supply function that considers the socioeconomic and demographic characteristics of the respondents. When the WTP is not directly sampled, the WTP estimate can be obtained both parametrically and nonparametrically. The fundamental assumption is that individuals will prefer an alternative if its utility outweighs that of another. Once the WTP is quantified, it can be aggregated to yield an overarching population value. This involves multiplying the mean or median value by the population. It is crucial to exercise care in selecting both the population and the time period, aligning them with aggregate values.

The CV method stands as the most prevalent valuation technique in environmental economics, predicated upon stated preferences. Nonetheless, considering potential pitfalls associated with CV analysis, an alternative approach emerged: discrete choice experiments.

Discrete choice experiments (DCEs)

Discrete choice experiments (DCEs)[9] involve presenting respondents with a range of alternative options, each varying in characteristics and levels. Respondents are then prompted to indicate their preferred choice among these alternatives. The underlying concept posits that the utility derived from the surveyed consumers can be individually captured based on the attributes of the options. Consequently, DCEs stand as the sole choice modelling approach that aligns with utility maximisation and welfare theory, especially when a status quo is present. In instances where a status quo is not available, respondents are compelled to select an alternative, potentially deviating from their actual preferences.

Constructing a DCE involves an initial step of selecting attributes, such as the level of environmental friendliness of a product and must include monetary costs among the attributes to enable willingness-to-pay estimation. By creating combinations of attribute levels, choice profiles are generated. In the final phase, choice sets are formulated for presentation to respondents, featuring two or more variants (choice profiles) for selection.

---

[9]   Kelvin J Lancaster, 'A New Approach to Consumer Theory' (1966) 74 *Journal of Political Economy* 132; Ian Bateman et al, *Economic Valuation with Stated Preference Techniques: A Manual* (Edward Elgar Publishing 2002) 480.

The acquired data serves not only for welfare estimations but also for assessing the impact of individual characteristics through econometric techniques. Within the context of DCEs, two distinct forms exist: simple choice modelling (CM) and conjoint analysis (CA).[10]

Choice modelling (CM) is typically used to determine the value of the total changes in a multidimensional good. Nevertheless, it can also evaluate changes of a multidimensional nature. Furthermore, the method presents advantages in the accuracy and reliability of the estimate, stemming from the inherent choice process.

The goal of conjoint analysis (CA)[11] is to determine which combination of a constrained set of attributes wields the most influence over choice or decision-making. Respondents are presented with a set of potential goods for this purpose. By analysing the decision behaviour of the respondents, the implicit valuation (utility or partial value) of the individual attributes composing the goods can be determined.

Other methods for modelling choices

Furthermore, there exist alternative methods for modelling choices.[12] Contingent Ranking Experiments[13] ask respondents to rank a selection of options distinguished by variations in multiple attributes.

In Contingent Rating, respondents are presented with scenarios and requested to rate them individually, using a semantic or numeric scale.

Paired comparison entails respondents selecting their preferred option from a pair of choices and specifying the strength of their preference on a semantic or numeric scale.

Advantages and disadvantages of choice modelling in expressed preferences

The various choice modelling methods are particularly suited for scenarios where changes are multidimensional and trade-offs between them are of specific interest. Discrete choice experiments can offer more informative insights compared to contingent valuation approaches, especially when dealing with

---

[10]   Ian Bateman et al, *Economic Valuation with Stated Preference Techniques: A Manual* (Edward Elgar Publishing 2002) 480.
[11]   John Mackenzie, 'Evaluating Recreation Trip Attributes and Travel Time Via Conjoint Analysis' (1992) 31 *Journal of Leisure Research* 171.
[12]   John Mackenzie, 'A Comparison of Contingent Preference Models' (1993) 31 *American Journal of Agricultural Economics* 593.
[13]   Vivien Foster and Susana Mourato, 'Testing for Consistency in Contingent Ranking Experiments' (2002) 44 *Journal of Environmental Economics and Management* 309.

trade-offs. They are also better suited for generalisations of results and adjustments.

Choice modelling generally avoids explicitly eliciting the WTP and instead relies on ratings, rankings, and choices among alternative attributes, from which the WTP can be indirectly inferred. This approach closely resembles real-world situations with which subjects are more familiar. However, a drawback of this method is the high complexity of choices and rankings involving multiple attributes or levels. Studies in economics,[14] and psychology,[15] have demonstrated natural limitations in how much information respondents can effectively process during decision-making. Moreover, increased complexity or depth in ranking responses introduces random errors, or at least imprecise responses. Outcomes and welfare estimates, however, can be very sensitive to study design. Therefore, conducting robustness analyses and thus analysing different study designs is advisable.

Subjective well-being valuation (SWB)

Subjective well-being assessment (SWB) measures personal well-being in relation to non-market goods, typically collected through surveys.[16] It encompasses three primary dimensions. Firstly, evaluative subjective well-being (or life satisfaction) involves self-assessing one's life based on a positive criterion. Secondly, eudemonic subjective well-being pertains to the pursuit of a fulfilling and meaningful life, realising one's true potential. The last dimension is momentary subjective well-being. In this dimension, feelings, affects, or moods at a particular point in time play a role above all and are influenced positively or negatively by current events.

The subjective assessment of well-being and sustainability are closely related. For instance, research demonstrates a correlation between achieving sustainability goals and self-reported well-being measures. Most Sustainable Development Goals are positively correlated with well-being, although the objectives of 'responsible consumption' and 'climate action' show a negative correlation. This suggests that environmental policy outcomes align positively

---

[14] Cf Jacob Jacoby, 'Perspectives on Information Overload' (1984) 10 *Journal of Consumer Research* 423.

[15] Cf George A Miller, 'The Magical Number Seven, Plus or Minus Two: Some Limits on our Capacity for Processing Information' (1956) 63 *Psychological Review* 81.

[16] Ed Diener, Shigehiro Oishi and Louis Tay (eds), *Handbook of Well-Being* (DEF Publishers 2018).

with SWBs, yet the process of achieving such policies is not necessarily positive.[17]

Further Measurement Approaches in Practice

The discussed methods are well-established in empirical and political research, yet practical constraints such as limited funds, time, or resources, can hinder their application.

In cases where values for a good or service have been estimated at one location, they can serve as proxies for similar goods or services at another site. Benefit Transfer (BT)[18] methods have been developed for this purpose, aiming to transfer study results to different contexts, provided comparability exists. This approach offers resource savings.

Additionally, leveraging findings from existing integrative studies and databases is an alternative. Numerous studies and databases compile impacts and social costs of emissions and other factors. An illustrative example is the Environmental Prices Handbook 2017 by CE Delft (CE Delft 2018),[19] which serves as a valuable resource for such analyses. These methods allow for informed assessments even when applying primary research methodologies may not be feasible.

OTHER ASPECTS OF THE CHOICE OF METHODS

In addition to methodological considerations, practical decisions regarding valuation methods are often influenced by various factors.

Evaluation by Policy Objective

Policy objectives can significantly impact the choice of valuation method.[20] When a regulatory framework utilises market-based instruments to achieve

---

[17]   Jan-Emmanuel De Neve and Jeffrey D Sachs, 'Sustainable Development and Human Well-Being' in John F Helliwell et al (eds), *World Happiness Report* (Sustainable Development Solutions Network 2020) https://worldhappiness.report/ed/ 2020/sustainable-development-and-human-well-being/ accessed 10 August 2023.

[18]   Randall S Rosenberger and John B Loomis, *Benefit transfer of outdoor recreation use values: A technical document supporting the Forest Service Strategic Plan (2000 revision)* (General Technical Report RMRS-GTR-72, USDA Forest Service 2001) www.fs.usda.gov/rm/pubs/rmrs_gtr072.pdf accessed 15 August 2023.

[19]   Available online at: https:// cedelft .eu/ publications/ environmental -prices -handbook-2017/ accessed 10 August 2023.

[20]   Cf Roman Inderst, Eftichios Sartzetakis and Anastasios Xepapadeas, 'Technical Report on Sustainability and Competition' (2021) DEOS Working Papers 2103 https:// ideas.repec.org/p/aue/wpaper/2103.html accessed 10 August 2023.

environmental goals, an implicit price or shadow value (cost) for the environmental good is established. This creates a market where none existed previously. In theory, if the goal is welfare maximisation, the price will fully internalise the environmental externality. In practice, however, this is unlikely since the shadow price typically results in partial internalisation.

This can be shown with the example of climate change through the pricing of changes in CO_2 emissions. Environmental targets are assumed to represent societal preferences, whether they involve trade-offs between different interests or the assessment of costs and benefits for a country's citizens. The total cost of climate change in an economy is usually quantified using a damage function as a percentage of the gross domestic product (GDP). The welfare costs of emitting a ton of carbon into the atmosphere are then expressed by the so-called social cost of carbon (SCC). These are defined as the present value of the social welfare costs of emitting a marginal unit of carbon into the atmosphere. Estimations of SCC can be determined on a global scale through specialised assessment models, such as Integrated Assessment Models (IAMs). A well-known example is the Dynamic Integrated Climate-Economy model, which defines welfare at any point in time as the benefit of per capita consumption multiplied by population size.

The SCC is highly responsive to the selection of various parameters, including the time frame, social discount rate, equilibrium climate sensitivity, and the potential existence of stochastic tipping effects. This sensitivity to parameters can cause large divergence between different models, which in turn can have very far-reaching effects on the overall assessment of the situation under consideration. Hence, it is essential adequately to substantiate the chosen SCC value. A vital reference point is the observable (shadow) price that might emerge as a consequence of the adopted target.

In the context of addressing climate change, specific targets were established, such as a maximum allowable CO_2 emission volume within a defined time frame. This framework gave rise to the EU Emissions Trading System (EU ETS), which determines the equilibrium price for CO_2 emissions, serving as a basis for carbon pricing. The allocation of allowances in this system can therefore reflect societal preferences concerning climate change.

Cost-Effectiveness Analysis (CEA)[21] is another approach for evaluating policy objectives. It involves comparing programmes or policies to identify those achieving a given goal at the lowest cost or attaining the maximum goal within a specified cost limit. CEA is suitable for comparing initiatives where

---

[21]   Louise B Russell, Dennis G Fryback and Frank A Sonnenberg, 'Is the Societal Perspective in Cost-Effectiveness Analysis Useful for Decision Makers?' (1996) 25 *Journal of the American Medical Association* 1172.

determining the output's value is challenging, but calculating the cost of delivering the output is relatively straightforward. Additionally, it is well-suited for situations with fixed targets, seeking the most cost-efficient path to reach the objective. This aligns with the discussion surrounding CO_2, where SCC estimates face model sensitivity. Within the CEA framework, targets can assess the societal benefits of a competition constraint. For instance, assuming that certain competition restrictions were unavoidable or highly likely to meet a specific goal, agreements could lead to emission reductions that might not be achieved otherwise. Evaluating such agreements, like the adoption of common technology in certain vehicle types, can be assessed by estimating the avoided abatement costs resulting from otherwise necessary traffic restrictions. Within the CEA framework, various options to achieve the set objective can be compared, including the estimated cost of consumer surplus losses due to price increases.

Time Preferences

Discounting, as previously mentioned, holds significant importance in accurately assessing welfare costs and benefits, especially when evaluating sustainability-related agreements among competitors. The welfare impact of price hikes on consumers and the overall welfare gain are subject to a temporal dimension, where gains and losses may manifest at different time points. To facilitate meaningful comparisons, these future gains and losses must be translated into present value terms. Discounting assigns less weight to the future costs and benefits of a unit of consumption compared to present ones. Various approaches exist for this purpose, such as utilising the social discount rate, often referred to as the Ramsey formula. This rate can be further refined by incorporating risk factors or incorporating diminishing discount rates over time. This discounting mechanism enables a comprehensive consideration of the time aspect when evaluating sustainability measures and their implications for competition.

Distribution Aspects

Apart from the time-related considerations, actions and policies impacting the environment inherently lead to distributional consequences.[22] Environmental policies favour (relative to the status quo) victims of pollution at the expense of

---

[22]   Roman Inderst, Eftichios Sartzetakis and Anastasios Xepapadeas, 'Technical Report on Sustainability and Competition' (2021) DEOS Working Papers 2103 https://ideas.repec.org/p/aue/wpaper/2103.html accessed 10 August 2023.

polluters. In addition, some policies may produce greater efficiencies for distributional outcomes. Notably, changes in consumer surplus arising from the rise in price due to competitive constraints (or increased costs of sustainable resources) and the change in environmental benefits may affect diverse income segments. In such a case, it may be desirable to adjust the weighting of changes in consumer surplus and environmental quality could be beneficial.

Table 12.1 provides an overview of the methods discussed, their respective attributes, and other aspects. The focus lies in the behaviours these methods reveal, the conceptual frameworks they embody, and the typical scope of applications for each method.

EXAMPLES OF THE MEASURABILITY OF SUSTAINABILITY SUCCESSES

In the following, the evaluation of sustainability advantages is demonstrated through the cases of CO_2 reduction, fair pay, and animal welfare. This analysis does not exclusively centre on economic quantification, as examined earlier, but encompasses broader valuation principles.

CO_2 Reduction as an Example of Ecological Sustainability Assessment

The evaluation of ecological sustainability considerations has been a prominent subject topic in research and practice for many years and is accordingly well advanced. Measurement typically proves straightforward for directly input- or output-oriented variables such as water and energy consumption or the output of materials or toxic substances, since direct physical measurement in physical quantities is possible here. Wherever this is not directly possible, more extensive efforts are usually required. With indicator 13.2.2 'Total greenhouse gas emissions per year', the Sustainable Development Goals describe a metric that can be relevant for society as a whole, but also in companies or for cooperations. A well-known player in this area is the CDP (previously known as the Carbon Disclosure Project), a non-governmental organisation that has been dedicated to collecting and publishing climate-relevant company data since 2002. In 2021, more than 13,000 companies with more than 60 per cent of global market capitalisation published data under the CDP.[23] Further prevalent initiatives and examples include the Global Reporting Initiative

---

[23] CDP, 'CDP reports record number of disclosures and unveils new strategy to help further tackle climate and ecological emergency' (14 October 2021) www.cdp.net/en/articles/media/cdp-reports-record-number-of-disclosures-and-unveils-new-strategy-to-help-further-tackle-climate-and-ecological-emergency accessed 10 August 2023.

Table 12.1   Overview of methods, revealed behaviour and framework

Method	Revealed behaviour/ aspect	Conceptual framework	Types of application
Revealed preferences			
Travel Cost Method	Participation in recreational activities at the chosen location	Household production; complementary goods	Demand for leisure activities
Hedonic Price Method	Acquisition of real estate	Demand for differentiated goods	Environmental quality
Avoidance behaviour, defensive spending, medical costs	Time costs, expenses to escape damage	Household production; substitute goods	Health, especially mortality and morbidity
Dose-response method	Relationships between input and impact	Estimation based on a value standard	Medical costs, agricultural yields, wages
Stated preferences			
Contingent Valuations Method	Willingness to pay	Survey, questionnaire	Consumer goods, environmental quality
Discrete Choice Experiments	Preferences for alternatives	Experiments	Consumer goods, environmental quality
Choice Modelling and Conjoint Analysis	Preferences and decision behaviour, also for, among other things, individual features of a product	Experiments	Consumer goods, quality characteristics
Subjective Well-being Valuation	Subjective well-being	Surveys	Life satisfaction, potential
Further measurement approaches and aspects			
Benefit Transfer	Monetary values for environmental goods	Comparability of goods	Environmental assessments where there is a need to conserve resources
Existing integrative databases	Issue costs	Use of existing databases	Social costs of various emissions
Social Cost of Carbon	Social welfare	Global application using Integrated Assessment Models	Marginal cost of one metric ton of CO_2 in the atmosphere; global cost

Method	Revealed behaviour/ aspect	Conceptual framework	Types of application
Cost-effectiveness analysis	Effectiveness of policies	Comparison of different policies	Health policy, CO_2 emissions
Social Discount Rate	Temporal dimension of welfare change	Weighting of future gains and losses	Welfare costs

(GRI) with its standards on corporate reporting on emissions and energy (GRI 302 and GRI 305), among others, the ISO 14064 standard on greenhouse gas accounting, and a wide range of models for calculating the CO_2 footprint.

However, even the collection of supposedly simple indicators such as CO_2 emissions is often a complex undertaking. Unlike water or energy consumption, for example, CO_2 emissions cannot be measured directly, but must be calculated. For example, the combustion of different substances releases different amounts of greenhouse gases. In addition, while CO_2 emissions are the commonly referenced term, their overall influence on climate change is paramount. The influence of other greenhouse gases on the climate is therefore mostly measured relative to the influence of CO_2. The factors for global warming potential are therefore '1' for CO_2, up to 30 for methane (CH_4) (i.e., methane has a global warming potential that is up to 30 times greater than that of CO_2) or up to 300 for nitrous oxide (N_2O).[24] In addition to this complexity in calculating CO_2 emissions, which is only hinted at here, there is also the question of where exactly corresponding emissions occur.

Following the Greenhouse Gas Protocol[25] and from the perspective of the company concerned, Scope 1 emissions are direct emissions from company-owned or company-controlled activities. These include, for example, emissions from production processes or equipment (e.g., vehicles, furnaces, or boilers). Both Scope 2 and Scope 3 emissions are indirect emissions, as they occur outside the boundaries of the respective company. Scope 2 emissions come from electricity, steam, or other energy sources used by the company but generated outside the company. Finally, Scope 3 emissions are all other types

---

[24]   Intergovernmental Panel on Climate Change (IPCC), 'Climate Change 2021: The Physical Science Basis. Contribution of Working Group I to the Sixth Assessment Report of the Intergovernmental Panel on Climate Change' (6 August 2021) www.ipcc .ch/report/ar6/wg1/ accessed 10 August 2023.

[25]   WRI and WBCSD, 'The Greenhouse Gas Protocol: A Corporate Accounting and Reporting Standard' (March 2004) https://ghgprotocol.org/sites/default/files/standards/ ghg-protocol-revised.pdf accessed 10 August 2023; WRI and WBCSD, 'Greenhouse Gas Protocol: Corporate Value Chain (Scope 3) Accounting and Reporting Standard: Supplement to the GHG Protocol Corporate Accounting and Reporting Standard' (September 2011) https://ghgprotocol.org/sites/default/files/standards/Corporate-Value -Chain-Accounting-Reporing-Standard_041613_2.pdf accessed 10 August 2023.

of indirect emissions that are upstream or downstream in the supply chain. They are a consequence of the activities of another company that is not under the control of the company in question.

In particular, the collection of data on Scope 3 emissions requires extensive and often very complex data from actors upstream or downstream in the supply chain, for example, on materials or processes. Obtaining such data is often difficult or fraught with uncertainties or inaccuracies. Nevertheless, a differentiation of the scopes mentioned is necessary, for example, to avoid double counting across different companies or to identify significant levers to reduce CO_2 emissions. The above-mentioned aspects illustrate only a few examples of the many challenges involved in making sustainability issues measurable.

In addition to physical parameters, it is also possible to translate certain ecological aspects into economic parameters in the sense of monetarisation. The methods mentioned above can help. In the case of CO_2 avoidance, this is particularly straightforward because there are prices for CO_2, for example, for the certificates traded in the EU ETS. Alternatively, CO_2 tax tariffs can be used as the value of CO_2 abatement. However, one question to be resolved is which CO_2 price to choose if there are several, for example, in the EU ETS and in the national emissions trading scheme (nETS).

However, such approaches are not always possible. For example, it is difficult to put an economic value on the loss of biodiversity. Moreover, other aspects of environmental sustainability are already subject to measurement problems at the physical level, where the necessary scientific and technical knowledge or the data situation are not yet available and/or sufficient.[26]

Fair Pay as an Example of Social Sustainability Assessment

The second guiding theme relates to the social aspects of sustainability. In contrast to the established approaches for measuring economic and environmental performance, the assessment of the social pillar of sustainability is still in the development phase.[27] With regard to the specific aspect of fair pay, direct points of contact can be found in the Sustainable Development Goal indicators, e.g., via the 'Average income of small-scale food producers' (2.3.2) or the 'Average hourly earnings' (8.5.1). Corresponding aspects of fair working conditions can be measured directly through monetary indicators (wages). However, here, too, the question arises as to what objective should be achieved

---

[26]   Linn Persson et al, 'Outside the Safe Operating Space of the Planetary Boundary for Novel Entities' (2022) 56 *Environmental Science & Technology* 1510.
[27]   Michael Kühnen and Rüdiger Hahn, 'Indicators in Social Life Cycle Assessment: A Review of Frameworks, Theories, and Empirical Experience' (2017) 21 *Journal of Industrial Ecology* 1547.

or when remuneration can be considered 'fair'. While there is no universally accepted definition or method for calculating living wages, there seems to be a consensus that living wages are those that allow workers and their families to meet their basic needs.[28] Some methods for calculating living wages assume a family of four and needs for food, clothing, shelter, health care, transportation, and other needs.[29] Other methods use national minimum standards with the addition that wages must be sufficient to cover basic needs and provide additional disposable income.[30]

Beyond aspects that can be expressed in economic terms, such as wages, measuring social sustainability tends to be more challenging. Unlike environmental aspects, there are no physical variables that can be measured, as output or input variables, for example. Instead, qualitative information must be used, at least as a complement. Qualitative and quantitative data can be obtained through site-specific data collection (e.g., site-specific data on working hours or wages), specialised databases or through general data (e.g., average wages in certain countries or regions). Typical data sources used in a corporate context, for example, in the context of life-cycle assessments, include general risk or reputation data, supplier self-assessments, social audits, employee surveys, focus groups, and interviews or observations. The quality of the data can therefore vary considerably. Even more so than for environmental aspects, such data can be subjective, based for example on reports from employees about the degree of control they feel they have over their working hours and environment. Despite their subjective nature, such sources may be appropriate if these reports are relevant to the social outcomes of interest.

The challenges of measuring aspects of social sustainability are exemplified by aspects of fair working conditions, which go beyond aspects of remuneration. For example, the Sustainable Development Goal indicator 8.2.2 'Degree of national compliance with labour rights based on textual sources of the International Labor Organisation and national legal bases' is no longer directly measurable and should be measured through qualitative assessments and benchmarks. Moreover, it is clear that while the Sustainable Development Goals provide a potential normative basis and reference point for capturing positive contributions to sustainable development, they are not designed as a performance measurement system for assessing contributions at the organisational level. Beyond issues of working conditions, there is no consensus

[28] UN Global Compact, 'Living Wage: Take the Living Wage Tool' (2021) www .unglobalcompact.org/what-is-gc/our-work/livingwages accessed 10 August 2023.

[29] Andrea Werner and Ming Lim, 'The Ethics of the Living Wage: A Review and Research Agenda' (2016) 137 *Journal of Business Ethics* 433.

[30] ETI, 'Base Code Guidance: Living wages' (18 May 2016) www.ethicaltrade.org/ resources/base-code-guidance-living-wages accessed 10 August 2023.

assessment category in social performance measurement concepts and frameworks that address, for example, sustainability impacts at the societal level or even at the local community level.[31]

Animal Welfare as an Example of Other Sustainability-related Aspects

As discussed, animal welfare is not directly part of the Sustainable Development Goal canon and is more relevant in a broader understanding of sustainability. Indeed, if the welfare of the animal as a living being is placed at the centre of the issue, it is immediately clear that direct measurability is not given, at least not at the moment. Although it may seem cynical, the suffering (or the well-being) of an animal cannot be directly expressed in measurable terms. This is the problem of measurability: just because something is not measurable or even monetizable, this does not necessarily mean that improving it is not possible or socially desirable.

Alternatively, measurable indicators of animal welfare can be found, such as the climate in the barn or the stocking density.[32] In this case, however, the link is indirect, as it is not animal welfare per se that is made measurable, but upstream indicators that are assumed to have a positive impact on animal welfare. If animal welfare is in turn a means to an end to achieve other sustainability objectives (e.g., climate change or biodiversity), then the relationships described in the previous sections apply.

---

[31]   Michael Kühnen and Rüdiger Hahn, 'Indicators in Social Life Cycle Assessment: A Review of Frameworks, Theories, and Empirical Experience' (2017) 21 *Journal of Industrial Ecology* 1547.

[32]   See Initiative Tierwohl, 'Criteria' https:// initiative -tierwohl .de/ tierhalter/ kriterien/ accessed 10 August 2023.

13. The legitimacy problem and its resolution

Charlotte Kreuter-Kirchhof

In the context of antitrust decisions and the decentralised application of Article 101(3) TFEU, the question increasingly arises as to where competition authorities and the undertakings called upon to self-assess can derive the legitimacy to balance competition concerns with non-competition objectives. A distinction must be made between the legitimacy of decisions made by an undertaking and the binding decisions of competition agencies.

DECISIONS OF UNDERTAKINGS

Undertakings[1] are free to make the decisions that they believe are right for themselves. Companies can, for example, base their business activities primarily on making a profit. Likewise, they can decide to pursue sustainability goals. While most companies strive for different goals and weight them differently, today there are also companies that set social and environmental goals as the core purpose for their business.[2] The purposes of these social enterprises are social or charitable goals.[3] Which sustainability goals are set as the goals of a company, what priority is given to the individual corporate purposes, how these goals relate to each other, and to what extent the company reviews the implementation of the goals is within the undertaking's scope for decision-making, which is protected by fundamental rights.

This freedom finds its limit in the law, especially in the freedom of others. It is an essential task of the legislator to define public welfare goals in a binding

---

[1] On the protection of fundamental rights of legal persons Charlotte Kreuter-Kirchhof, *Personales Eigentum im Wandel* (Mohr Siebeck 2017) 268 ff with further references.

[2] The term 'social enterprise' is used. See for Germany Social Entrepreneurship Netzwerk Deutschland (SEND), '4. Deutscher Social Entrepreneurship Monitor 2021/2022' www .send -ev .de/ wp -content/ uploads/ 2022/ 04/ 4 _DSEM _web .pdf accessed 10 August 2023.

[3] Cf definition of Social Enterprises by the European Commission, 'Social Business Initiative' (Communication) COM(2011) 682 final, 2 f.

manner, to determine the necessary steps to achieve them and to ensure their implementation. Thus, undertakings can focus their activity on profits; however, in doing so, the legal requirements which serve, for example, environmental protection and minimum social standards, must be respected. The undertaking is free to decide the extent to which it goes beyond these legal requirements in order to pursue Sustainable Development Goals. Binding legal requirements, however, set limits to this freedom of decision. Legislators can define strict environmental and social standards. If this is not done and the company acts within the scope of the decision-making powers limited by law, fundamental freedom is exercised. A company can pursue stricter sustainability goals beyond the legal requirements, but it does not have to do so.

In the case of self-assessment, undertakings would have to assess for themselves, within the framework of Article 101(3) TFEU, whether their agreements qualify for exemption. Undertakings themselves would therefore have to balance conflicting objectives to determine whether the sustainable development objectives they pursue outweigh the restrictions on competition. This balancing by the undertakings is not legally binding and therefore does not require the same democratic legitimation as a binding decision by an authority. Rather, the self-assessment is part of undertakings' freedom of decision. As a result, however, companies bear the risk of misjudgement. They cannot rely on a legally binding decision that their assessment is consistent with the applicable law and that competition concerns have been balanced with sustainable development objectives in a legally compliant manner. This uncertainty could impede agreements to protect Sustainable Development Goals. Judicial or regulatory confirmation at the request of companies could eliminate this uncertainty and would ease the path to regulation for sustainability agreements.

DECISIONS OF COMPETITION AUTHORITIES

The 17 Sustainable Development Goals may conflict not only with each other, but also with other goals. In individual cases, therefore, a balance must be found. For example, an effective climate protection measure (such as the construction of a wind turbine) may conflict with nature conservation concerns (such as the protection of rare bird species). If sustainability goals are integrated into antitrust decisions, the question arises as to who decides on this trade-off and thus balances the various goals – be they sustainability goals or the protection of competition.[4] Should climate protection for example take

---

[4]   Cf Jean Tirole, 'Socially Responsible Agencies' (2022) 7 *Competition Law & Policy Debate* 171.

priority, or the protection of biodiversity? What degree of supply security will be guaranteed with an increasing expansion of renewable energy?

If the competition authorities take binding decisions to balance competition concerns with non-competition objectives, they are bound by fundamental rights. If antitrust authorities weigh sustainable development objectives against other objectives – competition concerns or even other sustainability objectives – the question arises of to what extent the antitrust authorities have the legitimate right to make these decisions as part of the executive branch and to include sustainable development objectives in their balancing decisions. What needs to be clarified is the extent to which the legislature must legally structure the benchmarks for these decisions by law.

According to the Federal Constitutional Court, in case of interventions in fundamental rights, the legislature must make all essential decisions itself and cannot derogate it to other authorities.[5] Thereby, interventions in fundamental rights are democratically legitimised by decisions of parliament. All essential decisions are reserved to the legislature (theory of essentiality). As far as the reservation of the law extends, the executive power is prohibited from acting without an effective legal basis. The legislature can only transfer final decision-making powers to the administration within these limits. Final decision-making powers of the administration may not undermine effective legal protection.

For the further development of competition law, the antitrust authorities should be assigned balancing decisions on sustainability objectives only to the extent that these decisions are not reserved for the legislature. All essential decisions on balancing competition concerns with non-competition objectives should be made by the legislature. In this context, the decisions of the legislator can, in principle, be taken at Member State or European level. If the legislator has decided upon the essential decisions for balancing sustainability goals and competition concerns, the authorities enforce these legal regulations.[6] They then have to make the balancing decisions between competition concerns and sustainable development objectives on the basis of the law. In this context, Sustainable Development Goals have a different quality than traditional competition concerns. The legislator is called upon to develop standards of

---

[5]   BVerfG, 2 BvR 883/73, 28.10.1975, BVerfGE 40, 237, 248 f.; BVerfG, 2 BvL 8/77, 8.8.1978, BVerfGE 49, 89, 126; BVerfG, 2 BvR 228/12, 20.2.2013, BVerfGE 133, 112, 132, para 53.

[6]   It is conceivable that different authorities, each with their own expertise, will decide on different issues. A coordination procedure is then required between the authorities, e.g., the cartel authority could obtain the agreement of a nature conservation authority.

consideration that are manageable for the authorities in individual cases. The decisions of the authorities remain subject to full judicial review.

INTERNATIONAL DIMENSION

The legitimacy problem also has an international dimension, which is particularly relevant in the context of global sustainability issues. Suppose a national competition authority exempts the anti-competition decisions of an initiative to improve the wages of banana workers in Ecuador or to combat child labour in Asian countries. The case would first have to be decided at the national or European level. But with what legitimacy can a national or European authority or a business initiative then enforce the decision abroad? For example, in the case of fair pay in Ecuador, it can be argued that the sustainability initiative for banana workers is a unilateral economic intervention in the country's wage structure, which could potentially lead to distortions – banana workers are suddenly paid considerably better, but bus drivers in Ecuador are not. This could be viewed as a form of new 'benevolent' imperialism.

14. The danger of greenwashing

Rüdiger Hahn and Alexandra May

In the sustainability discourse, the danger of 'greenwashing' needs to be reckoned with. There are concerns that companies could use the cloak of sustainability to justify harmful restrictions on competition with no real desire to be more sustainable or that they present themselves as sustainable in the market when this is not actually the case.

DEFINITION OF GREENWASHING

The term 'greenwashing' is terminologically based on the term 'whitewashing'. Whitewashing describes behaviour that is intended to conceal grievances by an exaggerated highlighting of positive attributes. Accordingly, the term greenwashing covers whitewashing that specifically concerns sustainability factors. *Delmas* and *Burbano* define greenwashing as 'the act of misleading consumers regarding the environmental practices of a company (firm level greenwashing) or the environmental benefits of a product or service (product level greenwashing)'.[1] The term is composed of the colour green, which is regularly associated with nature and the environment, and the word 'washing'. Greenwashing thus refers to the special emphasis on (supposedly) positive environmental concerns to conceal a company's environmentally harmful behaviour or to misleadingly present it as sustainable.

Greenwashing, however, can extend beyond the environmental sphere to include other misleading claims about sustainability, such as social issues. More rarely, corresponding practices are also referred to as social washing[2] or 'bluewashing',[3] a term originating from the idea that companies use the United

[1] Magali A Delmas and Vanessa Cuerel Burbano, 'The Drivers of Greenwashing' (2011) 54 *California Management Review* 64.

[2] Francesco Rizzi, Natalia Gusmerotti and Marco Frey, 'How to Meet Reuse and Preparation for Reuse Targets? Shape Advertising Strategies But be Aware of "Social Washing"' (2020) 101 *Waste Management* 291.

[3] Daniel Berliner and Aseem Prakash, '"Bluewashing" the Firm? Voluntary Regulations, Program Design, and Member Compliance with the United Nations Global Compact' (2015) 43 *Policy Studies Journal* 115.

Nations blue logo to falsely signal their solidarity with sustainability issues through membership in the UN Global Compact. Furthermore, greenwashing can be engaged in not only by misleading consumers, but potentially also other stakeholders such as state actors.

GREENWASHING IN UNFAIR TRADING LAW

With the population's growing interest in environmental issues, environmental aspects are also playing an increasingly important role in the marketing of goods and services. In unfair trading law, greenwashing therefore covers statements by companies which suggest that they act or produce in a particularly sustainable, CO_2-saving or environmentally friendly manner, although this is incorrect or cannot be verified.[4] In particular, the provisions of Articles 6 and 7 of the UCP Directive 2005/29/EC and their corresponding national laws, which aim to prevent misleading behaviour towards consumers, have been the subject of case law decisions for many years. The courts have worked out that consumers are aware that advertising with sustainability aspects does not mean absolute sustainability, i.e., complete climate neutrality, but only sustainability in relation to comparable products. However, the content of this 'relative sustainability' must be communicated in a true, clear, specific, precise and unambiguous manner,[5] so that consumers can see in what respect the product is sustainable. This means that the company has additional obligations to provide information. This may not be necessary however, when in individual cases the average consumer can recognise the environmental benefit in question on his own.

In the United Kingdom, regulators can penalise companies for violating certain consumer laws based on the Green Claims Code. According to this code, companies must, among other things, 'not omit or hide relevant information' and they must take into account the 'full lifecycle of the product'.[6]

---

[4]   European Commission, 'Guidance on the interpretation and application of Directive 2005/29/EC of the European Parliament and of the Council concerning unfair business-to-consumer commercial practices in the internal market' [2021] OJ C 526/1, para 72.
[5]   European Commission, 'Guidance on the interpretation and application of Directive 2005/29/EC of the European Parliament and of the Council concerning unfair business-to-consumer commercial practices in the internal market' [2021] OJ C 526/1, para 76.
[6]   Competition & Markets Authority, 'Guidance: Making environmental claims on goods and services' (20 September 2021) www.gov.uk/government/publications/ green-claims-code-making-environmental-claims/environmental-claims-on-goods-and -services accessed 10 August.

Overall, the prohibition of greenwashing under unfair trading law is aimed at ensuring that consumers receive accurate information about the sustainability aspects of a product or service and can thus make well-informed decisions. Unfair trading law thus protects against competition distortions caused by false assumptions – especially with regard to sustainability aspects.

GREENWASHING IN ANTITRUST LAW

Greenwashing can also occur in situations relevant to antitrust law. In that case, this does not occur as a result of environmental statements made by a company to consumers, but in the context of cooperation between companies. Companies can try to greenwash agreements that restrict competition by making untruthful or exaggerated statements about sustainability benefits to prevent the authorities from investigating in the first place, or to falsely invoke the exemption of Article 101(3) TFEU or equivalent national laws.

This can manifest itself, for example, in agreements on the introduction of environmentally friendly production standards between companies at a uniform market level, which have only a minor positive impact on the environment but are accompanied by substantial price increases. Price fixing could thus be concealed under the guise of sustainability. It is also conceivable that a company could make certain criteria a condition for cooperation and use environmental concerns as justification, while in reality pursuing other interests that are not accepted as a justification in antitrust law.[7]

Risk Analysis

It is difficult to make a general risk analysis regarding the probability and quantity of greenwashing in antitrust law, especially in the case of sustainability cooperations. It should be pointed out that the protection by unfair trading law ultimately also reduces the risk of greenwashing in antitrust law. If companies conclude agreements for sustainability reasons, there is usually an interest in communicating the sustainability agreement to the outside world anyway. For statements towards consumers and other market participants, the principles of unfair trading law described above apply, so the validity of the statements and the agreements behind them must be reviewed. However, the obligations under the UCP Directive are enforced on a case-by-case basis – there is no comprehensive screening of sustainability claims in corporate

---

[7] Cf also Siún O'Keeffe, 'Sustainability and Competition Policy' (2023) No 1 Concurrences 14, 23.

communications. This is especially true for jurisdictions which do not have a public enforcement mechanism in unfair trading law, like Germany.

However, a risk analysis must be carried out anyway on a case-by-case basis, at best with regard to specific groups of companies and individual sectors. For this purpose, it must be determined what criteria play a role in the risk analysis and promote or counteract greenwashing. Greenwashing is particularly virulent when stakeholders are unable to assess the credibility of the respective claims. This can be the case when there is a lack of expertise, when claimed sustainability impacts arise only in the internal sphere of the company or can only be measured by the company itself. The most important factor here is how transparently the companies present the situation before and after the respective cooperation.

The legislative approach to greenwashing and the expectations of market counterparts also play a major role. On the one hand, a lax and uncertain regulatory environment reduces the risks associated with greenwashing for a company, while on the other hand an increasing demand from consumers or investors for more sustainable products increases the incentives for greenwashing.[8]

In addition, certain characteristics at the organisational level also influence the tendency to greenwash. For example, some industries and companies are more prone to greenwashing because they can potentially derive greater benefits from appearing more sustainable than they are (e.g., consumer goods companies). While greenwashing can be beneficial to a company if stakeholders do not recognise the false or misleading claims, it also carries certain risks. Again, this may be related to industry or company characteristics. For example, some companies are more likely to be the target of campaigns and media scrutiny than others (again, consumer goods companies, for example, are often singled out). For example, if an independent third party, such as a non-governmental organisation, exposes and publicly denounces greenwashing activities, this can have a negative impact on the reputation of the company in question. If a company fears such reports, the risk of greenwashing will also be lower. Furthermore, extensive greenwashing in some industries or for some product groups may even negatively impact the credibility of those companies that do not themselves engage in greenwashing if it leads to a general scepticism of all sustainability claims.

Finally, the fundamental orientation of a company, including its internal compliance mechanisms, also plays a role in the likelihood of greenwashing. Companies whose business model is directly geared towards sustainability, or

---

[8]   Magali A Delmas and Vanessa Cuerel Burbano, 'The Drivers of Greenwashing' (2011) 54 *California Management Review* 64.

that have strict internal control mechanisms, are probably less likely to engage in greenwashing. Nevertheless, this may again not be easy to assess from the outside.

To summarise, various factors contribute to the assessment of the risk of greenwashing in antitrust law. The decisive factors are the verifiability of sustainability impacts, the regulatory approach to sustainability agreements and statements, the demand from consumers and investors for sustainable products, and the visibility of the company in the economic structure. The better the verifiability of impacts, the stricter the regulatory framework; the lower the demand for sustainable offerings and the higher a company's market visibility, the lower the likelihood of greenwashing in sustainability collaborations. In contrast, poor verifiability, restrained legal supervision, and high demand for sustainable offerings increase the risk of greenwashing in the context of a sustainability cooperation just as much as a company's low visibility in the market.

Preventing Greenwashing in Antitrust Law

If greater consideration is given to sustainability aspects in antitrust law, the question arises as to how the risk of greenwashing can be reduced. Environmental reasons must not become an uncontrolled free pass for non-intervention by the antitrust authorities or an exemption under Article 101(3) TFEU or equivalent national law. Rather, it must be examined in the context of the exemption whether an environmental benefit is actually achieved. Are the efficiencies and advantages cited by companies as justification actually attained to an extent that benefits the environment and consumers, or does the agreement relevant under antitrust law only bring minor advantages that cannot neutralise the restriction of competition caused by the agreement?

The guidelines developed in unfair trading law can provide initial guidance for the standard of proof and the interpretation of terms such as 'climate neutral'. However, the court practice in this field regularly does not reach the depth of examination required for a balancing with restrictions of competition.

Greenwashing Test in the Context of the Exemption

In the context of exempting sustainability agreements from antitrust law, the characteristic of the indispensability of the restriction must be examined to determine whether corresponding sustainability effects arise. To this end, it must first be clarified to what extent the restriction is suitable for implementing the sustainability objectives at all and to what extent it provides sustainability benefits). In such a 'greenwashing test', it should be considered, for example, whether saved greenhouse gas emissions are instead polluted elsewhere, especially in connection with certificate trading, when other companies are allowed to emit the saved emissions instead on the basis of the certificates acquired.[9] After the basic suitability, the (expected) achievement of the target must be presented (prospectively, if necessary) and examined by the authority. This requires a level of technical knowledge which cannot automatically be expected from competition authorities, and which may also raise problems of legitimacy.[10] Once it has been established that the agreement achieves the sustainability objectives, the indispensability of the restriction of competition must be examined. It must be shown that the desired sustainability benefits could not be achieved unilaterally without cooperation.

It should be noted that further recognition of sustainability initiatives can only be considered if the risk of greenwashing is reduced as far as possible. To achieve this, it should be examined what incentives generally exist for certain companies and industries to engage in greenwashing. It must be examined on a case-by-case basis whether cooperation is being pursued primarily for marketing purposes, or whether significant gains for sustainability can actually be made. Whether the competition authority is actually able to properly examine each individual case is not easy to answer.

---

[9]   Andreas Heinemann, 'Nachhaltigkeitsvereinbarungen' (2021) 5 sic! 213, 223 f; Anatole Boute 'The Impossible Transplant of the EU Emissions Trading Scheme: The Challenge of Energy Market Regulation' (2016) 6(1) *Transnational Environmental Law*, 72 f www.cambridge.org/core/journals/transnational-environmental-law/article/ impossible-transplant-of-the-eu-emissions-trading-scheme-the-challenge-of-energy -market-regulation/BAF5CD9ECE08C610E348FAFA1F9D6772 accessed 18 August 2023.

[10]   See Chapter 13.

15. *Competition and Sustainability*: concluding remarks

BASIC ASSUMPTIONS OF THIS BOOK

In politics, business, and society, sustainability has become a key term. However, 'sustainability' is a legally clearly defined phenomenon. At best, it describes 17 global objectives with its targets and indicators. The idea behind this term is urgent and undisputed: the protection of the Earth's climate system, the preservation of biodiversity, the fight against hunger and poverty – these demands and the other Sustainable Development Goals are legally and politically central and recognised worldwide. Representatives of the younger generation, political decision-makers and also representatives of the business community are articulating more and more clearly that sustainability must be an essential component of corporate action as it is already for many companies. Legally, this is anchored in the multi-stakeholder approach of the Sustainable Development Goals. Corporate sustainability is also being increasingly rewarded in markets, be it in the decisions of consumers or through better investment possibilities of sustainable finance.

In this book, we show how the struggle for more sustainability relates to competition economics and law. In a market economy, competition is the central driver of market activity, and safeguarding it is a fundamental task of economic law. With competition law and the possibilities of enforcement, whether official or private, powerful instruments are available to channel entrepreneurial behaviour and to sanction undesirable activities.

This raises the question of whether competition law hinders measures taken by companies to achieve sustainability goals. It also raises the question of whether and how the powerful instruments of competition law can and should be used to better achieve sustainability goals.

Competition law is by no means the only way of controlling economic activities. Other laws and tools are of much greater importance for sustainability goals than antitrust-based interventions. The special appeal of competition, however, is that it relies on free market forces and the creativity of entrepreneurs. Competition law sets the framework within which these entrepreneurial initiatives can unfold. It may also occasionally prevent behaviour that promotes sustainability, since the goal of protecting competition is often, but not necessarily always, compatible with protecting sustainability.

If one examines the relationship between competition and sustainability, there is a significant underlying assumption in the very fact that these two issues are brought together: companies are central to the achievement of these goals. It is essential to harness their power, and thus the possibilities of entrepreneurial creativity and innovation, as well as the market mechanism, to advance the Green Deal and the Sustainable Development Goals.

This finding is in line with a key statement of sustainability research: companies are actors in sustainable development and can (like other social actors) both inhibit and promote sustainability goals. The construction of a fundamental opposition between corporate interests on the one hand and interests in sustainable development on the other is misguided.

So, our research is based on the assumption that sustainability goals can be achieved within the framework of market mechanisms and competition, and that these mechanisms should therefore not be undermined. Competition remains the central mechanism of the economy. We expect that in the future, the economic model will be further geared toward an ecological-social market economy that brings the power of markets together with awareness and support of sustainability.

OPERATIONALISATION OF THE CONCEPT OF SUSTAINABILITY

Sustainable economic activity is oriented toward intra- and intergenerational justice. The Sustainable Development Goals of the United Nations with their subgoals and indicators contour the concept of sustainability and break it down to more concrete goals. A consideration of sustainability impacts in antitrust application requires that the term be defined and operationalised for practice. This is partially accomplished by the Sustainable Development Goals. However, the concrete measurement and evaluation of business activities with sustainability in mind face limitations. All methods have weaknesses. Nevertheless, an assessment is often possible to a certain extent, using quantitative as well as qualitative evidence. While a final certainty may be lacking and the quality of measurements and assessments may well differ with regard to the different sustainability goals, this is often true for the 'calculation' of different competition effects.

The Sustainable Development Goals open the door for parties to make their case in competition law proceedings, based on a broad variety of aspects and factors. There must be some limits to this. Apart from the difficulty of measuring effects, there is a problem of competence and legitimacy for competition agencies in this respect. Therefore, we believe that it is impossible to use the existing framework without legislative steps in a way that could be called game changing. While we have shown that some improvements can easily be made under the existing legal regime, a bigger step towards sustainability in competition law requires intervention by the legislature. Lawmakers have to take key decisions on economic policy. This is not for the agencies to decide.

One way to operationalise the concept of sustainability more strongly would be to focus on a few selected aims: instead of a comprehensive approach, priority could be given to climate protection, for example. The concept of sustainability would then not be understood horizontally but would be differentiated according to objectives. For example, according to the proposals of the European Commission in the Green Deal, the climate protection goals of the Union are to be implemented by 2030 through concrete measures of the Union and the member states. With the Taxonomy Regulation, which is intended to promote sustainable investments, criteria for concrete measures were presented.[1] The regulatory technique of the Taxonomy Regulation could lead the example for a sustainable competition agenda: there must be certain positive effects that are clearly measurable and significant; there are core restrictions that must not be agreed under any circumstances; and there are technical specifications that must be met.

However, such prioritisation is viewed critically: the sustainability goals are closely intertwined and interact in numerous ways. Most sustainability scholars prefer a holistic approach. Why should climate protection be prioritised over the issue of biodiversity or social sustainability goals, such as the prevention of child labour? This makes the task complex. That is why we set out in this study to look into every detail of competition law and see what can be achieved by small and bigger steps.

In many aspects, we found that it will be difficult to come to a socially and ecologically fair market economy without value judgements. The (alleged) agnostic paradigms of efficiency with concrete numbers are challenged by this approach. We take some comfort from the fact that the ordo-liberal school that influenced European competition law heavily in its beginnings (and German competition law still today) was strongly based on certain values that went beyond a naked idea of efficiency.

EVALUATION OF CONTROL MECHANISMS

Today, numerous governmental control mechanisms are used to monitor and achieve sustainability goals. Roughly speaking, these can be divided into regulatory measures and pricing measures. Both types of government market inter-

---

[1] For more details see Chapter 10.

vention serve to steer competition in such a way that no conflict arises with public welfare objectives. In principle, these measures can also be designed to be competition-neutral in the sense that no distortions of competition arise between market players.

The application of competition law in the narrower sense, i.e., the prohibition of cartels, abuse control, and merger control, is generally not affected by state interventions. However, there are certainly reasons why such interventions (bans, regulations, minimum standards, taxes) may not always be sufficient to achieve the sustainability goals set by the state. In such cases, cooperation between companies can also serve the common good and promote the achievement of sustainability goals. Two constellations were identified here:

First, so-called 'policy failures' may result in too much consideration of short-term costs, such as investments in sustainability measures, and too little consideration of long-term benefits, so that governmental intervention alone may not be sufficient to achieve self-defined sustainability goals.

Secondly, at least some consumers themselves may be interested in higher sustainability standards than those provided for in the rules. This can make cooperation between companies particularly meaningful if the offer of higher sustainability standards is associated with economies of scale and a critical quantity must be reached in order to be able to offer products with higher sustainability standards to consumers at acceptable costs.

If economies of scale and scope, and possibly also network effects, mean that individual companies cannot implement certain sustainability measures on their own without incurring losses, cooperation between companies can be beneficial for sustainability, the common good, and efficiency in individual cases.

From an economic perspective, too, consideration should therefore be given to creating certain possibilities in competition law to enable sustainability cooperation. Nevertheless, this must not be a 'blank cheque' to 'disguise' any cartel as a sustainability measure and to engage in so-called greenwashing.

The competition authorities are reaching the limits of their technical capabilities, their legal competences and their institutional legitimacy when it comes to increasingly taking sustainability aspects into account, whether in cooperation agreements, in abuse proceedings, or in mergers. They were not created to enforce sustainability goals (outside of economic sustainability). At best, competition agencies can take environmental and social goals into account in their original field of activity if there is a connection with competition. Competition law can be shaped more in the direction of an ecological-social market economy, but its core remains the protection of competition. At the same time, it should be noted that many economic regulations take extra-economic ideas into account. This is also legitimate since horizontal clauses, fundamental rights, and other laws make it ever harder to claim a supremacy of 'pure' competition law. Many competition agencies worldwide have been transformed into market regulation authorities that deal with different rules, from competition to consumer law, from fairness to public procurement, from energy regulation to transparency. From the perspective of competition policy, integrating other regulatory topics into this institutional cosmos has the advantage that market-based paradigms are more in focus, and bureaucratic solutions without an understanding of competition are more likely to be averted.

OPENNESS OF THE CURRENT COMPETITION LAW

The analysis of the legal situation and case practice in current competition law has shown that it already addresses sustainability aspects in many ways.

So far, there has been little discussion of the consequences of the application of competition law to sustainability aspects in cases where the sustainability link is obvious, such as in energy or waste management. Cases from these areas regularly have at least indirect effects on sustainability goals, for example, when market foreclosures are broken up or mergers are only made possible with certain commitments. The application of competition law does not provide for any consideration of the consequences in this respect.

Sustainability issues recently gave rise to new competition rules for the agricultural sector in the Common Market Organisation. In other areas, too, there are legislative interventions in the universal application of general competition law against the background of sustainability aspects.

In the application of general competition law, it should be noted that the horizontal issues of the EU treaties have had hardly any practical impact so far. In view of the breadth of previous formulations, this is not the key to an increased consideration of sustainability goals in the application of competition law. The horizontal clauses and objective provisions of the treaties, in addition to fundamental rights, have so far not led to balancing the decisions of these objectives with antitrust objectives.

The *Wouters* case law does not indicate anything to the contrary. The relevant cases make it clear that these are special constellations within the framework of delegated competences. A general restriction of the prohibition of restrictive business agreements for the common good does not follow from this. At best, it can be inferred from the cases of this doctrine that an exception to the prohibition of Article 101(1) TFEU can only be considered in the case of a complete undermining of the respective goals. Having said that, it seems to become more difficult to ignore horizontal clauses or fundamental rights when applying EU competition law.

At present, the assessment of sustainability initiatives falls primarily within the scope of Article 101(3) TFEU. An older line of cases suggests that many sustainability initiatives can meet the high requirements of this exception. With the 'more economic approach', however, corresponding considerations become less visible, so that more recent decisions appear to be stricter. Where competition agencies grant an exception for sustainability cooperation, this is not really a revolution but a return to previous standards.

The essential requirements of Article 101(3) TFEU – improvements in the production or distribution of goods, and a fair share for consumers – can be fulfilled in individual cases. It is at least not excluded that sustainability aspects are recognised as benefits and that a fair share is given even if the benefits are achieved outside the market concerned. Thus, the concept of intra- and intergenerational justice could be recognised in competition law. However, the European Commission's 2023 horizontal guidelines fall short of expectations.

Self-assessment remains subject to major uncertainties for companies, which can lead to so-called hold-up problems in particular if not insignificant specific investments are required, i.e., investments whose value is significantly reduced or, in extreme cases, even zero if used in an alternative way than originally planned. Some sustainability initiatives will be characterised precisely by the fact that companies derive at least no immediate profit from the initiative. If the companies do not even have a significant prospect of profit, the risk of making an incorrect self-assessment is too big.[2]

Greater clarity, a 'safe harbour', and guidance from competition authorities would be helpful. In this context, the current framework needs to be consolidated. It would be possible to explore the case for a block exemption regulation further.

In other areas of competition law, such as the prosecution of abusive practices and merger control, there has so far been little awareness of sustainability aspects. Yet here, too, there are numerous obvious references. The concept of competition, which is used, for example, in the SIEC test of merger control, is in principle open to interpretation and could include a normatively charged concept (e.g., ecologically sustainable competition). In the prosecution of abuses, there have been recent cases in which non-competition rules have had a supporting role in establishing an abuse. This was exemplified, for example, by the *Facebook* case as interpreted by the German Bundeskartellamt. The violation of competition law was partly based on the violation of data protection rules. A competitive edge through the breach of other regulations, e.g., those of environmental law, could entail independent legal enforcement

---

[2]   Cf Ella van den Brink and Jordan Ellison, 'Article 101(3) TFEU: The Roadmap for Sustainable Cooperation' in Simon Holmes, Dirk Middelschulte and Martijn Snoep (eds), *Competition Law, Climate Change & Environmental Sustainability* (Concurrences 2021) 40.

under competition law. To date, it has not been recognised that the creation of negative externalities by a dominant company constitutes an abuse nor that the avoidance of negative externalities would be a possible justification for otherwise abusive behaviour.

The German ministerial approval of mergers that had previously been banned represents a particularly vivid, but also controversial case of intervention in the application of competition law in favour of public welfare considerations. Sustainability aspects have already been addressed in this context – in the *Miba/Zollern* case, which in our view, however, is not a very convincing example.

It would be conceivable to take sustainability aspects into account in the design of remedial measures or in the assessment of a fine. In view of the limited previous experience with this, however, caution would be advisable when introducing it for reasons of both proportionality and legality.

The competition agencies could also take greater account of sustainability aspects within the scope of priority setting for selecting cases.

With regard to the participation of third parties in proceedings, it should be noted that the assertion of a legitimate interest is sufficient. This interest does not necessarily have to be of an economic-competition-related nature. For example, sustainability aspects can be brought into proceedings by third parties. Even if there may be a lack of relevance to the decision in case of doubt, a certain degree of transparency is created in this way and a broadening of the agency's information base is achieved. The more sustainability aspects have to be examined, the more important cooperation with other institutions becomes for competition agencies.

To sum up: as is currently understood, competition law is not directly geared to examining and implementing sustainability goals. The substantive standard of review remains solely competition-focused and should not be completely altered in the future. However, sustainability effects do occur in many cases, which can be taken into account more consciously than before. Conceptually, the concept of competition can be further developed in the direction of socially and ecologically sustainable competition – this could form part of a concept of 'competition on the merits', as it is often referred to by the European Court of Justice.[3] Sustainability aspects can already be taken into account in numerous steps under current law. This means that competition law is not the main lever for achieving sustainability goals. But it can be shaped in such a way that it does not stand in the way of achieving such goals through entrepreneurial initiative and may even provide incentives for non-sustainable behaviour.

---

[3]   Case C-680/20 *Unilever Italia* ECLI:EU:C:2023:33 [2023], paras 37, 39, 41; Case C-413/14 P *Intel* ECLI:EU:C:2017:632 [2017], para 137.

RESPONSIBLE COURSES OF ACTION

In this study, numerous options for the further development of competition law have been explained. In doing so, the protection of competition remains the point of reference.

A first set of options is merely intended to sharpen an understanding of the role of competition in achieving sustainability goals (*sustainability awareness*). Where there is room for manoeuvre that can be used relatively freely under the law, such as in the case of priority setting, it is to be expected that competition-related sustainability issues will be given greater attention as a result of a heightened awareness. This group includes, in particular, the proposals on selecting cases, calculation of the willingness to pay, market definition with reference to sustainability, and the increased involvement of third parties.

A second set of options remains true to the competition logic and merely expands the scope for sustainability considerations through legislative clarifications. Here, in particular, those sustainability goals are promoted more strongly where there is a close connection to competition (*sustainability boost*). These options include proposals for legislative clarifications under the exemption, remedies and fines.

A third set of options is conceptually much more demanding, as it involves considerable further development of the concept of competition – at least from the perspective of competition law to date. Accordingly, the object of protection under competition law is to be ecologically and socially sustainable competition. Only those entrepreneurial activities that are designed for sustainable economic activity would be worthy of protection (*competition as sustainable competition*). The concept of competition is changing and, in particular, is moving away from the narrow efficiency orientation of the consumer welfare approach. Just as, to borrow from the *Facebook* case, in the digital economy the handling of data is a factor in competition, in a social-ecological market economy the handling of the planet, of other people, or of flora and fauna can be a factor relevant to competition. It must be admitted, however, that this implies both a transformation of the economy and a realignment of competition law. Options that fit into this category are, for example, the recognition of overall societal benefits in the exemption or sustainability as a balancing factor in the context of the prohibition of abuse.

A final set of options leaves competition untouched in its isolated system but recognises that extra-competition interests have a legitimacy out of their own right. Competition and non-competition interests are placed on an equal footing (*levelling approach*). This approach can either lead to the creation of areas of exemption from competition law, or to the recognition that noncompetition interests are to be set against competition law values. Examples of such options are proposals to create areas of exception, ancillary restraints in the context of Article 101(1) TFEU, or the ministerial authorisation in merger control.

The multitude of options and their very different intensity – sometimes the current state of the law is clarified, sometimes tools and procedures are introduced – already indicates the scope for the European legislator under this topic. How this leeway is used is the responsibility of policymakers. With increasing expectations for companies to assume greater responsibility for achieving the Sustainable Development Goals, it seems appropriate to further develop the legal framework. At the same time, two limitations should be considered. First, competition law is not the most important area of law for achieving sustainability goals. It can primarily facilitate or flank the achievement of goals and ensure that market failures do not undermine the transformation. Secondly, there are also problems in competition law that need to be solved – irrespective of the sustainability debate: the still insufficient international integration beyond the EU, the sometimes overly complex and lengthy procedures, the requirements of proof that occasionally seem excessive, or the integration of private law enforcement that could be expanded. These are just a few examples. A competition law that is to take on more far-reaching tasks must be 'fit for purpose' – this should not be overlooked despite all the enthusiasm for competition law instruments.

Hans Jonas formulated the 'principle of responsibility' as the imperative of sustainability as early as 1979: 'Act in such a way that the effects of your actions are compatible with the permanence of genuine human life on Earth.' This imperative also applies to entrepreneurs and decision-makers in competition.

Annex: brief description of all options

SCOPE OF APPLICATION OF COMPETITION LAW (SC)

SC 1: Create areas of exemption from competition law for certain industries, certain types of agreements, or certain sustainability goals.

PROHIBITION OF RESTRICTIVE AGREEMENTS (RE)

RE 1: Recognition of ancillary restraints in sustainability agreements if the restriction of competition is only a necessary secondary purpose of an agreement that is neutral in terms of competition since it aims at achieving sustainability goals or serves to open up markets.

RE 2: Exception for sustainability agreements to Article 101(1) TFEU within the meaning of the *Wouters* doctrine due to legitimate non-competition objectives, namely sustainability.

RE 3: Better visibility of agreements on sustainability-relevant competition parameters by presenting corresponding case groups in guidelines.

RE 4: Assumption that anti-competitive agreements that harm sustainability have an appreciable effect.

RE 5: Extension of guidelines on standardisation agreements with a focus on criteria for environmental and social standards.

EXEMPTION UNDER ARTICLE 10(3) TFEU (EX)

EX 1: Modified willingness-to-pay analysis to identify sustainability benefits in the context of a classic consumer-welfare approach.

EX 2: Recognition of overall societal benefits within the exemption, even if they are out-of-market efficiencies.

EX 3: Moving away from the solely economic criteria of Article 101(3) TFEU and introduction of a more normative balancing.

EX 4: Individual exemption of model cooperation agreements that aim to achieve significant sustainability impacts and serve as a model for statutory rulemaking.

EX 5: Introduction of a statutory exemption clause (along the lines of the Austrian model) or an exemption along the lines of Section 3 of the German competition act for the cooperation of SME on sustainability.

EX 6: Creation of a block exemption regulation for sustainability agreements.

PROHIBITION OF ABUSE (AB)

AB 1: Capturing changed preferences in market definition.

AB 2: Recognition of the possibility of externalisation as a market power factor.

AB 3: Consideration of sustainability in the context of justification of an abuse.

AB 4: Expansion of the abuse provisions by a category of cases regarding 'infringement of non-competition regulations' (based on the *Facebook* case) to include sustainability-related infringements of the law.

AB 5: Viewing unsustainable behaviour as exploitative abuses, especially for social sustainability goals (e.g., fair pay).

AB 6: Exploitation of public goods as abuse of market power.

AB 7: New exclusionary abuse case groups tied to Sustainable Development Goal violations.

MERGER CONTROL (MC)

MC 1: Changes to the criteria for taking up cases so that mergers that are particularly relevant to sustainability can be examined under merger control law.

MC 2: Further development of the SIEC test in terms of environmentally and socially sustainable competition.

MC 3: Consideration of non-competition goals in the context of a trade-off.

MC 4: Extension of the efficiency argument to include the sustainability impact.

MC 5: Strengthening sustainable remedial action.

MC 6: Correction of the regulatory merger control decision in a separate procedure (e.g., ministerial approval) in which sustainability considerations are examined.

PROCEDURES AND SANCTIONS (PR)

PR 1: Stronger consideration of sustainability interests within the framework of the authorities' priority setting.

PR 2: Further entitlement to informal advice (e.g., through 'comfort letters') in sustainability-related cases.

PR 3: Establishment of a Sustainability Sandbox (based on the Greek model), i.e., a controlled testing of sustainability-promoting collaborations.

PR 4: Enabling sector inquiries into issues of environmentally and socially sustainable competition.

PR 5: Better integration of third parties in proceedings who contribute sustainability-relevant aspects (e.g., NGOs).

PR 6: More intensive cooperation between competition agencies and other authorities.

PR 7: Increased transparency of sustainability considerations on the occasion of decisions by competition agencies through sustainability checks (e.g., climate check) or ex-post evaluations.

PR 8: Consideration of sustainability effects as a mitigating or aggravating factor in the setting of fines.

PR 9: Increasing and limiting the private risk of damages if the violation was committed with sustainability damages or with good intentions for sustainability goals.

Index

Printed and bound by CPI Group (UK) Ltd, Croydon, CR0 4YY

23/04/2025

14660986-0001